Frontier Historian

Edward Everett Dale

FRONTIER HISTORIAN

THE LIFE AND WORK OF
EDWARD EVERETT DALE

EDITED BY
Arrell M. Gibson

with introductory essays by

ARRELL M. GIBSON
ANGIE DEBO
JOHN S. EZELL

University of Oklahoma Press : Norman

Library of Congress Cataloging in Publication Data

Dale, Edward Everett, 1879–1972.
    Frontier historian.

    Includes bibliographical references.
        1. Dale, Edward Everett, 1879–1972—Addresses, essays,
lectures. 2. Frontier and pioneer life—The West—
Addresses, essays, lectures. I. Title.
E175.5.D22A25 1975   978'.007'2024 [B]   75–11774
ISBN 0–8061–1305–7

Contents

I. Life

Edward Everett Dale: The Historian

Arrell M. Gibson

Few persons live long enough to see themselves become the central figure in a timeless regional legend. Edward Everett Dale was one of these. Most men of consequence dazzle others with the force of personality. Edward Everett Dale dazzled those about him with the force of utter simplicity and confident ingenuousness. The richness, human flavor and commanding attention which pervade many Dale essays are derived not from overpowering research, detached synthesis, and conceptualization, but from honest reporting, personalized sharing of intimate grass-roots feelings, aspirations, experiences—in short, from humanized history.

The reservoir of knowledge, insight, and understanding from which Dale artfully composed his essays was only minimally derived from formal academic training and research. Most scholars follow a sequential progression in their preparation to produce new knowledge and share it with the reading public. In their youth they customarily move promptly through the Bachelor of Arts, Master of Arts, and Doctor of Philosophy degrees, then devote years of study and research to accumulate the essential command in breadth and insight of their special interest before they attempt to transmit this knowledge through articles and books.

Dale followed a different course. He seasoned himself with frontier living, observing firsthand its social ferment and change. Belatedly he reached the decision to undertake academic training to sharpen his native intellectual talents and to learn the technique of transmitting this frontier experience legacy. At the age of twenty-six he faced squarely the question of whether to punch cattle or go to college. Friends scorned this proposed step reminding him that he would be thirty-one by the time he was graduated. Dale concluded with simple, direct logic that in five years he would be thirty-one anyhow and the real question was, did he wish to reach that age with a college degree? He did not complete the Ph.D. at Harvard until the age of forty-two, which left him a professional life of thirty years to share his frontier experience and heritage through college teaching and writing. And he used the academic degrees as credentials to command the forum for transmitting that heritage. Therefore, in assessing Dale's bibliographical impact on Western history, his social milieu more than his academic training shaped his values, commitment, writing bent, and productivity as a professional historian.

Most of what Dale wrote was autobiographical in that he had lived a prototype of virtually every incident, movement, and circumstance contained in his essays. The principal elements in the Dale legacy were pioneer family, the Cross Timbers nester culture, the prairie-plains stockraising culture, his early private and public education and, finally, with Frederick Jackson Turner's assistance, Dale's discovery of the West as substantive American history. All of these elements colored his performance as a Western historian. And as one reads Dale's essays, he may be troubled by the difficulty of categorizing him professionally—at times the serious, scholarly, research-bent historian looms, but more often he shows as the folklorist, humorist, a perceptive on-the-spot frontier reporter, and a poet.

Dale's early life in the Texas Cross Timbers yields compelling bibliographical clues to the genesis of "Two Mississippi Valley Frontiers" and other agrarian-centered essays. His family was dominated by a stern, tough-minded father, the frontiersman archetype. Born in Kentucky in 1829, the elder Dale grew to manhood on the north Missouri frontier. He made the Gold Rush to California in 1850, driving an ox team across the plains, mountains, and deserts to the lodes of the Sacramento. Returning to Missouri via Panama with a comfortable stake, Dale settled on the Nebraska frontier for a time, then moved to Texas, taking a farm in the lower Cross Timbers of Tarrant County. He lived by the doctrine of the Primitive Old School Hardshell Baptist Church, which helped to toughen him to meet the challenges of frontier living.

Edward Everett Dale was born in 1879 in a log cabin on this north Texas farm. At the age of five the boy labored at his father's side clearing brush to open more cultivable land and working the fields of corn and cotton. Young Dale's knowledge of the frontier, imparted by his father, extended back to the time of Andrew Jackson. His father's role in the drama of expansion of American settlement from Kentucky to Missouri, into Nebraska, and on to Texas provided for Dale a very real genetic and cultural connection with this epic.

The force of the pioneer family in Dale's experience included a frontier mother who listened attentively to the prattle and puerile poetry recitations of her young son and who taught him to read at the age of four. Her tender devotion imparted to Dale an awe for pioneer womanhood which he romanticized in *Prairie Schooner* verse. She died when

Dale was five, leaving him to the care of a brother, George, five years his senior.

George was young Dale's interpreter of the universe, the source of all wisdom, patiently answering the many questions raised by the very curious little brother. When Dale read from the poem "Paul Revere's Ride,"

> A hurry of hoofs in the village street
> A shape in the moonlight, a bulk in the dark;
> And beneath from the pebbles in passing a spark
> Struck out by a steed flying fearless and fleet . . .
> And the spark struck out by that steed in his flight
> Kindled the land into flame with its beat.

he asked George the meaning of these lines. George replied, "It means just what it says. You've seen sparks fly when we'd hit a rock a glancing lick with a hammer. Well, Old Paul's horse was shod, so his iron shoes knocked sparks from rocks and set the whole country a-fire." Dale acknowledged his debt to George, recalling in his unpublished autobiography that his brother was his "guide, philosopher and friend . . . . Always to me he was the fountainhead of all wisdom, and everything he told me was accepted as Gospel truth."[1]

Until the age of thirteen, Dale commented that he had not had "any schooling to amount to anything," probably in attendance no more than twelve months altogether. Most of the years of his early youth Dale worked with his father in the fields of the Cross Timbers farm. In his autobiography he explained why the school term began in late November and lasted only a few months. "As in many other parts of the South at this time cotton picking had a distinct priority over

[1] Edward Everett Dale, *The Cross Timbers: Memories of a North Texas Boyhood* (Austin: University of Texas Press, 1966), 140, 148; and Edward Everett Dale, Autobiography (unpublished), in possession of Mrs. Rosalie Dale, 27.

education. There was ample reason for this. Few local school districts had enough money for more than a three to five-month term of school. To begin it in September when the cotton-picking season was just opening and let the children remain idle during the latter part of the winter and early spring did not make sense" to Cross Timbers farm parents.[2]

Dale was in school for a short period at the age of eight, and advanced to the fourth then, in a few weeks, to the fifth grade reader group. For the most part Dale had to content himself with reading the Bible, his father's church paper *Signs of the Times, Pilgrims' Progress, Longfellow's Poems*, and *The Farm and Fireside*.

The quickening awareness of a special sense of being, in which he included George, came to Dale at an early age. He recalled, "I began to feel that George and I were not quite like the other boys of the neighborhood. This did not mean a feeling that we were better or worse than the other kids of the community but only that we were *different*. Just how or why we were different never occurred to us, but it seems clear to me now that because we both read a good deal we lived, to some extent, in a make-believe world, into which few of our boyhood friends could enter."[3]

The Cross Timbers in the 1880's was a zone of blending cultures as people from the Deep South, Middle Border and a few from the East settled the country. "Speech of the Pioneers" and the twelve collected essays in *Frontier Ways*, all recapitulated by Dale in his autobiography as swatches of childhood flashbacks, depict the cultural cross-fertilization occurring on this agricultural frontier.[4]

[2] Dale, Autobiography, 46.
[3] Dale, *The Cross Timbers*, 46
[4] Edward Everett Dale, *Frontier Ways: Sketches of Life in the Old West* (Austin: University of Texas Press, 1959).

Sunday visits in the homes of members of the Hardshell Baptist Church centered on women quilting, patching worn clothing, and sewing garments, and the "women's tongues often moved faster than their fingers as they discussed the local news and gossip." Local superstitions and taboos, powerful individual and group behavior determinants, were rich grist for the folklorist's mill. Dale reported the injunction against killing frogs in a pond, for such an act would cause cows using the water to give bloody milk. The pain of an infant at tooth-cutting time was eased by the mother tying a mole's foot around the baby's neck. And old men in the community often carried potatoes in their pockets to ward off rheumatism.[5]

The puritan values of Cross Timber society hallowed certain female parts and functions and banned them as subjects of public discussion. A "woman did not break her leg but a 'lower limb.' " Dale commented that with "floor-length skirts and the use of the term 'limb' it almost seemed that it was a social error for a woman to admit that she had legs. . . . To refer to an unmarried woman's future children was a grave social error . . . . Such words as 'belly,' 'boar,' and 'pregnant' were never used in mixed company." When a woman was pregnant the euphemism "in a family way" was used to describe her state.[6]

Dale related the pathos and compassion of Cross Timbers society by the instance of how the community cared for an ancient blind woman, left alone by the death of her son. Rather than see her committed to the county poorhouse, the members of the local Primitive Baptist Church agreed to keep

[5] Dale, *The Cross Timbers*, 144–45.
[6] *Ibid.*, 157.

her in their homes as long as she lived. She resided with the Dales for two months.[7]

Cross Timbers settlers were mobile. Businessmen in nearby towns served the pioneeers' travel needs by operating wagon yards. The wagon yard included a stable and camp house. The traveler paid fifteen cents to board his horse at the stable and for cooking and sleeping use of the camp house. Dale collected a series of stories centering on this frontier establishment and titled them "Tales of the Wagon Yard." If at evening there was no wagon yard closeby, pioneers slept on the prairie. Another transportation service for the settler which Dale reported was the immigrant car. After railroads laced the Southwest, the trains included immigrant cars which in many cases replaced the covered wagon for transporting settlers to a new territory. The immigrant car was the familiar boxcar that the settler leased from the railroad and in which he loaded his family, provisions, plow, and other tools and implements, seed and livestock for the journey to the wilderness homestead.[8]

The workings of Cross Timbers nester culture exposed Dale to extra-legal practices which he later reported to Turner, confirming for the eminent frontier historian that which had been largely theory on an inevitable American pioneer response. Dale observed neighbors substituting simple arbitration for "going to the law" to settle disputes over land, property boundaries, or stock ownership. His father was called upon several times to assist in this process. The two parties to the dispute beforehand agreed to settle that matter by private arbitration. The local arbitration panel consisted of three men, each party to the dispute appointing

[7] *Ibid.*, 156.
[8] Dale, Autobiography, 137.

one man, and these two choosing a third. The extra-legal frontier tribunal investigated the matter in dispute, heard the evidence, and rendered a decision which both parties had agreed to accept as final.

And Dale had a sensitive ear and congenial spirit for the occasional humor which emanated from the Cross Timbers milieu. Some of this humor was dry and grim, illustrated by the story of Brother McKelvey, a member of the Primitive Baptist Church whom Dale described as an entertaining talker. He had served four years in the Confederate Army and participated in many battles and bore the scars of many wounds. McKelvey recalled, "When I enlisted in the Southern army soon after the war started, I thought that to get shot meant to be killed, but after being wounded half a dozen times, I learned that this was not true." During one battle he received a severe wound and was carried to the "dead house" with the dead and dying. When the funeral party came to bury him next morning he was alive and protesting. After a short stay in the hospital McKelvey returned to his regiment for combat. Dale's propensity for humor and judicious use of witty allusions flavored his essays.[9]

At the age of thirteen, Dale left the Cross Timbers. His father had decided to become a stockman, using the money from the sale of the farm to buy a tract of Greer County, Texas, grassland and a small herd of cattle. Young Dale moved easily and enthusiastically from the agrarian routines of the Cross Timbers farm to ranching on the prairie-plains. He quickly learned the technique of handling range cattle and horses, helping his father on the family Greer County ranch and riding as a cowboy for neighboring ranchmen. Also Dale occasionally worked as a trail driver, moving herds

[9] Dale, *The Cross Timbers*, 145.

from north Texas ranches to new ranges in the old Cherokee Outlet near Woodward in Oklahoma Territory.

Dale gloried in the free life of the cowboy. Later in essays on life in the prairie-plains environment, he stressed the easier existence in this region, both for ranchmen and the intruding nesters, permitting a more *simpatico* life style than was possible in the Cross Timbers. People in this new land had more leisure than had been the case for the early settlement frontiers to the East. He found the prairie-plains a more permissive region, its mores permitting dancing, card-playing, and other forms of frontier entertainment which were banned in the puritan-Primitive Baptist culture of the Cross Timbers.

Dale explained that the pioneer on the prairie-plains had more leisure because of environmental conditions which to a large degree determined the economic enterprises conducted there. Stockmen had considerable leisure because their industry required during the year only short periods of intensive hard labor and close attention, at roundups and winter feeding made necessary by occasional blizzards. Otherwise the herds required only casual attention, the rich grasslands and mild climate making it possible for the animals to shift for themselves. This allowed ranching families much time for visiting, dancing, and other recreations.

The intruding nester also had more leisure on the thick grass-carpeted prairie-plains. He had no forests to clear and was liberated from his eternal contest with the ubiquitous sprouts, which each planting season had to be grubbed from the soil after the trees had been removed. Also the one-crop emphasis of the agrarian frontier extension into the prairie plains in cotton and wheat production required only intensive seasonal attention, permitting the nester during certain periods of the year time for other activities which had not been the case in the multi-activity, self-sufficient agrarian frontier of the East. The settler in the prairie-plains faced the admitted handicap of very limited timber resources for obtaining wood for fuel and constructing dwellings and fences. The few trees on this frontier grew along the watercourses and in the canyons. Dale explained the adjustment to this problem in his essay "Wood and Water: Twin Problems of the Prairie Plains."

In his autobiography, Dale stated that "My years as a cowboy and ranchman . . . taught me many things that vitally affected my future. They made me an ardent conservative in all business matters . . . even more important, they . . . instilled in me a cowman's philosophy of life or, more correctly, perhaps, his attitude toward life. Every man who has worked cattle understands what this means."[10]

From the leisure available to the pioneer in the prairie-plains environment Dale drew the opportunity to continue his education, and the description of his first contact with adult education, drawn from his autobiography, provides a vista on another frontier institution—the Camp School. T. E. Jones, "an ardent prohibitionist and very much a promoter," was a Greer County school master. Each summer he conducted a camp school for adults near Granite. The site for the camp school was on the south side of a mountain in a "beautiful grove and a gushing spring of pure, cold water." The camp school extended for four weeks. The curriculum consisted of instruction in oratory, singing, and temperance. Jones' payment for instruction was derived from the enrollment fee of three dollars from each student, and income from the franchise issued by the town of Granite for operating the

[10] Dale, Autobiography, 149.

concessions at the three-day graduation ceremonies and picnic which concluded the camp school term.

Students camped near the shady grove, where the out-of-door classes were conducted, or boarded with families in Granite. During the 1897 session which Dale attended, fifty students enrolled for the camp school. The learning-teaching day began each morning at seven-thirty when Jones sounded "assembly" on a trumpet. Dale recalled that Jones was a vigorous bachelor with the "appearance and manner of a top sergeant." After the students had endured twenty minutes of rigorous calisthenics, Jones distributed songbooks and the student body sang for half an hour. A stanza from one song went:

> Somewhere tonight in a cold, dreary world
> wanders a boy I cherish so,
> treading the dark and unbidden road
> Leading to misery, pain, and woe.
> Once he was pure as the saints in white,
> Noble and manly, my joy and delight,
> Facing a future so happy and bright
> But now, oh my God, he's a drunkard tonight!

The day's academic instruction then began. Jones passed to each student a book containing temperance speeches. One-half of the class remained at the platform and received guidance from the instructor. The other half of the camp school student body scattered to various parts of the grove, each finding some secluded spot in the shade to memorize his speech and practice delivery. Jones instructed each student on voice, enunciation, emphasis, and gesture. The four-week camp school session closed with graduation program, ceremonies, and a three-day picnic. Most of each commencement day was spent in the students delivering their best orations.

Jones awarded to the three students rendering what he judged to be superior performances a silver medal, a gold medal, and a "grand gold" medal. Pioneer famlies gathered from fifty miles around for the closing exercises of the camp school. They sat in rapt wonder at the fiery utterances of Jones' pupils. Businessmen from the town co-operated. They provided lumber to build a large platform and seats. The local school board loaned the school organ for group singing. It was also agreed that Jones should sell concessions for the merry-go-round, cold drinks stands, doll racks, a shooting gallery, and venders of peanuts and popcorn. The concessions opened during the morning and afternoon recesses between orations, and in the evening. Dale commented that "the audience listened with rapt attention" to the orations, "but it is doubtful if our efforts had the slightest effect upon the consumption of liquor."[11]

As 1900 approached, Dale's frontier seasoning had nearly been completed. A concatenation of incidents led him to a teaching career in the prairie-plains pioneer schools, which ironically began as a means and became, in a sense, an end, in that this was the beginning of a formal two-step process for him to transmit his legacy of frontier experience. He and his brother George were eager to become independent ranchmen on a partnership basis. Beginning with a small tract they had inherited from their father and a small herd of cows, they leased additional range and attempted to stock their expanded pastures with cattle purchased by money borrowed from a local livestock commission company. Needing additional money to maintain their expanded operations, Dale decided to prepare himself to teach school.

For about two months he attended the school at Navajoe,

[11] *Ibid.*, 153.

a settlement in Greer County serving the nesters, ranchmen, and Indian trade from the nearby Kiowa-Comanche Indian Reservation. Then he applied for and passed the territorial examination, receiving a certificate stating that he had completed the equivalent of eighth grade school work. Next he enrolled in a four-week county normal institute for teachers at Cloud Chief, a town situated to the north in the Cheyenne-Arapaho Country, a vast tract recently opened to homesteaders. Dale said in his autobiography that teaching "appealed to me for, although I had no thought at this time of making teaching my life work, it seemed that it might be interesting to teach three or four terms and use my savings to buy calves. This would help me achieve my real ambition which was to join George in the ranching business." The normal institute was held in the Cloud Chief schoolhouse. On enrollment day, teacher candidates rode in from all directions, extra clothing and a few books tied in a sack behind each saddle. Dale and several other students at night spread their blankets on the prairie near the Cloud Chief schoolhouse. At the end of the four-week term Dale submitted to the territorial examination which, if he passed, would entitle him to a certificate stating that he was qualified to teach in the schools of Oklahoma Territory. The county superintendent, who graded the examinations for certification, "tempered justice with mercy" and Dale passed, receiving his teacher's certificate in 1898. His first school was at Clabber Flat near Navajoe on a contract calling for a three-month term at twenty-five dollars a month. The Clabber Flat School functioned in a building twenty by thirty feet. Dale taught fifty-eight pupils, ages six to twenty, with one student twenty-four. At the time, for added income, he held a commission as deputy sheriff.

In 1900, Dale and his brother went broke in the ranching business, wiped out by limited pasture, a harsh, killing winter, flooded cattle markets, and low beef prices. They sold their land, cattle, most of the horses, household and even personal effects to settle their debt with the livestock commission company. Dale lamented that while the brother partners had "paid the last dollar of our debts," they faced a "grim and bleak future." Broke and homeless, Dale returned to teaching to support George and himself.[12]

Dale had one last experience in pioneering before his frontier legacy was completed. In 1901, the federal government opened the Kiowa-Comanche country to the settler. After survey and reservation of town sites there were 13,000 homesteads in the new settlement tract. It was to be opened by lottery, the homesteads to be assigned to registrants at drawings held at Fort Reno and at Lawton. Dale and George regarded the Kiowa-Comanche opening an opportunity for them to make a fresh start. They registered for homesteads, agreeing that if only one drew a claim, he would divide the land equally with the other. On the day of the lottery, George's name was drawn. Dale and he were then permitted to enter the settlement zone and select their 160-acre homestead. Dale's ecstatic recollection of their search and discovery of the homestead was a reiteration of the pioneer's land lust lyric which had sounded time and again since the 1790's. They reconnoitered the territory, finally coming upon "a lovely valley about a mile and a half wide and extending approximately the same distance north to where Otter Creek emerged from a deep canyon in the mountains. The valley was open to the south but was hemmed in by low mountains on the east and west. We turned east and

[12] *Ibid.*, 161

crossed the crystal clear stream flowing over a colorful mosaic of many colored pebbles. As we looked to the north we were fairly dazzled by the prospect before us. Clearly this was it! A quarter of a mile farther east was a small tributary of Otter Creek. It came through a wide gap in the mountains to the northeast and between it and the main stream lay the loveliest valley we had ever seen. It was level as a floor and covered with grass reaching to our stirrups."[13]

Dale returned to teaching to earn a stake to develop the Otter Creek homestead. He taught at the Red Fork, Duke, Headrick, Roosevelt and Blair schools of southwestern Oklahoma Territory. In 1905 he enrolled at the Oklahoma Territorial Normal School at Edmond to strengthen his credentials, attending fulltime in 1908 and graduating the next year with a two-year associate degree. Additional formal education had disturbed his pioneer moorings and quickened his desire for further study. He enrolled at the University of Oklahoma in 1909 and was graduated two years later with a Bachelor of Arts in history. That summer he was hired to teach history at the Edmond teachers college. Determined to do graduate work, he applied for and received admission to Harvard University and an Austin Teacher's Scholarship for $250. At Harvard he fell under the spell of Frederick Jackson Turner. Dale stated in his autobiography that Turner's course on the American West "opened to me a new Heaven and a new earth in the field of American History. When Turner spoke of the lack of respect of the law, *per se* on the American frontier I recalled that even ministers of the Gospel living near Navajoe cut and hauled wood from the Indian reservation across the North Fork of Red River,

---

[13] *Ibid.*, 168.

keeping an eagle eye out for the United States marshals or Indian police."[14]

Turner's discussion "of extra-legal associations brought to my mind memories of the livestock associations that existed in Southwest Oklahoma which employed livestock inspectors, to check on brands, stop the theft of cattle and horses, arranged roundups, and made rules with respect to them. The mention of settling disputes by arbitration reminded me that two of our neighbors in the Texas Cross Timbers came to my father and asked him to join them in settling a dispute between two men in the community. Turner's mention of the fact that a man on the American frontier frequently worked at various vocations called to mind that I, myself, had engaged in half a dozen types of work. It was a shock to realize that all of these things were a part of history."[15]

After completing the Master of Arts degree at Harvard in 1914, Dale was appointed instructor of history at the University of Oklahoma. Five years later he returned to Harvard to work on the Ph.D. degree, which he completed in 1922. Thereupon he resumed his place at the University of Oklahoma in the Department of History and in 1924 became chairman, a post he held until 1942. The University of Oklahoma continued his academic home until his retirement in 1952 with the rank of George Lynn Cross Research Professor of History.

Sharpened by academic study and Turner's influence, Dale proceeded vigorously to the formal dissemination of his frontier experience heritage. The corpus of Dale's literary

[14] *Ibid.,* 173.
[15] *Ibid.,* 174.

production centers on eighteen books, sixty essays and articles, and six volumes which he edited. Many of his writings were braced with scholarly research, but all of them were seasoned with his frontier heritage. Of his books, *The Range Cattle Industry* (1930), *Cow Country* (1942), *Indians of the Southwest* (1949), and *Frontier Ways* (1959) loom as the strongest. The essays which dominate the Dale bibliography are "Old Navajoe," "Two Mississippi Valley Frontiers," "The Speech of the Pioneers," and "Cow Country in Transition."

Dale's value to Western historiography is less that of a stern scholar producing new knowledge from intensive research, and more that of a participant in much of the drama of frontier development sharing his experiences with a vicarious reading public. His best, most engaging, compelling, and significant writings were derived from his legacy of frontier experience. This does not mean that Dale did not himself engage in serious research and expect the same from his students. He successfully established pre-eminent Western history research collections at the University of Oklahoma in the Phillips Collection, which became the core for the University Library's Western History Collections, and at the Oklahoma Historical Society where he served as a Director on the governing board for nearly fifty years. The important thing about Dale is that he did not need to do research to write important books and essays, but simply to share what he already had experienced. Dale must be regarded less a hard-nosed professional historian and more of a romantic interpreter of the frontier milieu. He was never the bitter, carping cynic, but always the enduring optimist, a living witness, a vibrant participant to what he interpreted, taught, and wrote about. If Dale required a professional identity, he could be classed as a social historian, more interested in the people than presidents.

Edward Everett Dale was a bridge, a sparkling spirit and genuine link connecting the simplistic frontier past and the complex technological present. With splendid poise and sensitive response he provided exciting, living connective tissue between these two eras through a long and distinguished career as teacher and writer.

Edward Everett Dale: The Teacher

Angie Debo

His life and his work were all of one piece. They were like his characterization of the homely verses that formed so readily in his thoughts, "They all lie in one realm—the realm of plain western people." Thus an evaluation of his teaching must go deeper than a description of his classroom lectures.

He was born in Texas in 1879. His forebears had followed the frontier from Virginia through Kentucky and Missouri (with a side trip by his father to the California gold fields) to the "Cross Timbers" of North Texas, where his father literally hacked a productive farm from the postoak-blackjack jungle that covered the thin, sandy soil. Here the boy's mother died, and when he was nine years old, his father and the two sons still at home spent some months with older members of the family in the frontier community of the present Jackson County, Oklahoma, then claimed by Texas. Four years later they returned to settle there, where the father established a small ranch.

To the boy Ed it was an exciting new environment. Here the town of Navajoe had sprung into lusty but short-lived existence. Three miles away across the river was the reservation of the Kiowas, Comanches, and Apaches; and these hunters and warriors of the Plains, subdued only thirteen years before, came often to pitch their tipis while they traded at the store owned by his older brother and brother-in-law. Three or four miles to the west was the great Western Trail of the cattle drives from far down in Texas to the railhead at Dodge City, Kansas; and the trail boss might drive over with the chuck wagon to replenish his provisions before crossing the unsettled lands to the north. Also the Kiowa-Comanche-Apache Reservation was leased to cattlemen, and cowhands from remote line camps might ride in to attend a party in town or a box supper at the schoolhouse. All around were settlers trying to establish farm homes on the bare prairie. One of the Dale brothers was improving a claim near the townsite, living in a half-dugout with sod walls.

Thus the boy came into early contact with the Indians, cowboys, and homesteaders of his future lifetime interests and with the ambitious little towns and institutions they were establishing. When he was seventeen, following a supreme court decision, the area—formerly claimed by Texas—was joined to the Territory of Oklahoma. Ironically it was through a legal technicality that he became a citizen of the state to which he would render such distinguished service.

The State of Texas provided schooling for pupils from eight years old up, but long before Ed reached that age he had taught himself to read and was devouring every book he could lay his hands on. This was supplemented by some sketchy attendance at brief terms of school. Everything he read was fixed in his memory, from the grandiloquent pages of Barnes's grade school American history to the King James Bible, so that their words passed half humorously into his later classroom lectures. When he was eighteen he took an examination prepared by the Oklahoma territorial board of education and received a diploma stating that he had completed the common school course.

The next year he decided to become a teacher. In those

days each Oklahoma county held a four weeks' "Normal Institute" every summer, where teachers came to review the common school subjects with the addition of some pedagogical principles. Young Dale took this course at the new town of Cloud Chief, then the county seat of Washita County. This was in the former Cheyenne and Arapaho Reservation. It had been opened to homesteaders six years before, but for a time it remained largely a cow country with grass free for the grazing. Now settlers were coming in and schools were springing up. Cloud Chief was too small and its primitive dwellings too crowded to accommodate the forty teachers, actual and prospective, at the institute. Dale slept on the prairie and took his meals at a near-by house. At the close he took the territorial examination and received a teacher's certificate. He was then employed by a rural school for a three months' term at twenty-five dollars a month.

But typhoid fever struck the Dale family. The father died and the two sons—Ed and his brother George, five years his senior—were ill for months. The school got another teacher. Then since the two brothers were experienced cowhands, they decided to go into the cattle business on a scale larger than their father's operations. They went to Kansas City and borrowed money with which they bought cattle to stock their range.

Nobody who has ever listened to Dr. Dale's classroom lectures in which he discoursed expertly on the duties of a line rider, the equipment of the chuck wagon, or the techniques of trail driving will ever forget this stage of his career. "Handling a trail herd was very much like teaching school," he used to tell his students; "you had your fast cattle at the point, then your average strung out following, and your slow ones at the drag. And no cowboy ever liked to ride

23

the drag."* When he was a graduate student at Harvard, a woman once said to him, "Mr. Dale, you look as though you have spent your life bending over dusty documents." As he related it, "I didn't tell her I got that bend in my shoulders from sitting days and nights in the saddle."

But the brothers' career as stockmen ended, as many others at that time ended, in disaster. The cow business was about over in Oklahoma, for even its western land was rapidly filling with homesteaders. The Dales, unable to meet their obligations, were obliged to sell at a loss. When their debts were paid, they each had a horse and saddle and a joint capital of fifteen dollars. Jobs were not plentiful on that bare frontier, and Ed Dale could not be particular. He began picking cotton at fifty cents a hundred pounds. The lank young cowboy found it difficult to fold his long legs to the stature of the stubby Oklahoma cotton plants; the first day he netted seventy-five cents and went to bed too tired and stiff to sleep. But he soon began to earn $1.25 a day—a very good day's picking for a grown man unaccustomed to the work.

One day a man came riding by looking for a school teacher. Dale remembered his interrupted teaching career and expressed his willingness—not to say his eagerness—to abandon the cotton field. Thus he began his work as an educator in a one-room country school at thirty-five dollars a month for a three months' term. He discovered a great joy in teaching—the same release of creative energy that an artist finds in his work. All his life he proudly spoke of himself as "a school teacher," innocently unaware that many

* Here and at other places in this essay I have quoted with the permission of my publisher from a biographical sketch I wrote of Dr. Dale in *Oklahoma: Foot-loose and Fancy-free* (Norman, University of Oklahoma Press, 1949).

college professors avoid that title by every device known to snobbery.

The Kiowa-Comanche-Apache Reservation had just been opened to settlement, and there was a homesteader on every 160 acres. Dale taught in one of the schools that these settlers with characteristic frontier courage were establishing in a region that had so recently been virgin prairie. He lived with a homesteader's family in a one-room sod dugout. Dale taught in the rural schools of this area for four years, and established a reputation as an outstanding teacher—a much more difficult achievement than to attain similar recognition in a university. Teaching thirty or more pupils from beginners of five or six, or even four, years old up to independent-minded young adults of sixteen or older required skill and understanding.

In 1906 he began to serve as superintendent of the schools in the growing towns of the region: first Headrick, which had obtained a railroad and absorbed Navajoe; then Roosevelt, in the former Kiowa-Comanche-Apache Reservation; and finally Blair, a few miles from Headrick. These promotions required more academic preparation; thus at the age of twenty-seven he began to attend summer sessions of the territorial Normal School at Edmond. This town was all of seventeen years old, so that he did not have to sleep on the prairie. He stayed with other young men at a boarding house, where "We paid ten dollars a month for bed and board and could hardly tell which was which."

The college itself had opened with twenty-three students only fifteen years before, but to the earnest young man from the range and the sod dugout, it represented an academic dream come true. He never forgot his impression of the "magnificent" building of native red sandstone and brick burned near the campus, the "great" library of more than one hundred volumes (only to see so many books together!), and the "scholarly" faculty, some of whom even had degrees. As he had never been to high school, he was enrolled "in what was very appropriately called the sub-Normal department." By attending when he could during summers and an occasional winter session he made up his high school deficits and completed the two-year college course in 1909; then went on to the University of Oklahoma, receiving his bachelor's degree with a history major in 1911. He went back to southwestern Oklahoma the following year to his super-intendent's position at Blair, meanwhile serving as special instructor at what was now the Central State Normal School at Edmond during the summers of 1912 and 1913.

Like the great and simple people from whom he sprang he had always been fascinated by the power of the printed word. At the University he had been enrolled in a course where he was expected to write a series of papers on the territorial acquisitions of the United States. (It was with James S. Buchanan. I inherited it myself a few years later.) To him this was no required assignment, but an outlet for creative powers he had barely suspected. The advance of American conquest across the continent became to this son of the frontier a great heroic epic; he had the naïve, uncon-scious imperialism of the pioneer who went out into the wilderness with the innocent intention of owning it all. With a pride too sincere for modest posing, the superintendent of the school at Blair realized that he had done a good piece of work and employed the local newspaper editor to print it.

This first published writing reveals Dale's developing phi-losophy of history. He was still influenced by the uncritical nationalism of Barnes's grade school text; he began by saying that the territorial expansion of the United States is a "very wonderful story," and closed by observing that the coming quarter century would doubtless see its continuation and that "in the light of past experience, the sovereignty and protection of the United States cannot fail to prove an unmixed blessing to any people that may come under its jurisdiction." He was to learn in later years that American expansion was indeed a *mixed* story of sordidness and heroism, but it never ceased to be for him a "very wonderful story," with the creative forces always in the ascendant.

More significant were the traits that Dr. Dale's later students learned to regard as characteristic. There was the penetrating humor that was never sarcasm. There was the clear-cut organization for effective teaching that he had learned while instructing thirty children of all ages and degrees of advancement in a one-room school with no equipment: the choice of simple words and sentence structure, and the careful transition from one chapter to the next that was so marked a feature not only of his later writing, but even of his classroom lectures. There was the happy confidence that American history was not finished and that the future chapters would be even more inspiring than the past. Most significant of all was the instinctive feeling of this undergraduate— who had not yet discovered Frederick Jackson Turner—that not all of it had occurred along the Atlantic seaboard.

He had of course received no instruction in methods of research. There was no one to call his attention to sources or to instruct him in the techniques of documentation. The University of Oklahoma was also a beginning institution. Its history faculty consisted of good classroom teachers, largely self-educated, but of sound scholarship. They at once recognized Dale's ability, and Buchanan in particular en-

couraged him to enter more advanced study. In 1913 he left
Blair and began his graduate work at Harvard, receiving his
master's degree in history in 1914. Here he learned historical
techniques, a fascinating discovery that he followed the rest
of his life with an interest that never flagged.

The history faculty, especially Turner, encouraged him
to carry on his studies in his own way without attempting to
prune his exuberance into a standard form. At the same time
he gained insights through their more mature interpretations.
One of his last books (*Frontier Ways*, 1959) was dedicated
to Turner in these revealing words:

He brought me into pastures fresh and green
By waters still he led me by the hand,
[Here his students will note the unconscious Biblical quotation]
And things, which I in youth had often seen
As meaningless, he made me understand.

To Turner's thesis that American history furnishes a con-
crete illustration of social evolution through various stages
from savagery to a complex industrial civilization, he added
from his own experience this significant particular: that only
in Oklahoma was the process rapid enough to take place
within the memory of one still living generation.

With his new degree from Harvard he came to the University of Oklahoma in 1914 as an instructor in the history
department. When I entered the University as a freshman
a year later, the students in that small frontier institution
(enrollment, about 1500) had already discovered that his
history lectures were sheer enjoyment. I saw him on the
campus, an unprofessorial figure, with his cowboy walk, his
soft voice, and his alert far-seeing eyes. I even took my required semester of American government with him during
my freshman year—a course wished off on him as a lowly

instructor—but although I found him an excellent teacher, this was not the field of his special interest. I came directly under his influence when as a junior I changed from a science to a history major. By this time he had risen to the rank of assistant professor.

He was still joyfully conscious of the research techniques he had acquired during his one graduate year at Harvard, and he instructed his students in historical methodology with all the zeal of a new convert. The term paper required in the course was a *term* paper. Every week he inspected our notes, pointing out faulty techniques, requiring the painful fixing of citations, seeing that everything went down on paper. At a final conference with each student he showed us how to organize our collected material and to follow an approved system of documentation. Then and only then did we write our paper. For myself, I can say that the method I learned from him has served me throughout the years; and it is my belief that much of the bad historical writing we read comes from faulty note-taking and note-organizing techniques. So much, for his happy confidence that a group of unpromising undergraduates were eager to enter the field of historical authorship.

I came again under Dr. Dale's direct influence as a student when I returned to the University for graduate study during 1929–31. By that time he had become well established as a scholar. He had gone back to Harvard and received his doctorate in 1922. Although he knew all phases of the westward movement, the fields of research he chose for his degrees are significant of his major lifetime interests. When he was a student at the University of Oklahoma all candidates for a bachelor's degree were required to present a thesis; he chose as his subject, "The Location of the Indian Tribes in Oklahoma." (This of course was long before the scholarly works of Grant Foreman and others in the Indian field.) At Harvard he chose as his master's thesis, "The White Settlement of Oklahoma," and for his doctoral dissertation, "The History of the Ranch Cattle Industry in Oklahoma."

Now he saw the development of the West as a larger movement than his personal observations on the Oklahoma frontier. To his practical experience in "working cattle" he had added a knowledge of the whole range industry through a research assignment from the United States Department of Agriculture. He had enlarged his early day acquaintance with Indians ("Yes, I knew Quanah Parker; he was a good man") by serving as a member of the Meriam survey staff that visited reservations throughout the United States during 1926–27. At that time he had advanced steadily in the history department: to associate professor in 1922 (the year of his Harvard doctorate), to professor in 1923, and to head of the department in 1924. But the qualities that had made him beloved of students when he came to the campus as an instructor had never changed. Everything, even in his larger field of knowledge, was reduced to human terms.

Gray-haired men and women throughout the state and the nation still remember even his mannerisms with affection. He was never known to meet a class on time, not because he was negligent but because it was so difficult to tear himself away from the delightful activities that centered around his office. Even so, there was no watching of the clock by students hoping it would soon be legal to "cut class." As he hurried in, he wolld select some carefully arranged papers from his battered brief case—for notes were sacred and had to be handled with order and system—and lay them precisely on the desk, where they would remain untouched through-

out the period. He never began immediately; the presence
of a class in the room was such an unexpected pleasure that
he needed to spend some time in greeting. Then suddenly he
launched into his lecture.

His first word swept his hearers into an enchanted land—
a land of wild and virgin beauty as it lay brooding through
the centuries. Over it moved the soft-footed native, loving
and merging with the setting; the cowpuncher, watching his
herd beneath the lonely splendor of the stars; the rugged
settler, with the bare poverty around him and the light of
the future in his eyes. And there were conquistadores, explorers, mountain men, prospectors—every one an individual person. And all through the lecture was a sparkling
thread of joyous humor that differed from the professorial
"joke" as the mountain stream differs from the fireplug. At
the exact end of the period he would come to a complete
and rounded conclusion, and the sentence pointing to the
subject of the next day's lecture was delivered with the
sound of the closing bell. Any person who has ever come
under the spell of his narrative is forever disqualified from
making an unbiased estimate of the man's life and work.

Almost as important as his lectures were his individual
contacts with his students and the people of the state. "I have
yet to be convinced," he once said, "that a grouchy temper
is a sure indication of scholarship." People poured into his
office in streams and overflowed into his seminar room—all
kinds of people, youngsters in trouble, returned alumni,
important looking official delegations, Indians, graduate students in grim pursuit of knowledge. And always he was the
same—listening more than he talked, but talking a great deal,
courteous with the courtesy of unaffected interest. And
Oklahoman that he was, he nearly always found some com-

mon ground of experience: "Of course I remember your
mother; she used to live in—" or, "And so you come from
Blair; do you remember Old Man—."

Once I was working in his seminar room when he brought
in a fullblood Kiowa couple: a very pretty woman who
spoke good English, and her older husband who sat impas-
sive, apparently not understanding a word. Dr. Dale and the
woman fell to talking about Indian costumes. He showed her
a photograph he had used in one of his books—a beautiful,
graceful girl with rich fringe and beadwork dripping from
her buckskin dress. The tears rushed into her black eyes; she
cried, "That's my picture. Where did you get it?" The
professor was almost as excited as she. He had picked it up
somewhere and had never expected to meet the original. He
carefully autographed a copy of the book and courteously
presented it. One knew how she would treasure it. Then
other Kiowas drifted in and they began to talk of Satank, the
proud old war chief who raided in Texas back in 1871 and
then chose death to captivity. The old man still sat propped
against the wall. Suddenly his voice boomed out in a wild
chant. He was singing Satank's death song! The very song
the old warrior had sung just before he forced his captors to
kill him! The others translated it excitedly. It went somewhat
like this:

> "O sun, you remain forever;
> But we warriors must die.
> O earth, you remain forever;
> But we warriors must die."

Such contacts added together made up the sum of his
approach to history. Even an issue like the need of the trans-
Appalachian frontiersmen to navigate the Mississippi was
seen through an individual experience. One of his Kentucky

forebears packed a flatboat with the year's produce and painfully moved it down the river, only to have it confiscated by Spanish officials at New Orleans. He returned on foot, and one could understand how he cursed Spain and the indifference of the Eastern Establishment at every step.

Thus to Dr. Dale, historical events were not abstractions, but human motives in action. He not only gave his regular courses from that perspective, but he introduced innovative ones. At the present time Indian history is being offered in many colleges, but he anticipated this movement by more than forty years. As early as 1930 he alone among academic historians saw that "Throughout the tapestry of American history there is woven the red thread of the Indian," and he added that course to his department—a subject as foreign to contemporary historical interest as a history of Kazakhstan. He also encouraged his graduate students to choose Indian studies as research assignments, from seminar papers to doctorial dissertations.

He trained these same graduate students in habits of intellectual integrity. Although his most extensive influence was with the undergraduates who crowded his lectures, his graduate students were special. He urged them to make a critical evaluation of sources. "Be like the cowboy, who said, 'The devil may not be so bad; the Other Fellow wrote the Book.' " He told them to broaden their techniques. Again a cowboy made the point, this time as a bad example. He had recently married, and someone inquired about his wife. "You know I feel bad about that woman," he answered. "She broke her leg, so I had to shoot her." And always backing up his methodology was his comprehensive scholarship. His students discovered that their independent findings simply filled in the outlines, but never changed the facts of his over-all view.

Even so, his viewpoint both in its breadth and its limitations was the viewpoint of the American pioneer. In spite of his careful discipline as a research historian he remained the "Average Man" of his verses. This gave him a strength that many historians lack. He was able to read a Government document and visualize instantly what its translation into action would mean to the individual people whose lives would be affected. He could penetrate human motives with an accuracy impossible to one whose training had been mainly academic. He had a shrewd grasp of economics based on sympathy with individual struggles to make a living. His commitment to democracy was not a theory, but a Jacksonian reality.

On the other hand, although he knew European history, he saw it only as a series of personal narratives like a historical novel. Diplomacy and world politics for him did not exist; he could visualize people, but not peoples. Imperialism, if he thought of it at all, was the march of civilization across the waste places of the earth. Even in his interpretation of the frontier spirit he seemed to ignore the predatory forces that warped its creative urge.

The disillusionment of modern thinkers awakened his amusement and surprise: it seemed so artificial and insincere. In 1924 I visited him in his office after a year of graduate study in a great Northern university. There I had found the history faculty in a state of shock. They had put their faith in the international idealism of Woodrow Wilson, and the American people had deserted him. They saw the ordered life of Europe in collapse, and at home Harding scandals were breaking every day in new headlines. They were convinced

that nothing could be learned from the past; the only reason
for studying history was the intellectual pleasure of knowing
it. There was no human progress. When I told Dr. Dale that
they denied the idea of progress, his face lighted up in a
smile of utter incredulity. "What nonsense," was all he said.

For his whole philosophy of history was summed up in
that one word: Progress. The whole course of human life
moved upward toward the stars; and Oklahoma, because of
the rapidity of its development, occupied the most interesting place in the procession. Unlike Turner, who could
explain the influence of the frontier, but was somewhat
vague about the next stage, he regarded the future as the
most interesting advance of all. The material forces had been
conquered; the dream of the pioneer had been realized; it
was the next task to make similar conquests in the realm of
culture, the kingdom of the spirit, the achievement of the
larger life. Perhaps he erred in assuming that this final development would be automatic. Perhaps the exposure of the
corrupt acts he largely ignored is necessary in attaining this
better society. But he was confident that the hardihood
developed in taming the wilderness would win this greater
battle, and he had full confidence in its ultimate triumph.

Possibly this "Average Man" sensed more truly than the
despairing intellectual the course of history. But whether his
philosophy were true or false, he voiced the deepest feelings
of the society that formed his faith. He knew that dreams
come true; he had seen the dramatic power of their fulfil-
ment. The homesteader's "claim," with its unturned sod, its
family dwelling a dugout in the creek bank, and its tethered
team and cow became a prosperous farmstead. The raw new
town with boundless ambitions became a pleasant community center with tree-shaded streets and civic spirit, or a busy

city cutting the clear air with its skyline. He himself had come up from the aspiring would-be teacher sleeping on the prairie to a scholar whose word was heard beyond the seas.

For his fame soon traveled to other schools, and he received many invitations to serve as a visiting professor or a special lecturer. First in 1926 he went to the University of Texas, an institution very similar to his own. But next came William and Mary, where he fairly reveled in the atmosphere of the old colonial capital of Williamsburg. "I was a new sort of professor to them," he said whimsically, "but they seemed to like it." (He served there twice.) Also there were the universities of Nebraska, Missouri, Ohio State, Duke, Michigan, Wyoming—and so on.

In 1952 he reached the age when he became emeritus professor of research at Oklahoma. But the following year he spent in Australia as Fulbright lecturer at the University of Melbourne, where he conducted courses on "The American West" and "American History and Institutions." He also lectured widely at universities and to other groups throughout the Commonwealth, making the same Oklahoma-type of friendships on the other side of the world.

He served as visiting professor at the University of Houston during 1954–55, and went back later as the M. D. Anderson Professor of History through 1958–59. Eventually his activity was curtailed by advancing age, but he always spent some time in his office. He was immensely gratified when the new history building on the Oklahoma campus was given his name. The last time I ever saw him he led me to his front window and pointed out the tower clearly visible from his home.

Thus his long career as a teacher came to a fitting end. But his words are echoed not only from classrooms in that building but in many classrooms and from many typewriters. Once I discovered to my chagrin that in several places in my own writing and even in the title of a book I had been guilty of flagrant, though unintentional, plagarism. I wrote to him to express my regret. He answered:

"I feel flattered that you should find yourself unconsciously using my own words in your writing. I really appreciate your feeling that I have been able to contribute something to your work. Let me know how it comes on and if I can help you in any way you know you have only to ask me. It is a great satisfaction to see my former students doing things worthwhile because the time is fast coming when you are the ones who must carry the torch."

He could have said the same—and no doubt did say it—to a vast concourse of men and women he had taught. Thus his teaching goes on.

Edward Everett Dale: The Man

John S. Ezell

In December, 1947, as a young historian in my first semester of teaching, I attended my first meeting of the American Historical Association. Like most neophytes, I hoped to see, hear, and perhaps meet some of the leaders of the profession, known only as authors of books I had read and admired. The crush of historians boded well for the celebrity seeker, but faithful attendance at numerous sessions quickly brought home one lesson of conventioneering—the patriarchs of the clan seldom give papers, other than presidential addresses!

Consequently, my wife Jean and I bought tickets to the banquet. In the large hall we found scores of tables rapidly filling, and quickly slipped into two empty chairs. One of our companions was most conspicuous: a commanding personality with a high-pitched voice, silver hair, and finely-chiseled features. He first smoked a cigar, then numerous cigarettes, before finally settling down to obvious enjoyment of a well-worn pipe. Throughout the meal the entire table listened to his stories which seemed to flow from an inexhaustible store.

At the conclusion of the dinner and the presidential address, our unknown table mate showed no haste to leave, but relit his pipe and turned to us. "I am E. E. Dale from the University of Oklahoma," he said, and with that began our long association with one of the finest men of the profession. I was not a western historian, but no student of American social and intellectual history could fail to recognize the author of *The Range Cattle Industry* and *Cow Country*. His role as "Two-gun Dale," while a graduate student at Harvard during the Boston police strike, was also a familiar one.

It soon became obvious that this gentle man wanted to talk about us. He was not being polite or condescending, but was genuinely interested. My wife was born in Texas, and he had been also; he and I had degrees from the same graduate school. He knew most of my professors, and had even gone to school with some of them. When he asked how we liked our present position and if we would be interested in a move to the University of Oklahoma, we quickly assured him that we would. He then suggested that I send my file to the chairman, and that he would "put in a good word" for us. Although I sent the papers as promised, I considered his words a mere gesture of kindness and did not believe either of us to be seriously committed. To my utter amazement, a few weeks later I received, not a request for an interview, but a firm offer of employment! I now suppose that I am the last man employed by this University who had never been on the campus and who had been seen by only one member of the faculty. Moreover, on my side of the story, all I knew about the school was that it was the home of E. E. Dale and the University of Oklahoma Press. Afterward I claimed that I was not hired because of my credentials, but because he liked my lovely redheaded wife. He never denied it, but always smiled at this joke between us.

The year 1948 was a boom one at the University of Oklahoma, and housing was at a premium. We learned of a new apartment that might be available, and Jean immediately wrote to Dr. Dale promising to bake him a cake if he would recommend us. His reply was a poem in which he vowed to put a hex on the landlord if we were turned down. Thus, we learned once more that our newfound friend put in "a good word" for us and that he was a poet of no mean ability. Of course, we got the apartment, he got the cake, and another strand was woven in the web of friendship.

Needless to say, our first social contact upon arriving in Norman was with the Dales. From the first time we met E. E. Dale's wife, Rosalie, we began thinking of them as "the Dales." We learned that she had been a student assistant in French at the University when Dale was a history instructor. They met when he attended a French class that she taught. Later, he arranged to have her tutor him for his French examination at Harvard. Three years later, when he was forty, he persuaded her to give up her own career as a high school teacher and to marry him.

Hardly had we unpacked our bags than we experienced the first of countless numbers of memorable hours in their homes. First in the large, rambling, white frame house on Norman's Main Street, with its spacious, shaded yard and flower beds, fruit trees, and grapevines; then, later, in its modern brick replica close to the campus. The large, book-lined rooms, highlighted by Indian arts and crafts and Rosalie's antiques, exuded an air of comfort and fellowship. The large dining table groaned under the weight of good food. Whether at that table, or the bridge table (later canasta), free and easy conversation was the order of the day. No topic was foreign to Dale's interest, and, inevitably, he was able to add some little-known historical fact, a personal experience, or tell a humorous story which enlivened the discussion. His experiences as a farmer, cowboy, teacher, and as "Many White Horses," the name bestowed upon him with his adoption by the Blackfeet, gave authenticity to any story which he told.

Playing cards with him was an experience to remember. Rosalie generally "played by the book," and her partner could predict her actions. But Dale played cards as he did most things—with gusto and daring and "by the seat of his pants," often to the discomfiture of his partner and opponents. He loved to win and seemed to defy the law of averages in that respect. This is not meant to suggest that he was single-minded in his playing, for I soon concluded that his almost steady stream of anecdotes was part of his strategy. I must confess that often I could not remember which cards had been played; but then I didn't care.

As wonderful as a visit to their home was, something even more enjoyable was an invitation for a weekend at their cabin in the Arbuckle Mountains in southern Oklahoma. This structure, which they owned for over thirty years, was located at the top of a steep cliff overlooking a stream. Spacious and comfortable, it was not cluttered with modern conveniences like running water and indoor plumbing. Besides chairs and numerous beds, it was dominated, naturally, by a large table for eating and card-playing and a wood-burning cast-iron cooking range. To arrive at this aerie, however, one first had to climb—and I do mean climb—the seventy-two steps leading up to the kitchen door. Up these steps also were carried the supplies, fireplace wood, and water which was fetched from a spring below. I still remember with admiration the long-legged ease with which Dale ascended these heights, although he was nearly forty years my senior.

These expeditions usually began on a Friday afternoon after school. Following a drive of a couple of hours, there was usually only time for hauling supplies up those steps. So Saturday was the big day, and that meant that fishing was the principal item of business if the weather permitted. As one would expect, Dale always had enough tackle for everyone. Always the perfect host, he would point out the best fishing places along the free-running stream and invite young and old to try to outdo the monster that he had caught "right there" on some previous expedition. Like his card playing, he fished for "fun," and so a good time was had by all, even if the fish did not always co-operate. But if they did, then there was fresh fish for supper or breakfast.

Dale was the cook on these occasions, and his menu, though varied, usually featured the dishes he had cooked when a cowboy on the range. Two specialties were pot roast and baked beans done in a style of which he was justifiably very proud. His cooking chores were usually punctuated by observations that what was wrong with this country was "too damn many one-egg men in it!" Or if his boiled coffee seemed overpowering, he always stoutly maintained, "There is no such thing as too-strong coffee—only too-weak men." But while Dale was "long" on cooking, dishwashing was not one of his favorite chores. The "volunteers" were usually decided by a game of pitch, and Dale seldom was a loser. It should be said in his behalf, however, that "cleaning up" his dishes always seemed like fun.

In later years, when the steps became too steep for even Dale to climb, the locale of these weekends shifted to the family farm on the edge of the Wichita Wild Life Refuge. This land had been won by Dale and his brother in the lottery for the Kiowa-Comanche lands. As the saying goes, "getting there was half the fun." Driving through miles of timbered hills and rolling meadows, past herds of buffalo, elk, and longhorns and prairie dog towns, one arrived at the homestead of this man who so epitomized the Old West.

Here was the same comfort and warm companionship which characterized his home and Arbuckle cabin. There was a large pond for fishermen, horses to ride and baby animals to enchant the children, and acres of cotton or wheat that encouraged elders to talk about weather, insects, crop prices, and what the countryside was like sixty years before. A trip for groceries to one of the nearby small towns was a fascinating glimpse into the world of the farmers and a lesson in the ease with which Dale could fit that role also.

It was a wonderful experience for a young historian to work in a department with a person like Dale. Here was a man, who, in the vernacular, "had it made." Already he had achieved the highest honors that his University had to offer. His position in the profession was secure, and he had been president of the national societies in his areas of interest. When I arrived on the campus, I can recall no one telling me that I must "publish or perish." Likewise, I cannot remember anyone using a twelve-hour teaching load to excuse a lack of research. My office was across a narrow hall from Dale's, and all I had to do was look through his door—which was never closed—and see him working at his desk or hosting visitors who took advantage of his open door.

One thing I quickly learned was that apparently everyone who came to Norman knew Dale, or wanted to, and that most of them were future or former students of his. Once you were his student, you were likewise his friend, and he would remember you and never be too busy to reminisce, congratulate you on your major and minor triumphs, and counsel with you on your problems and future. He suffered bores, if not gladly, at least patiently. Unlike Will Rogers, he perhaps could not say that he had never met a man he did not like, but he certainly tried to like them all. I can recall too many times for comfort, however, when in the brashness of youth I was critical of a colleague, and he gently reproved me, not by glossing over the fault of which I complained, but rather by pointing out mitigating circumstances or strong points that I had ignored in my assessment.

His common ploy was to tell of a more serious error he had made or an amusing tale of some friend in like predicament, thus easing the sting. Several of my favorite Dale stories, which have become a part of my own philosophy, illustrate this facet of his character. In the first, a young professor, whom I will call Joe, was struck by the fact that as his colleagues became older many lost the spark of vitality that had made them good teachers and productive scholars. Joe and some of his friends discussed this phenomenon with intensity, and the matter ended with Joe extracting a promise from his comrades that they would tell him when he "began to slip." With the passage of time, age came to Joe, as to all men, and he began to show it. His friends talked about his decline and their promise concerning it. Finally, one of their number was deputized to break the news to Joe. He began, "Joe, you know that you have always said you wanted to be told when you began to slip." Whereupon Joe interrupted with, "Yes, and I want you to be sure and tell me the minute I start!"

One of the stories that Dale told with the greatest glee concerned his own official retirement, if he ever could be said to have really retired. On the occasion of his becoming a professor *emeritus*, his friends decided that the event deserved special recognition, and so a little ceremony was planned at which they could pay him honor. After the usual accolades, the formal program ended. One of those in attendance, a local shopkeeper, rushed up to Dale, shook his hand

44

and declared: "I want to congratulate you upon this great honor. They should have done it for you years ago."

If Dale ever "slipped," his colleagues were none the wiser. Although he was past seventy when he received his "great honor," he later taught in Australia for a year and several more at the University of Houston. At home, he was always ready to "pinch-hit" at any time, to the unfailing pleasure of the lucky students involved. Even when his official teaching days were over, he shamed the rest of us by appearing at his office in the early morning and working through the day until he was usually the last man to leave. And this, mark you, was during his eighth and ninth decades.

Aside from an increasing appearance of frailty, about the only concession that Dale made to age was the loss of some of his hearing. As those who knew him were aware, he held no "truck" with such things as bi or trifocal glasses and merely accumulated separate pairs which were rotated into position as the occasion required. When his hearing began to fail, he had an aid built into the frame of one set of his glasses. The friendly joke, which he enjoyed, was that after this addition you watched until he put on the glasses with the aid to ask a question or make a comment; otherwise, without that particular pair, he talked uninterruptedly.

Although he was a stern taskmaster as far as his own labor was concerned, he was never too busy to help others. I recall with pleasure the many occasions when he would lay aside his pen—only in his later years did he dictate to a secretary—to discuss a teaching or research problem with a colleague. He was literally a walking gold mine to be exploited for thesis topics, articles, or books. As he had taught a broad spectrum of courses, his knowledge of bibliography was phenomenal in many fields. His standards of scholarship were inspiring, and his listeners were left no doubts that the historian was of a special breed and by the nature of his profession had a greater responsibility for care and honesty. This was not only the hallmark of his career, but it also elicited his special commendation when it was obvious in the work of others.

Certainly one of the most endearing personal characteristics of E. E. Dale was that he never took himself too seriously. A large portion of his humor found him the butt of his own jokes, although usually, as with most of his wit, a good point was made. I remember many years ago when the campus was going through one of its recurring spasms of trying to come up with ways and means of improving teaching, some of the younger faculty decided to hold a seminar to discuss how this greatly desired end might best be accomplished. One afternoon as we were leaving the building that housed the history department offices, Dale was approached by one of the ringleaders of the seminar and asked: "Aren't you going to the teaching seminar?" Upon receiving a negative reply, the unwise professor pressed the issue: "Don't you want to be a better teacher?" Dale's answer has given me food for thought ever since. "Hell, I am not half as good a teacher now as I know how to be!" How many of us are half as honest?

Another classic story occurred in his class on western history in which one of his books was used as a text. One day he made a correction in the book and remarked to the class that he felt sure it would be all right with the author for them to change the material. One of his female students expressed the view that perhaps they should not make this alteration without first checking with the author to see if he approved. Dale agreed, and she was delegated the responsibility for contacting the author and letting him know that they believed he had made an error. She promptly wrote to the publisher to forward this message to Edward Everett Dale. In time she received an answer from the author in the same circuitous manner stating that their professor was right and thanking her for bringing the matter to his attention. Dale then asked her to read the letter to the class and it was not until she read it aloud that the sameness of E. E. Dale, her teacher, and Edward Everett Dale, the author, became red-facedly apparent to her!

As I have mentioned, Dale was a versifier of no mean talent. I would like to quote one of his efforts because of its subject matter and because it is so typical of his gentle irony.

THE HISTORY PROFESSOR'S LAMENT

Dear distant friend, I seat myself
To write a little line
And ask the news of you and yours
And tell of me and mine.
There isn't very much to tell
Except of grief and toil.
The wheels of Time go round as though
They're greased with lightning oil.
I rise each morning with the lark
And eat my egg and prune
Then work until it's almost dark
With just a snack at noon.
My wife remains at home all day
To sweep and dust and scrub
She boils and fries and bakes the pies
And cooks the daily grub.

Before my class I talk for hours
Of presidents of mighty powers
And tell how old King Ferdinand
Sent young Columbus out to land

Upon our shores in search of spices
That he could buy at cheaper prices.
I fairly rave and saw the air
And students doze in every chair
And while they dream of college shops
Where swarthy fuzzy-headed fops
Hie back and forth with glasses tall
Of lemonade or coke for all.
Between my classes chaps come in
And park themselves and then begin
To tell their troubles, grief and woe
And ask me why they're flunking so.
They talk until the world looks flat
And I don't know just where I'm at.

But on the days I give a quiz
I square the score, for then it is
Each student wrinkles up his brow
And tries to answer when and how
The Vandals, Hottentots and Huns
Spiked all the Romans' heavy guns
Or how the Yankees one by one
Took nostalgia at old Bull Run.
The perspiration you can bet
Rolls down each face in gobs of sweat
And falls on names of kings and queens
In drops as large as pinto beans
And groans galore and many a sigh
To grief and sorrow testify.

Too bad!—their troubles soon are done
And mine, alas! have just begun.
I lose religion, temper, sight
In reading what these heathens write
Scan every line and read between
And try to figure what they mean
If anything—and what they've made,
For I at last must make the grade.
So when at last the sun goes down

Below the prairie bleak and brown
And I start for home with dragging feet
To get a little bite to eat.
I feel too tired to sally out
And with the giddy gad about.
So wife and I sit home and chat
Of him and her and this and that
And very often talk of you
And wish that you could be there too
To tell us jokes and laugh with us
And oftentimes the weather cuss,
But since you're not, quite soon we say
"I guess we'd better hit the hay,"
Then sleep until the rooster crow
Bids me arise again and go.
So goes each day for me and wife.
O say, ain't that an awful life?

Perhaps the nearest that Dale ever came to summarizing the forces that made him such a unique person was in 1952 when the University of Oklahoma selected him for its highest honor—a Distinguished Service Citation. In accepting the award, he said: "My philosophy of achievement embodies only these two points: that one devote whatever talents and abilities he may have to unselfish service, and to continue his efforts so long as he is blessed with sufficient health and strength to do his work because I am sure that one who does that can have no fear of life—nor of death." So he kept on working, tirelessly. Twenty years later when death took him away, true to his creed, he was putting the final touches on his autobiography.

In retrospect, in the classroom he was a stimulating teacher, attracting large undergraduate enrollments and graduate students from many states. His personal warmth, quick wit, sharp memory, and endless supply of stories made

49

him appealing to people in all ranks of life. His great popularity was enhanced by a willingness to share his time and knowledge with all who asked, and the fact that even his oldest acquaintances cannot recall his ever making a disparaging remark about anyone. Edward Everett Dale personified what the terms "friendship," "Old West," "model teacher," and "historian" should mean. To use one of his own terms, he rode tall in the saddle.

II. Work

Cowboy Schoolmaster*

The great land lottery of 1901 ended on October 4th but for several months more the land offices at Lawton and El Reno were kept busy. Many persons who drew "lucky numbers" and filed on homesteads were town or city dwellers who knew nothing of farming and had no desire to learn. Most of these sold their claims before the end of the six months period which the law gave them to make actual settlement on the homestead. Tracts of 160 acres were sold for five or six hundred dollars that were eventually worth fifteen to twenty thousand.

If George and I had gone into the real estate business we might have done very well, but our only desire was to get settled on our own beautiful claim and start improving it. Obviously our first task was to build a house, so we drew the rest of the money due us from the sale of our Greer County land. We then hauled the necessary material from Hobart, twenty-five miles north of our claim, and hired a "jack leg carpenter" who lived near Navajoe. With our help he built us a box house sixteen feet long and fourteen feet wide. The site was some fifty yards from the middle of the west line of our land and about the same distance from the bank of the creek. We bought a small cook stove which we felt would also provide enough heat. Other furnishings included beds, chairs, a cupboard, cooking utensils, and dishes we brought

* From Edward Everett Dale's unpublished autobiography.

from our former home near Navajoe, for Jay and his wife had their own furniture and did not need that of our father's.

By the time we were settled in our new home it was mid-November. George's leg was again troubling him so he returned to the hospital at Mangum. He was gone for three weeks and the next day after he left, a fierce blizzard struck bringing sleet and snow. As a result, I lived alone in our new home for that entire time without seeing another human soul! We had neighbors less than a mile away but the weather was so bad that no one ventured out if it could be avoided.

Fortunately, I had laid in an ample supply of food and by staying close to the little stove it was possible to keep warm. The first couple of days were lonely ones but I soon became adjusted to living alone. Three or four books including a thick, one volume history of the United States and a copy of Longfellow's poems were read and studied with great care. When tired of reading, I sometimes found entertainment in writing verses of my own. Some of these were published a quarter of a century later in my little volume of verse, *The Prairie Schooner and Other Poems*. I would also occasionally venture out with my little Remington rifle for a brief and slippery stroll along the timber-bordered stream hoping to bag a squirrel. Sometimes I was successful and found squirrel stew with drop dumplings a refreshing change from a diet largely of bacon, beans, sour dough biscuits, syrup and dried fruit.

The long period of bitter cold ended at long last and the snow and sleet were quickly melted by the warm winter sun. George came home in high spirits for his bad leg was much better, and I was delighted to see him after my three weeks of living by myself.

As we checked our resources, however, we found that building our new home and paying George's medical bills, added to living expenses, had left us again virtually penniless. Moreover, there seemed to be no way of earning money as cotton picking was over and in the winter months neither farmers nor ranchmen needed help.

The long period of cold weather had reduced the fuel supply of many of the settlers in Greer County and some of our former neighbors soon came to us asking that we sell them some wood. Living for years on the prairie of Greer County had given both George and me a love for a growing tree fully equal to that of Joyce Kilmer. There were many dead or half dead trees along the creek, however, and some dry logs or branches on the ground. These we gladly sold, and while we were not paid much for a wagonload of wood our income from this source was enough to keep us supplied with groceries for a few months.

In addition to reserving a 320 acre tract of land at the county seat towns of Lawton, Hobart, and Anadarko as townsites, the federal government had set aside three or four other townsites of 160 acres each. One of these was about three miles southeast of our place. Here the thriving village of Mountain Park had grown up. By November it had three or four general merchandise stores, a hotel, blacksmith shop, meat market, barber shop, and a population of nearly a thousand.

One day I rode over to Mountain Park to get the mail and have my hair cut. The barber had just finished with me and I was putting on my coat when a long, lanky chap came in and said to him:

"Jim, if you're goin' up to Hobart this week I wish you'd ask that County Superintendent of Schools to send us a teacher. Our school house is just about finished and we want to start school a week from Monday if we can find a teacher."

"Here's a teacher right here," said the barber, "and he's a good 'un. Mr. Dale, this is Dick Robinson."

As a matter of fact, Barber Jim did not know whether I was a "good 'un" or not but only that I had taught a short term of school in Greer County. The rest of his statement was only guess work.

Mr. Robinson explained to me that he lived about twelve miles southeast of Mountain Park and was one of the three trustees of the Deep Red School District. He added that the other trustees were in town for they had all come up to get a load of feed for their cattle. If I would consider teaching their school we could go and see them and settle the matter at once.

The idea appealed to me very much especially after meeting the other two trustees who seemed to be men of high type. Within fifteen minutes it was agreed that I should teach their school for three months at a salary of forty dollars a month to be paid in district school warrants. These would probably have to be discounted at a bank although they drew six per cent interest until they were paid.

When I asked about a place to board, Dick Robinson said that he and his wife didn't have much room but if I didn't mind that, they would be glad to have me board with them. He added that they lived only a quarter of a mile from the school house. I assured him that I was not accustomed to "much room" and it was agreed that the Robinsons would board me for eight dollars a month which included payment for pasturage and feed for Steve.

George received the news of my school teaching job with

mixed feelings. Naturally, he hated to be left to bach all alone, but realized that we had to eat and with the coming of spring we would not be able to sell enough firewood to replenish our supply of groceries already alarmingly low. So the offer of forty dollars to teach school came like manna from Heaven.

On the Sunday afternoon before the Monday set for the opening of school, I mounted Steve and with a sack holding my spare clothes and a few books tied behind my saddle set out for my new job. It was easy to find the Robinson place but a bit shocking to realize that when Dick said he "didn't have much room" he had told the truth—and how! His house was a single room about eighteen feet long and fourteen feet wide. It was on the south side of a small hill and the rear half was largely underground although the floor was level with the front yard.

The furniture consisted of two double beds extending along the west wall. Between the footboards of these there was only room for a couple of trunks. The cook stove was in the northeast corner of the room with a cupboard beside it. The dining table on the east side, half a dozen chairs and a shelf east of the door held a water pail, tin dipper and washpan.

Dick and his wife gave me a most cordial welcome and introduced me to their sister-in-law who was visiting them. They brought forward their three children, Geneva, about eight years old, Elmer, who was six, and Clarence, four.

After a good supper we sat and visited for a couple of hours. The Robinsons were from Wise County, Texas where Dick's father owned six or seven hundred acres of land and a cotton gin. Dick had farmed some of this land as a renter but wanted a home of his own so had come out and registered for the lottery. Failing to draw a number below 6,500 he had bought this place for four or five hundred dollars.

About nine o'clock Clarence was asleep on his mother's lap and Dick suggested that he and I go out to the well and get a cool drink before going to bed. He drew up a bucket of water and after drinking we sat down on the well curb and continued our conversation for about ten minutes. During this time we could hear the women moving about in the house and dropping shoes. Finally all was still inside and the light shining through the window grew dim so he remarked that he was sleepy and we'd better get to bed.

When we got inside, I saw that the two women and Geneva and Clarence were in the north bed and the south one, next to the door had the covers turned back for Dick and me with young Elmer crosswise at our feet. Dick got in bed next to the wall and I blew out the lamp, hung my outer garments on a chair within easy reach and slipped into bed on the front side. As was customary at that time and for many years more, all men and boys slept in their underwear. No one in that region had ever heard of pajamas and only an occasional very old man slept in a nightgown and cap.

The last thing I remember before falling asleep was wondering about how to get my pants on the next morning. It proved very easy. When I woke it was broad daylight and Dick was up and outside doing the feeding and milking. The women were both up and cooking breakfast, diligently keeping their backs toward my bed. I reached and retrieved my trousers, slipped them under the covers and hunched up my knees to make a small tent of the covers. Under this it was easy to pull on my pants and then sit up to put on shirt, pivot around to get my feet on the floor, and slip on socks and shoes. I was then fully dressed and needed only to wash and comb my hair to be ready for breakfast.

It might be said now that for the next three months this was my method of dressing. By that time it had become a fixed habit and even when there was no necessity for it, I continued to dress in bed.

Immediately after breakfast Dick and I went to the school-house. Except for a chair and small table for the teacher supplied by one of the school board members it had no furniture. The twenty by thirty foot room had been swept clean, however, and there was a water bucket and long-handled tin dipper in one corner, and a wood burning stove in the middle of the room. There was also an axe and a pile of wood outside. Dick said that the children had been told to bring chairs or stools as seats and the big boys would chop wood and bring water from a nearby neighbor's well. He added that the board would have some benches made as soon as the neighborhood carpenter could get around to it.

The lack of a blackboard troubled me a little but I had brought a thick pencil tablet with me and when Dick left me for his own work, I nailed this to the wall behind my table. Figures and exercises could be written large on this with a soft pencil and the sheet torn off when something else was needed. I also had a small bell, a relic of my Clabber Flat teaching, to be used in summoning the kids to work.

About eight-thirty I saw through a south window two tall, lean teenage girls coming. Each had some books under one arm and was carrying an empty red powder can, evidently tossed aside by the construction crew building a railroad a couple of miles to the west. When they came through the door the girls both curtsied most politely to me. They then placed their books on the floor, seated themselves on the powder cans and were apparently ready for school.

Other children soon began to arrive each carrying a chair, stool, or short bench. In one or two instances parents brought the youngsters and chairs for them in a wagon, but as a rule the children came alone bringing their lunches in a tin pail and an assortment of text books. At nine o'clock I rang the bell and those playing outside trooped in. Two boys had failed to bring anything to sit on, but I found a couple of nail kegs and a short board outside which provided a precarious bench.

A count revealed that there were thirty-two pupils ranging in age from six to sixteen. From them I learned that the former home of most of them had been Texas. The Hash and "Widder Grubb" families that were closely related, however, were from the mountainous part of Virginia, the Mounts from Colorado and the Thompsons from Indian Territory where Mr. Thompson owned and operated a large general store. He was regarded as well-to-do by his neighbors, most of whom were quite poor.

It was not possible to do much the first day except get the names and ages of the children, find out how far they had gone in school and organize classes. None of the very young had been in school before or knew the letters of the alphabet, and some of the nine or eleven year olds had attended school only three or fourth months and had not gone beyond the First Reader. Some of the older ones would now be classified as the fourth or fifth grade and two or three might have reached the sixth. Without exception, however, every one of these thirty-two children was very intelligent, and eager to learn.

Within two or three days we had settled down to work

in happy fashion. I liked these kids and they liked me. Their text books from various states were sent to town and the book dealer gave a generous price for them in an exchange for the adopted texts used in Oklahoma Territory. In a couple of weeks the local carpenter delivered us ten long benches which solved the problem of seating. We still had no desks and no blackboard but we got along very well without them. Two of the benches were put in front of my table for the use of classes when called, and a thick pencil tablet nailed to the wall served in lieu of a blackboard. The other long seats were placed well to the rear of the room in order that my hearing classes would not interfere too much with the studies of the other pupils.

About the first of May came a startling interlude, when a tornado from the northwest struck the schoolhouse, moving it some thirty or forty feet to the southeast. Fortunately, it remained upright but the seats were overturned and the kids and I all fell flat on the floor. The south side of the roof was split and a heavy rain which came behind the wind poured in. The youngsters, all crying and wailing as they got to their feet, earnestly asked me:

"Perfessor, will there be another 'un?"

I assured them that there would not be and looked them over to see if any were hurt. One boy had a small knot on his forehead and a little six-year-old girl was sobbing that her back was hurt. I sat down, took her on my lap and unbuttoned the back of her little dress and found a blue spot about the size of a dime between her shoulders. I rubbed it a bit, told her that she was not hurt, and she stopped crying. With the help of the boys we moved all the seats to the dry side of the room and when the children's parents arrived, white-faced and trembling, they found their offspring running and sliding on the wet floor near the south side of the room!

School was dismissed for a couple of days while the men got the building back on its foundation and the roof mended. For the rest of the term, however, when a dark cloud appeared to blot out the sun, all the kids in the room became so fidgety and nervous that I had to call a recess and send them outside. Once out of the building where they could keep an eye on the clouds, their nervousness vanished as if by magic and they instantly began to play with enthusiasm a game of town-ball, shinny or "blackman." Feeling that they were "playing me for a sucker," I would ring the bell and call them in, but immediately their jittery nervousness returned and there seemed nothing to do but either to give another recess or dismiss school for the day and send them home.

Most persons today would view with horror the prospect of living for three months with a family of five in a home of only one fairly large room. They would feel that life under such conditions must be a sordid and unhappy one. Nothing could be further from the truth. Mrs. Robinson kept the little home scrupulously clean and provided us with three meals of plain, substantial food every day. The children were always quiet and well-behaved when in the house but they were playing outside most of the time until dark and were put to bed soon after supper.

I have never known a more modest, kindly, and considerate family than the Robinsons. Once accustomed to dressing under the bed covers every morning and going to the well each evening for a drink of cool water while Mrs. Robinson retired, it became quite natural. Any preparation of lessons, reading or grading of papers could be done at the schoolhouse after four o'clock when the children had gone home. As far as a bath, nobody in the entire region took more than one a week, usually Saturday night, and very few that often. I usually went home on weekends where I could take a dip in the creek or in a wash tub if the water in the stream was too cold.

Teaching at Deep Red was a most happy experience. The children were good as gold and even the beginners made a remarkable advance in this brief term of three months. The three or four to whom I had to teach the alphabet could read quite well by the end of the term and spell correctly every word in the Primer including "cylinder" which is more than can be said for some of my former students in college!

The school term ended about the first of June. I bought about twenty pounds of mixed candy as a "treat" for the children, and hid it in the barn. After the Robinson kids were sound asleep I brought this in and poured it out on the table. Mrs. Robinson and Dick helped me to put it into the small paper bags which had been given me. These were placed in a large wooden box and concealed under a bed, with Dick voicing some regreat that Elmer could not have seen the "big pile of candy on our table."

School ended the next day with classes as usual until afternoon recess but this final period was devoted to a program of readings, songs, and the awarding of some prizes. These were attractive books with colored pictures that I bought to be given for excellence in spelling or arithmetic and to the child who had made the most progress in all studies. Then the bags of candy were distributed and goodbyes were said, sometimes accompanied by tears of some of the older pupils and more or less sticky kisses from a few of the small fry. They were comforted a bit when told that I had promised the school board to come back the next term which they hoped would be for at least four or five months.

Pleasant as my three months in the Deep Red community had been, I was very glad to get back to our Otter Creek home again and resume baching with George. He had been a bit lonely at times in spite of my frequent weekend visits and the fact that we now had good neighbors all about us. The past six or eight months had brought great changes in this area and others soon followed.

The railroad extending south from northern Oklahoma had been completed to Vernon, Texas, and the village of Mountain Park grew rapidly. A little later a branch of the Frisco had been pushed southwest from Oklahoma City to Quanah, Texas, crossing this earlier railway line about three miles south of Mountain Park. At this intersection, a new town called Snyder had been established which soon outstripped its neighbor to the north. Some ten or twelve miles west of Snyder, in Greer County, the Frisco also founded the town of Headrick. To this Navajoe, only seven miles northwest, quickly removed "lock, stock and barrel" leaving only the schoolhouse. This was torn down a few years later and only the little windswept cemetery remained to remind the old timers of the flourishing little town that for over fifteen years had been an important trade center for a huge area.

These changes came very fast but meant little to George and me. Our most pressing problem was how we were going to eat for the next few months! My so called "salary" of forty dollars a month had been paid in school district warrants but there were no funds to pay them. In consequence they had to be sold and, although they drew six per cent interest until paid, the banks refused to take them for less than a twenty-five per cent discount.

This meant that my forty dollars a month was reduced to thirty dollars and after paying for my board and lodging I had left only twenty-two dollars a month. It is true that little money was required, for bacon was only about ten cents a pound and twenty-five cents would buy enough steak to serve a family of four or five persons. Even so, all I had left of my teaching pay could hardly be stretched far enough to buy our groceries from June until cotton picking began in September. Until that time, getting a job was virtually impossible.

Luckily, we happened to meet an old Yankee claimholder who sold us a second-hand mower to be paid for in six months. The bluestem grass on our valley land across the creek was almost waist-high, so we made a wooden bullrake and began cutting and stacking hay. We put up several stacks, did a little cutting for others farther down the creek, sold two or three loads of wood and pulled through until autumn. The fare was a bit slim sometimes but wild currants, plums, and fish we caught from deep holes in the creek added something to our diet so we were never hungry.

About the first of September Mr. Jenkins, whom we had known in Greer County, came to see us. He said that he had accepted a job as manager of a cotton gin in Washita County but had about thirty head of cattle on his claim some twelve miles south of us and asked George to live in his house and take care of them during the ginning season. This would be about three months, and, although the pay was low, George was glad to take the job for the work would be light and Jenkins gave him the first month's payment in advance!

My term of school at Deep Red did not begin until the first of November so I was again left alone to keep bachelor's hall. It was not so lonely as it had been the year before, as the weather was lovely and there were now convenient neighbors who were frequent visitors. One of these had a large field of cotton and during October I joined Uncle Mike Smith's three boys in cotton picking. To save time, I took a lunch to the field and one of my clearest memories is of how good the food tasted at supper after picking cotton from soon after sunrise to sundown with only a cold lunch at noon. The sourdough biscuits, bacon, fried potatoes or canned corn, and sorghum had a flavor that only a long day of hard work in the crisp October air can give.

Of course, I often rode down to see George on Sundays. He was looking after the cattle and cutting and putting in shocks of a little feed from time to time, but his most difficult task was keeping a few of the more perverse old cows from breaking through the pasture fences and raiding the nearby farmers' fields of feed crops. He was quite comfortable most of the time, but Mrs. Jenkins had insisted on taking most of the furniture with them, including the cookstove. This made it necessary to build a campfire in the yard to prepare a meal and to bake biscuits in a Dutch oven. Cooking outside presented no problem most of the time, but was difficult on rainy days which were fortunately few.

George was still at the Jenkins place when my school term at Deep Red began about the first of November. Mrs. Robinson's health was bad so I boarded with Mr. and Mrs. Worthy who lived about a mile northeast of the schoolhouse. Their home of five rooms seemed very commodious compared with the Robinson's one-room dugout, and although they had three young daughters, ranging in age from eleven to six, they were able to give me a small room and still have ample space for their own family.

I was very glad to get back to the Deep Red school again.

My former students and their parents all seemed delighted to see me and I quickly became acquainted with the half dozen or so new pupils who came. I rode over to see George once or twice at weekends but in less than a month Mr. Jenkins sent his family home and George returned to our Otter Creek cabin. After that until the term ended about the first of March many of my weekends were spent with him there.

As was the custom, I dismissed school for a week as Christmas drew near, after giving the children a treat of candy and apples. The holiday was as welcome to me as to the youngsters for I had not been with George much for three or four months. We had Christmas dinner with our brother, Henry and his family, who had sold the hotel they had been operating in Cordell and removed to Mountain Park. Most of that holiday week, however, was spent on the claim, hunting a little along the creek but mainly only visiting.

My school closed about the first of March with the same type of exercises as at the end of the first term, treats for the children and the awarding of prizes. Money had been available to pay my warrants, and the school board had promised to give me a six months term the following year at forty-five dollars a month so I agreed to return.

It was good to be home again and my first task was to plant a big garden on a plot of ground across the creek which we had plowed the preceding September. If we ever had any doubts as to the fertility of the soil, they speedily vanished. Everything I planted grew amazingly. We had far more onions, potatoes, beans, cantalopes, watermelons, and other "garden truck" than we could use, so we gladly gave the surplus to our nearby neighbors.

The months slipped by quickly. We cut and stacked a

little more hay, sold a few loads of wood, and so bought enough groceries to enable us to eat fairly well. Yet we both had a constantly growing feeling that we were in our own language, only "spinning our wheels and getting nowhere fast." Here we had lived for nearly two years on one of the most beautiful and fertile 160 acre tracts of land we had ever seen. Clearly, it could be made a most productive farm by the expenditure of a few hundred dollars, but we had no money and apparently no means of securing any. We could not give the land as collateral for a loan because a homesteader must live on a claim five years in order to get a patent to it free of charge except for a small clerical fee. Until he received such patent, the title was held in trust by the United States government.

One evening near the end of summer, George came up with a surprising suggestion. Under what was known as the "commuted provision" of the Homestead Act, a homesteader might receive a patent or fee-simple title to his claim after fourteen months residence by paying a dollar and a half an acre to the federal government. George proposed that we do this instead of wasting some three years more to get the land free.

My first reaction to this proposal was little short of horror. We had borrowed money before with tragic results and "a burned child dreads the fire." As we talked it over, however, my objections began to vanish. Unlike our short time cattle loan, this one would be for several years during which the land was certain to increase in value and the advance would be even greater because the money would be used for improvements.

Once we had agreed on this course, we became quite enthusiastic to put it through as soon as possible. It took some time to take care of all details but it was easy to get a loan of eight hundred dollars to be paid in five years. George made the trip to Lawton, paid the $240.00 at the land office, and received his patent. This left us $560.00 which would seem a pitifully small sum as this is written in 1963, but was important money in Oklahoma Territory sixty years ago.

One of our first tasks was to move the house nearly a quarter of a mile south to a spot only a couple of hundred yards from the section line road along the south side of the land. This was done to avoid having to cross a short west branch of Otter Creek which had caused us trouble after a rain. The move was not difficult as the neighbors helped us and the task was finished in a few hours.

Before we were able to get much done toward improving the land, it was time for my school to begin at Deep Red. I boarded with Mr. and Mrs. G. D. Thompson who lived a mile east of the schoolhouse. They had three sons and two daughters in school and a baby boy at home. They were a lovely family with an attractive two-story house. There were three beds upstairs where the boys and I slept.

School started off in excellent fashion for I now felt very much at home in the Deep Red community. It was about the middle of September and the weather was lovely. When I rode home at the end of the first week, George and I talked about a farm hand to break sod, build fences, corrals and sheds.

Here I was able to help. The Hash family from the mountains of Virginia had, in addition to three children in my school, two grown sons at home. The older of these, Alex, impressed me as a nice quiet chap who would be just what George needed. When I got back to Deep Red, I rode over to the Hash home to see him and explained our situation. He did not seem to mind eating bachelor's cooking and when I asked what wages he would expect, he said he "would try it a month for sixteen dollars."

No better choice could have been made. George and Alex liked each other from the first day and soon became fast friends. Alex was a tireless worker and by the time my school closed the first of March, large fields had been plowed, pastures fenced, corrals and sheds built, a well drilled, and the yard fenced. For the next three years George had Alex with him a large part of the time and always declared that he had never seen a better farm hand.

While George and Alex were improving the farm, I was busily engaged in trying to improve the learning of the youngsters of the Deep Red school. The number of pupils had now risen to about forty. We formed a live literary and debating society, held a box-supper to raise money for the church, and attended other such suppers or debates at the Hilltop School six miles west of ours.

The Thompson home was a very pleasant one, but Mrs. Thompson was expecting a baby so a few weeks before it was due I moved to the home of Mr. and Mrs. Dysart for the last two months of the term. They were a lovely family and living with them was very pleasant. The children in the household were two sons of Mr. Dysart's first wife, Wesley about fourteen, and John, twelve. A couple of years after their mother's death, Mr. Dysart had remarried and the second Mrs. Dysart had borne him a daughter, at this time hardly more than a baby.

My decision not to return to Deep Red was reached only after long deliberation and considerable soul searching. The community was very close to my heart and for my pupils I felt a deep affection which it seemed that they returned in full measure. With very few exceptions they had studied hard and made remarkable progress. Some ten or eleven-year-old youngsters could barely read at the beginning of my first term of teaching the Deep Red school. Yet, after only thirteen months of schooling, they were equal to most sixth grade students in reading, spelling, writing, arithmetic, and geography.

It would have been a real pleasure to continue working with them, but it seemed that if I continued teaching it should be as principal of a school large enough to require two or three teachers. The members of the school board seemed deeply disappointed by my decision but did not blame me in the least.

The exercises of the last day included the usual treat for the children and the awarding of prizes. A number of parents came and seemed to enjoy the program very much. When it was over, however, and the time had come to say goodby, a good many tears were shed not only by the smaller fry but by some of the older girls and boys. It must be confessed that my own heart was deeply touched and every summer for the next two or three years I paid several weekend visits to friends in the Deep Red community and always received a most cordial welcome.

Two Mississippi Valley Frontiers*

In recent years we have heard much of the "American Way of Life." Those who use that expression must be thinking in terms of those fundamental rights guaranteed to us by the Constitution, or of that equality of opportunity and the right to live our own lives in our own way which is the precious heritage of every American. For if they mean the manner in which we live, the *mores* of a people or the social, economic and cultural pattern of life the phrase becomes meaningless. Because the American way of life in New England is quite different from that of the Deep South and in neither of these areas does it bear any marked similarity to that of the Great Plains, the Spanish Southwest, or the Pacific Coast.

This nation of ours is made up not only of states but of regions each with its own ways of life, its own customs, traditions and manner of thought. These regional cultures grow from definite roots. Some, as geographic conditions, lie close beneath the surface while others are deep in the background of history.

One of these regions is the area west of the Appalachians and east of the Mississippi between the Ohio River and the Gulf states—or Kentucky and Tennessee, the first states formed in the Mississippi Valley. The other is the former

*Read by the author during the annual meeting of the Mississippi Valley Historical Association, Cleveland, Ohio, December, 1947, and published in *Chronicles of Oklahoma*, XXVI (Winter, 1948–1949), 366–84.

Indian Territory now Oklahoma—the last state in the Mississippi Valley to be admitted to the Union. The influence of the first area upon American history has been enormous and that of the latter comparatively slight, though the story of its settlement and development is unique in the annals of America.

Population maps of the United States showing the peopled area at any time between 1790 and 1810 will reveal that a long tongue of settlement extended westward from the Appalachian Mountains to the Mississippi with its northern border the Ohio River and its southern one the northern limits of the present states of Mississippi and Alabama and western Georgia or roughly Kentucky and Tennessee or portions of those states if the map is one of the earlier dates named. For the purposes of this discussion, New Orleans and the tiny islands of French settlement in Louisiana or beyond the Ohio in Indiana or Illinois may be disregarded. Most of these latter were mere outposts in the wilderness as was Detroit, founded in 1701 by Cadillac, to be developed more than two centuries later by Ford.

The reasons for the early establishment of this wide frontier west of the mountains and south of the Ohio are not far to seek. When the English colonists of the tidewater region began the march westward they soon found their further advance toward the interior barred, or greatly hindered, by two forces. One was the formidable barrier of the mountain wall and the other was the resistance of many powerful tribes of Indians. When the advancing tide of population reached the mountains opposite Kentucky, however, both of these barriers gave way. Eventually Cumberland Gap was discovered offering a comparatively easy passageway through the mountains and beyond and extending as far west as the

Mississippi was a broad region which was not inhabited by any tribe of Indians. Kentucky and much of Tennessee constituted virtually a "no man's land." North of the Ohio were the fierce Shawnee, the Potawatomi, Sac and Fox, Miami, and other tribes, while in Georgia, Alabama and Mississippi were the Cherokees, Creeks, Choctaws, and Chickasaws. Far to the south in Florida were the Seminoles who formed the fifth and smallest of these so-called Five Civilized Tribes. Many of these Indians used the middle region as a hunting ground but no tribe of importance occupied it permanently.

In 1769 Daniel Boone pushed westward through Cumberland Gap to view with delight the verdant meadows and beautiful groves of Kentucky. Those who have visited the blue grass region and above all those born and bred there are not surprised that Boone lingered on this "long hunt" for nearly three years. They only wonder why he should ever have returned to Virginia! The lure of the West was too powerful, however, to permit him to remain long in his old homeland. In 1775 he led a party of settlers back to Kentucky and founded Boonesborough.[1]

Daniel Boone was a type. Perhaps others like him did as much as he to explore and open up this middle region to settlement but above all others he has caught the popular fancy. Boone and those of his kind, as Kenton, Harrod, Bryan, Crockett and others, loved pioneering for its own sake. They sought new lands not so much for the purpose of settling and developing them as to escape from what they regarded as the penalties and inconveniences of civilization. They were of the type described by Kipling when he wrote:

> He shall desire loneliness
> And his desire shall bring

[1] R. G. Thwaites, *Daniel Boone*, p. 118.

Hard on his heels a thousand wheels
A people and a King
He shall go back on his own track
And by his scarce cold camp
There he shall meet the roaring street
The derrick and the stamp.

A thousand wheels did not follow in the wake of these vanguards of the frontier because the mountain trails were for a long time impassible for wheeled vehicles. But there did come a people with their scanty possessions loaded on pack horses. Moreover, if these people did not bring in a king they eventually brought those things which a king is supposed to typify—law, and constitutional forms, and more or less orderly government.

Following the first pioneer explorers there poured through Cumberland Gap in the years of the Revolution and thereafter thousands of settlers eagerly seeking homes where they might improve their worldly condition and build up a heritage for their children. Some floated down the Ohio River. This was a long voyage during which the scow or keel boat was kept in the middle of the current to avoid attack by bands of Indians lurking in the forest along its northern bank. These immigrants came across the mountains or down the river in ever increasing numbers with the result that by 1792 Kentucky's population was sufficient for its admission as a state. Four years later the settlers of Tennessee formed a constitution without bothering to ask the consent of Congress and it was also admitted to the Union.

The people who came to occupy this exposed frontier prior to the admission of Kentucky and Tennessee to statehood and long thereafter and who survived to develop that region all had the same characteristics. As a rule they were young and were of the strongest and most hardy and aggressive type. It required courage to set out on the long journey across the mountains or down the Ohio River to occupy this remote land behind the Appalachians. Also when they had arrived, it was necessary to maintain themselves in a region where, as Felix Grundy said: "Death lurked behind almost every bush and every thicket concealed an ambuscade."

When Longfellow referring to the settlers of Plymouth wrote:

> God had sifted three kingdoms
> To find the wheat for this planting
> Then had sifted the wheat
> The living seed of a nation

he was but voicing a general truth as applicable to the settlers of all later American frontiers as it was to the militant Pilgrims. The bold, hardy, and adventurous migrated. The timid, weak, and satisfied remained at home. As a later writer has put it: "The cowards did not start; the weaklings did not survive." Or, as an old ranchman in the Far West once said with true frontier modesty: "We were a picked bunch in those old days. The wilderness cut out the culls."

Be that as it may, few will deny that the pioneers who occupied each successive frontier of America were of a bold and aggressive breed but conditions made this especially true in this area of Kentucky and Tennessee. Cut off by the mountains from any support from the East, the people of this long salient of settlement were, to use a military term, enfiladed by hostile Indians. Among the tribes north of the Ohio River were some made up of as savage and warlike Indians as could be found on the North American Continent. It was not merely blind fury which prompted them to write the story of Kentucky's history in blood for so many years.

Such leaders as Tecumseh were astute, far-seeing men. They realized the danger to their people of this long tongue of white settlement extending far out into the wilderness. Unless these settlements could be destroyed they would inevitably grow larger, be extended across the Ohio, and continue north until they met and merged with the population steadily advancing westward from New York, Pennsylvania, and eastern Ohio. Then the Indians would be dispossessed of their lands and those who survived driven beyond the Mississippi to face an uncertain future. It was not enough to fight a defensive warfare. These presumptuous whites must perish or be driven out. With tireless energy these Indian leaders led their painted warriors against the little settlements of Kentucky in a desperate attempt to blot them out and "let in the jungle." The struggle continued for many years and in this period the "wheat was truly sifted." Eternal vigilance was for these pioneers the price of survival. They established forts and palisaded stations, carried their guns to the field, and learned every art and trick of savage warfare. They matched skill with skill, cunning with cunning, and at times cruelty with cruelty.[2]

Coupled with the ever-present danger from the Indians beyond the Ohio to the people of the northern portion of this frontier area, however, was an almost equally grave danger to those settlers in its southern portion from Indians to the south. The great tribes south of Tennessee, as the Cherokee, Creek, Choctaw, and Chickasaw, were far more civilized and perhaps less warlike than were the Indians north of the Ohio. On the other hand they were much more numerous. Moreover, they viewed these white settlements

[2] See Theodore Roosevelt, *The Winning of the West*, (4 vols.) for detailed accounts.

with suspicion and were always ready to resist any encroachment, or threatened encroachment, on their lands. While they did not engage in as many bloody forays as did the Shawnee and some other northern tribes, they were a powerful barrier to the advance of population to the south. Also bands sometimes attacked the settlers and always they were a potential menace to the whites.

The situation of these westerners was rendered more perilous by the fact that behind the Indian tribes on either side of them lay the colonial possessions of two great European nations. Far to the north lay Canada and for a long time there were also British posts on the American side of the Great Lakes. That British officials deliberately encouraged the Indians to attack these settlements seems doubtful but they encouraged the savages to resist any expansion of population northward. British traders unquestionably sold guns and powder to the Indians just as did American traders half a century or more later in our own western territories. It is not surprising therefore that a deep resentment toward the British should have grown up among these people of the West.

To the south the Spaniards also sought to cultivate friendship with the Indians of the Five Civilized Tribes. Traders in Spanish Louisiana sold these Indians arms and ammunition and Spain's officials in Louisiana urged the Indians to oppose any advance of the American pioneers southward.[3] Hemmed in on both sides by Indians who were backed by these great European powers, the position of the pioneers of the Kentucky-Tennessee area was truly perilous. Only a people of rare courage, fortitude, and remarkable intelligence could survive in such a situation.

[3] *Ibid.*, Vol. IV (Sagamore Edition, 6 vols.), pp. 153–156.

Yet the fact that the colonies of these two European nations hung on the flanks of these western settlements was not an unmixed evil. It prevented the people of the long salient behind the mountains from becoming provincial backwoodsmen. Cut off by the mountains from a market in the East for their surplus products, these westerners felt an urgent need for the free navigation of the Mississippi which Spain for many years denied them. The man dwelling in a log cabin on the banks of the Ohio, Tennessee, Cumberland, or any one of many other rivers had a personal interest in Jay's treaty with England as well as in the political situation in Spain and in the acts of the Spanish government. Whether or not Manuel Godoy remained the chief minister of Spain, or Charles IV abdicated in favor of his son, Ferdinand, were to the Kentucky settler matters of vital importance. He and his fellows loudly demanded that Spain be persuaded or forced to grant to them the right to navigate the Mississippi. This they secured by the Treaty of San Lorenzo in 1795.[4] They felt, however, that their tenure of this right was most precarious and as additional settlers poured in, the demands grew for the Federal government to make it secure by the purchase of a portion of Louisiana. This log cabin dweller was therefore deeply interested in the transfer of Louisiana to France by Spain and in the negotiations of Livingston and Monroe culminating in the Louisiana Purchase.[5]

With access to markets thus assured and lands provided for further expansion westward, the population rapidly increased. The Indian menace still remained, however, and the newcomers were also of a hardy and adventurous type. Yet a differentiated society eventually began to develop. Men of

[4] Hunter Miller (Ed.), *Treaties and Other International Acts of the United States of America*, Vol. 2, p. 337.
[5] *Ibid.*, pp. 516–523.

means began to acquire the best lands and to cultivate them with slave labor. Some earlier settlers who sold their lands crossed the Ohio. It was plain that expansion in that direction would in time reach the lakes and demands grew for securing a northern outlet to the sea just as the southern one had been acquired. Resentment against British support of the Indians increased and some men began to dream of the acquisition of Canada.

These westerners played a conspicuous part in the Indian war against Tecumseh but by this time they had become powerful enough to wield an influence upon national politics. As the old Revolutionary War statesmen passed out of the picture, many of them were replaced by new leaders from this area. Henry Clay was chosen Speaker of the House in 1811. On the question of war with Great Britain the western representatives in Congress voted unanimously in favor of it, joining with the South for a war which New England strongly opposed and on the question of which the middle states were divided.

The frontier leaders, however, had no intention of favoring a war for others to fight. Kentucky-born Richard M. Johnson elected to Congress at the age of twenty-five left Washington and hurried west to lead a regiment of volunteers in the invasion of Canada. Having been granted his commission by Governor Isaac Shelby of that State, he and the Governor both played a conspicuous part in the Battle of the Thames. Johnson then returned to his seat in Congress.[6] Many of Harrison's soldiers in this invasion were Kentucky or Tennessee men just as were many of Jackson's in the South in his campaign against the Creeks and at New Orleans. In fact, about the only important American vic-

6 B. J. Lossing, *Eminent Americans*, pp. 99 and 368.

tories of this war were won in the West and that region furnished its only military heroes—Jackson and Harrison—together with a number of lesser lights.

Great as was the influence of this frontier Kentucky- Tennessee area on the war, it also had its influence on the peace. Henry Clay of Kentucky together with Gallatin, Bayard, Russell, and John Quincy Adams negotiated the Peace of Ghent and for once we seem to have done better around the peace table than on the field of battle. It might almost be said that in the second conflict with Great Britain we lost a war and won a peace. If there is some element of the truth in the old saying that "Waterloo was won on the cricket fields of Eton," there is also some justification for asserting that the Peace of Ghent was won about the sales stables, race tracks, and poker tables of Kentucky. The British commissioners, Lord Gambier, Sir Henry Goulburn and William Adams were second-raters since the talents of Britain's leading diplomats were required for solving the problems of the Congress of Vienna. Certainly these three commissioners were no match for Clay, Adams, and Gallatin. Henry Clay's influence with his colleagues was great and he brought to play in the negotiations all the skill of the western horse trader and poker player. With rare skill he made the American offers appear attractive, and alternately bluffed, "stood pat," "raised the ante," or "called the bluff" of his opponents. When a deadlock was reached, the Americans again and again said: "Consult your government" and Britain desperately weary of war repeatedly yielded. As a result a treaty was at last negotiated far more favorable to the United States than our people had any right to expect.[7]

[7] See Henry Adams, *History of United States*, Book IX, Chs. 1 and 2, for discussion of the negotiations at Ghent. For the treaty, see Miller, *op. cit.*, p. 575.

After the close of the war, western migration greatly increased. The Kentucky-Tennessee area was soon fully occupied and the population began to spill over its borders in ever-increasing numbers. The southern portion of the region north of the Ohio was settled by people from this area. Also the Southwest below Tennessee received a flood of settlers from this region while others crossed the Mississippi to occupy Missouri and portions of Arkansas.

While part of the increased population of the Kentucky-Tennessee region was due to immigration, a high birthrate was responsible for much of it since a dozen children was hardly an exceptionally large family. Now with the danger of Indian attack removed, and with increased prosperity, the people of this first frontier beyond the mountains were free to give more attention to national affairs. No longer forced to carry on Indian campaigns, they turned their attention to political campaigns. Moreover, they brought to political conflicts all of the aggressive qualities, hardihood, and strength developed by long conflict with the wilderness and its savage inhabitants. Soon it was apparent that a new political power had appeared and was eagerly reaching for the reins of government.

The election of 1824 brought to an end the era of the Virginia Dynasty which for thirty-two of the thirty-six years of government under the Constitution had occupied the executive mansion. Only the aggressive individualism which led them to fight among themselves prevented the people of this first trans-Appalachian frontier from securing the Presidency in 1824. Able as were the Adamses of New England, however, their personal qualities did not appeal to the people of the New America that was so fast developing. These people felt that four years was as long as they would tolerate an Adams in the White House. Then with Jackson's triumph in 1828, the political dominance of this first Mississippi Valley frontier had to be recognized. Moreover, from this time forward for a generation the states of Tennessee and Kentucky and their colonies largely ruled the nation.

Perhaps few will deny that this was true during the eight years of the "reign of Andrew Jackson" but a question may be raised as to his successor. If so, it should be pointed out that Van Buren was the "heir apparent" to the throne, or the creature of Andrew Jackson. Moreover, Van Buren's running mate was Colonel Richard M. Johnson, veteran soldier and statesman of Kentucky.

Van Buren's successor, William Henry Harrison, was not from the Kentucky-Tennessee area but he had all the qualities which the people of that region most admired. He was every inch a frontiersman and it might be said that upon his shoulders had fallen the mantle of Jackson. He had endeared himself to the people of Kentucky by his work in the Northwest and had led many of them at Tippecanoe. In 1812 he had been commissioned a major general in the Kentucky militia and as has already been said, many Kentuckians were with him at the Battle of the Thames including Colonel Johnson and Governor Isaac Shelby.[8]

His successor, John Tyler, was an accident and may be disregarded here just as he usually was when President. Then came James K. Polk of Tennessee, who defeated the perennial candidate, Henry Clay of Kentucky. Polk was not colorful enough for the westerners. Happy as they were over his acquisition of territory, he apparently had little sense of humor and it was difficult for either the first or secondary

[8] Lossing, *op. cit.*, pp. 240–243.

frontier to grow enthusiastic over a dour Scotch Presby-
terian. Zachary Taylor, or "Old Rough and Ready" seemed
a far more attractive figure. He was a professional soldier
born in 1784 in Virginia while his parents were journeying
west to settle in Kentucky. In 1785 he was brought to the
vicinity of Louisville when Zachary was only eight months
old and here he grew to manhood when this region was
truly a "dark and bloody ground." Not until he was twenty-
four years old did he leave Kentucky after accepting a commission in the Army. From this time his life was largely that
of a frontier soldier. His character and characteristics were
formed, however, during the nearly twenty-four years of
life in frontier Kentucky.[9]

Fillmore was another accident and Pierce an incident.
Then the American people decided to try again the nearly-
forgotten experiment of electing to the Presidency a man of
ample training and experience in government, politics and
diplomacy. This they did when they chose James Buchanan.
Soon convinced of their mistake, they in 1860 elected a
Kentucky-born, former rail splitter Abraham Lincoln, two
of whose opponents were John C. Breckinridge of Kentucky
and John Bell of Tennessee. Moreover, it will be remembered that Jefferson Davis, President of the Confederacy,
was also Kentucky born, and that Andrew Johnson of Tennessee succeeded to the Presidency when Lincoln was mur-
dered. With Johnson came the end of an era and the beginning of the period of the political supremacy of the Old
Northwest, especially Ohio and Indiana, which is another
story.

It has been possible to mention only a few of the men

[9] *Dictionary of American Biography*, XVIII, p. 349; also Lossing, *op. cit.*,
p. 353.

important in national affairs contributed by this first trans-mountain frontier region. Among others were Hugh White, Felix Grundy, Thomas Hart Benton, George Rogers Clark and his younger brother William, J. J. Crittenden, George Croghan, and many more.

In addition many men from this area pushed out into the great Southwest especially Texas. These included David Crockett, one-time member of Congress from Tennessee whose restless love of adventure took him to Texas to die at the Alamo. Also William Walker, the filibuster, and Sam Houston who resigned the governorship of Tennessee and journeyed westward to the Indian Territory. Here he lived with the Cherokees for some years before going to Texas to command its armies in the war for independence. Most men regard election to Congress, the United States Senate, or the governorship of a state as the crowning achievement of a lifetime. Sam Houston was Governor of two states, member of Congress from one and United States Senator from an-other, was Commander-in-Chief of the armies of a nation and twice President of a republic.[10] In addition, he married three wives and his youngest son Temple was born when Sam was seventy years of age. Surely if the Cow Country could boast that its "men were men" Tennessee might well retort that some of her own sons also had some claims to manhood! As a matter of fact, many of the militant pioneers of Texas and other parts of the Trans-Mississippi West were transplanted from Kentucky or Tennessee soil and the spirit of daring and toughness of fiber revealed in the land of their adoption had been developed in the land of their birth.

That this Kentucky-Tennessee region, which was the first

[10] See Marquis James, *The Raven*, for a very interesting biography of Houston.

important Mississippi Valley frontier, has exerted an influence upon the history of the United States out of all proportion to its size seems reasonably apparent. It is clear that the reason for the political dominance of this area must be sought in the type of settlers who migrated to it and to qualities developed in them by their experiences during the formative years of these states. The second area to be discussed is the last frontier region of the Mississippi Valley, or the present state of Oklahoma.

A survey of the population map of the United States as it was a hundred years after the adoption of the Constitution will show a pattern of peopled and unpeopled lands exactly the converse of a population map for 1800. A map for 1889 shows that settlement stopped short at the western boundary of Arkansas but in Kansas and south of the Red River in Texas continued westward to about the hundredth meridian which forms the western boundary of Oklahoma. East of this meridian between the southern line of Kansas and the Red River, which marks the northern limits of Texas, a broad salient of Indian lands thrust far back into a sea of settlement just as three-quarters of a century earlier such a map showed a long tongue of settlement in Kentucky and Tennessee reaching far out into the Indian country.

This peninsula of Indian lands over two hundred miles wide and with an area approximately that of all New England, or slightly less than the combined areas of Ohio and Indiana, was the Indian Territory now the state of Oklahoma. In 1888 no white person held legal title to a single acre of land within its limits and the total Indian population was only some 75,000 of which more than four-fifths belonged to the Five Civilized Tribes.

The reasons for the formation of this long salient of near

wilderness extending back into the lands occupied by a white population are as definite as are those for the extension of the Kentucky-Tennessee area of settlement far out into the unpeopled lands of the Mississippi Valley. Virtually this entire region had been granted to the Five Civilized Tribes of Indians and they had been removed to it from their old homeland in the Gulf Plains between 1820 and 1840. This area had been promised to them for "as long as grass grows and water runs" and whites were forbidden to live within the limits of the territory of any tribe except by the consent of the Indians themselves. Thus a wall had been placed about this great Indian Territory by governmental decree—an intangible wall —but none the less real because of that.

Even at the time of their removal four of the five great tribes to which this territory had been granted had attained a considerable degree of civilization due to long contact with the whites. These four tribes, the Cherokee, Creek, Choctaw, and Chickasaw had for centuries occupied in their old homeland east of the Mississippi what might be described as a strategic region. They held the headwaters of the tributaries of the lower Mississippi, as well as of those streams which flow south into the Gulf and they also guarded the passes through the southern Appalachians. It was inevitable, therefore, that any nation which sought to hold the mouth of the Mississippi and the shores of the Gulf of Mexico must reckon with these powerful tribes.

Three European nations sought to do this—the Spaniards in Florida, the French in Louisiana, and the English in Georgia. The colonists of these nations early sought alliances with these tribes and zealously sought to secure their favor. As a result the Indians soon learned to play one nation off against the other and to secure presents, concessions, and favors from all three without the slightest intention of allying themselves with any one of them. In the practice of this crude but effective form of diplomacy the Indians received training in the arts of diplomacy and political intrigue which they later used with telling effect against officials of the United States in negotiations for the removal of these tribes to the West.

By the time of removal there had been considerable intermarriage of Indian women with the white men who made their homes in the Indian country, and as a result every tribe except the Seminole had a number of mixed-bloods. The mixed-bloods as well as some fullbloods were in many cases well educated—some having attended schools or colleges in the East. Commissioners of the United States government sent to make removal treaties urged that in this new land beyond the Mississippi there was an abundance of game and the Indians might there continue the old hunting life of earlier days. Yet, paradoxical as it may seem, it was the well-educated Indians, including many mixed-bloods, who signed such treaties against the bitter opposition of the unlettered fullbloods. The latter who clung most closely to the old Indian life of hunting and subsisting on native products were the ones most reluctant to leave the land of their fathers.

Bitter criticism has been heaped upon those Indians who negotiated treaties for the surrender of all lands in the East and removal to far-off Indian Territory. There is evidence, however, that these men were motivated solely by a desire to advance the welfare of their people. Here they saw the untutored fullbloods subject to the influence of the worst element of the frontier whites who encroached upon their lands, plied them with liquor, and corrupted their women. Unable to understand this strange new civilization, these bewildered fullbloods were in a fair way to become a race of drunken outcasts. What the leaders felt was urgently needed was time—time to establish schools to educate their unfortunate kinsmen and teach them the ways of white civilization. Given two or three generations in a land remote from the corrupting influence of whites, this might be done and these people made competent to maintain themselves in the midst of a white civilization once it had again overtaken them.[11]

On no other basis can be explained the provision for large funds for education which the Indian negotiators insisted must be included in the removal treaties, nor the feverish energy with which they established schools once the new homeland was reached. Each of the larger tribes set up an educational system immediately upon its arrival in the Indian Territory. Boarding schools or academies were created modeled upon those of the South and supported by funds from the tribal government. All instruction was in English and the teachers were the best qualified men and women that could be found.

In 1846 the Cherokee had established two national seminaries—one for men and the other for women. In these were taught Greek, Latin, English literature, higher mathematics, music and science. Many young men and women received in these, or the Choctaw academies, the beginnings of a classical education which they completed in some eastern college as Princeton or Mount Holyoke.

The establishment of an educational system was made possible because these so called "Indian Nations" after their removal westward were hardly Indian tribes in the com-

---

[11] See Ralph H. Gabriel, *Elias Boudinot, Cherokee, and His America*, pp. 141–155, for evidence that this was the attitude of the Cherokee signers of the Treaty of New Echota.

monly accepted use of that term. They were very small republics under the protection of the United States. Each of them, with the exception of the Seminole, had a written constitution and written laws. The tribal governments had power of life and death over their own citizens and almost complete authority to administer the affairs of their people.[12] In fact, these tribes were independent nations except for such limitations as were expressed in the treaties of cession and removal. Lands were held in common as a public domain but with individual use guaranteed to every citizen.

Here, for some three-quarters of a century these little Indian nations lay like an American Balkans set down in the midst of the United States. Slaves were held in every tribe and with the outbreak of the War Between the States these Indian republics all made treaties of alliance with the Confederacy. As a result they were at the close of the war compelled to free their slaves and make provisions for them to share in the tribal lands. In addition, they were forced to surrender the western half of the Indian Territory in order to provide a home for other Indian tribes.[13]

Between 1866 and 1885 more than a dozen tribes from various parts of the West were brought to these ceded lands and given large reservations there. The Indian Territory thus became divided into two parts of nearly equal size. The eastern half was occupied by the quasi-independent nations of the Five Civilized Tribes while the western half consisted largely of great Indian reservations assigned to tribes brought in from Kansas or other parts of the Prairie West.

During the war the lands of the Five Civilized Tribes were so ravaged by the armies of both North and South, that at its

[12] For the tribal constitutions see *Oklahoma Red Book*, I, p. 201–237.
[13] For Treaties of 1866, see *Ibid.*, pp. 341–379.

close these Indians were in a deplorable condition. One-third of the adult Cherokee women were widows and an almost equal fraction of the children orphans. In the other tribes the situation was little better.

All educational progress was stopped with the outbreak of war and during its course most of the school buildings were burned or badly damaged. With the coming of peace, however, these buildings were rebuilt or repaired and the Indian leaders resumed with vigor the task of educating their people sufficiently to enable them to live and compete with the whites on equal terms once the advancing flood of settlement should overflow their little nations.

The advance of white population, however, was more rapid than the Indian leaders had believed to be possible. In the twenty years from 1870 to 1890 the population of Kansas increased from 364,000 to 1,427,000 and Texas from 818,000 to 2,335,000 with corresponding increases in most of the neighboring western states.[14] It was inevitable that as fertile lands subject to settlement grew increasingly scarce, many persons along the border of Indian Territory should view its attractive lands with covetous eyes and demand that they be made available for occupation by white settlers. By the middle 1870's such persons were urging Congress to devise some means by which the treaties guaranteeing their lands to the Five Civilized Tribes might be abrogated or so modified as to permit the entrance of whites. Loudly they demanded that the tribal governments be abolished, each Indian allotted a tract of land from the common holdings, the remaining lands opened to white settlement, and a territorial government established.

The Indian leaders felt that at all hazards this must be

14 Figures are from the Census.

prevented. Some have asserted that this was due to their reluctance to give up their offices in the tribal governments and the economic advantages accruing to them by virtue of the communal land system. This may have been true in the case of some but there were others whose reasons for objecting to such changes were far more altruistic. Educational progress, even though interrupted by the war, had been great but the majority of the fullbloods were not yet sufficiently advanced to live among whites and compete with them economically in a white man's world. Time, and yet more time was needed and to secure it they determined to resist to the utmost the efforts of the whites to destroy their governments and overrun their country. Moreover, they brought to the task all the political wisdom and statecraft accumulated in conducting their own governments plus all the skill in diplomacy which they had acquired during the long period in which Spain, France, and England had sought alliances with them in a struggle for supremacy on the North American Continent.

The Indian leaders braced themselves in the struggle and for a quarter of a century fought desperately to hold the line against the population that strove to break it down and let in the white man's laws, government, and way of life. The situation, curiously enough, was the exact opposite of that in the Kentucky-Tennessee area a century earlier when painted warriors for so long stormed against this long peninsula of white settlement seeking to break it down and let in the wilderness. In both cases the Indians were foredoomed to defeat. Yet despite the small population of the Five Civilized Tribes their long experience in diplomacy and political intrigue enabled them for a quarter of a century to resist the ever-increasing pressure of the whites upon the intangible wall about the Indian country.

Each of these tribes maintained a delegation in Washington to look after relations with the United States and seek to prevent any action by Congress or the executive branch of the Federal Government prejudicial to the interests of its people.

In their struggle against white invasion the Five Civilized Tribes received little help from the Indians on the reservations in western Indian Territory. Most of these tribes were small, unorganized, and little civilized. In consequence it was in this region that the barrier to entrance by settlers was first broken. In 1889 an area of some two million acres was opened to occupation by homesteaders.[15] The following year Oklahoma Territory was created.[16] Then one by one these western tribes agreed to take allotments of land in severalty and sell the surplus to the United States to be opened to white settlement. Within a dozen years after the first opening in 1889 virtually all of these lands ceded by the Five Civilized Tribes in 1866 as a home for other Indians had been occupied by white settlers. The western half of the former peninsula of wilderness had been blotted out and the territory of the five Indian republics had become an island in the midst of white civilization.

Still the Indians of the Five Tribes carried on their losing struggle to maintain their national integrity. By this time, however, there were forces within to lend aid and encouragement to those without. Prior to the War Between the States many Indians in each of these tribes were slave owners.

[15] *Oklahoma Red Book*, I, pp. 423–425.
[16] *Ibid.*, pp. 426–437.

The communal land system made it easy for some of these to develop large plantations which they cultivated by slave labor. Eventually a plantation aristocracy grew up not unlike that of the Old South.

When the slaves were freed, these men were left without labor to farm their extensive holdings. After the ravages of war had been somewhat repaired, some of these plantation owners sought for a new source of labor and found it in the poorer whites of Arkansas and Texas. At the request of the planter, the tribal government issued permits to whites to come in for a year to work as laborers. These laborers frequently received a share of the crops grown by them instead of a cash wage and so became in reality sharecroppers. Their permits were renewed from year to year until they became virtually permanent residents. Permits were issued to others to live in the Indian country and operate stores, mills, or cotton gins. The building of railroads brought in railway employees and the opening of coal mines brought in still more "citizens of the United States" as they were called.

Before the close of the Nineteenth Century, the whites in the Territory of the Five Civilized Tribes far outnumbered the Indians. Yet the latter owned all the land, operated the governments and were in consequence the ruling class. The whites were merely tenants subject to the will of the tribal authorities. Except in the case of intermarried citizens, they had no public schools for their children, could not own land, vote, or share in any way in the Indian governments. In short, they were merely residents and might be removed at any time by the tribal authorities. The need for their services was so great, however, that the time came when a whole-

94

sale removal of them was unthinkable.[17] Yet their presence made the struggle of the Indians to preserve their tribal forms and system of common land holding more difficult since to assaults from without were added the activities of this enormous "fifth column" within. The story is far too long to give in detail. In 1893 a commission was created by Congress to negotiate agreements with the Five Civilized Tribes looking to the distribution of their lands in severalty and the abolition of the tribal governments.[18] The Indians flatly refused to negotiate but the sands of time were fast running out for their little republics. Congress clothed the commission with additional powers. The tribal lands were surveyed and classified and rolls of the citizens of these tribes made up in preparation for an equitable distribution of the common property. The jurisdiction of the Federal courts was extended over the Indian Territory and the tribal courts forbidden to function. At last the Indians yielded to superior force, signed agreements to accept all that had been done, and agreed to the allotment of the tribal lands in severalty.[19]

In 1906 Congress passed an enabling act providing for the joining of Oklahoma and Indian Territories to form the State of Oklahoma and authorizing the election of delegates to a convention to make a constitution for the new state. The constitution was formed, ratified by an overwhelming majority, and state and county officers elected.

November 16, 1907, was the date set for the inauguration

[17] It is quite impossible to list all of the numerous articles that have appeared in *The Chronicles of Oklahoma* dealing with matters referred to in the latter part of this paper. Earlier issues should be consulted by the reader interested in details of life in the Indian Territory and relations between Indians and whites.

[18] See *Oklahoma Red Book*, I, pp. 481–485, for the various acts with respect to the Dawes Commission.

[19] *Ibid.*, pp. 559–617.

of the Governor and the officials and on which the new state government was to go into operation. On that day the inagural ceremonies held at the capital were witnessed by a huge throng of people while every important town in the state also arranged for a celebration in honor of the coming of statehood. Each of these was attended by swarms of happy people coming for many miles from every part of the surrounding country. Only one group was absent. Within the limits of the former republics of the Five Civilized Tribes many of the older Indians remained at home to mourn the passing of the old governments and the old order under which they had so long lived and which they so much loved.

Thirty years later a Cherokee woman married to a white man said that her husband had asked her to go with him to attend the statehood celebration at the nearby town but she had refused. Late that evening he returned home and said: "Well, Mary, we no longer live in the Cherokee Nation. All of us are now citizens of the State of Oklahoma." After the lapse of more than thirty years there were tears in this woman's eyes as she recalled that never-to-be-forgotten day. She said: "It broke my heart. I went to bed and cried all night long. It seemed more than I could bear that the Cherokee Nation—my country and my people's country—was no more."

Though the Indians had lost the cause for which they had so long battled, the years of struggle had done their work. It had given to their leaders a training in politics, statecraft, and diplomacy which has made them among the cleverest and most able politicians in the state of Oklahoma or almost any other state. This training had, moreover, been built upon a heritage of political skill dating back to the eighteenth century.

Conscious of their political ability and of the fact that they had long been owners of all land tilled by their white tenants, these Indian leaders had no intention of accepting an inferior status for themselves or their people in the new state. The President of the Constitutional Convention was not an Indian but he was an intermarried citizen of the Chickasaw Nation and in consequence, his children were of Indian blood. A number of Indians served as members of this convention and may have been in part responsible for the section in the Constitution defining races which says: "Wherever in this Constitution and laws of this state the word or words 'colored' or 'colored race' .... are used, the same shall be construed to mean or apply to all persons of African descent. The term 'white race' shall include all other persons."[20] Thus every Indian, no matter how dark his skin, is a white person as defined by the Oklahoma Constitution.

At the time of Oklahoma's admission as a State in 1907 slightly less than five per cent of its population was of Indian blood and about that ratio has been maintained for forty years. In 1947 the number of Indians in the state was some 120,000 of a total population of around 2,300,000. Yet these people of Indian descent who are but five per cent of Oklahoma's total population have contributed to the state leaders and prominent men and women, especially in the field of politics and government, out of all proportion to their numbers. None of the thirteen governors of the state to 1948 has been of Indian blood but two were intermarried citizens so their children are of Indian blood. One of the first two United States Senators was Indian, the late Robert L. Owen, and every Oklahoma delegation in Congress has had at least one member of Indian descent, sometimes two, and occasion-

[20] *Oklahoma Constitution*, Art. XXIII, Sec. 11.

ally three. Two speakers of the lower house of the state legislature have been Indians and many of its most prominent members as well as many state senators have been of Indian blood. One of the three members of the Corporation Commission in 1948 is Indian and Indians have served as members of the Supreme Court and as district judges. With but one exception, every county superintendent of schools of one eastern Oklahoma county for forty years has been Indian and most other officials of this and other counties have been of Indian descent.

It is not alone in the field of politics and government that these Indian people have made important contributions. Among them have been writers, artists, musicians, teachers and ministers, as well as prominent lawyers, physicians, editors, bankers, and merchants. They have also been active in many organizations. The late Mrs. Roberta Lawson, one time President of the American Federation of Women's Clubs, was the granddaughter of a famous Indian. It is also significant that the two statues which Oklahoma has placed in the Hall of Fame in our national capital as those of her two greatest sons are both of Cherokee Indians—Sequoyah and Will Rogers. A people numbering less than five per cent of Oklahoma's total population have given to the state perhaps twenty to twenty-five per cent of its best known men and women.

It may be asserted that most of these prominent individuals have been mixed bloods and should not be designated as Indians. Yet they are all included in the five per cent of the state's population of Indian descent. Also, ever since Oklahoma's admission to the Union, the state's politics have been dominated by the people of its eastern half, the area of the Five Civilized Tribes.

Enough has been given to show that the early history of Oklahoma—the last state created in the Mississippi Valley—has been as colorful as that of the first two states formed beyond the Appalachians. That the settlers of the Kentucky-Tennessee area for a generation were in constant conflict with the Indians and during the succeeding generation wielded an enormous influence in the national government few persons will deny. Most students of Oklahoma history will also agree that the Indians of the Five Civilized Tribes fought desperately for a generation to preserve their status as independent nations and for another generation have had an enormous influence in Oklahoma politics and government.

Whether or not the historian will accept the view that in both cases political power and influence stemmed from the strength developed in earlier conflicts is another matter. Yet few things worthy of recording in the annals of a nation merely happen. The multiple threads which make up the fabric of history have always been woven by vital forces in such fashion as to reveal a more or less distinct pattern. If the conclusions here suggested should appear unjustified, it is hoped that they may at least be deemed worthy of consideration.

From Log Cabin to Sod House*

In recent years we have heard much of Americanism and
the American way of life, as though they were both static
and standardized, though anyone who has traveled extensively in various parts of our country knows that they are
neither the one nor the other. Politically our nation is made
up of states, but so far as the pattern of economic and social
life is concerned, it is even today made up of regions that are
in many cases very unlike one another. Perhaps there is a
fundamental Americanism which is essentially the same
throughout the nation but the American way of life in New
England is very unlike that of the Deep South, and in neither
region does it bear much resemblance to that of the Great
Plains, the Spanish Southwest, or the Pacific Coast. The life
of any of these areas, moreover, is very different today from
what it was half a century ago, so it is plain that both time
and place must be considered in seeking to determine conditions in any portion of America.

The cultural and economic pattern which, broadly speaking, is the life of the people of any region, grows from certain
distinct roots. Some of these, as climate and geographic
conditions, lie close beneath the surface while others are
deeply rooted in the subsoil of history. From these grows a

* Read by the author during the annual meeting of the Illinois State
Historical Society, Springfield, Illinois (October, 1945), and published in
The Journal of the Illinois State Historical Society (December, 1945),
XXXVIII 383–413.

pattern of life which reaches full flowering and eventually produces fruits. It would seem that if these fruits produced by various regional cultures could be gathered and placed in a great wine press and the juice could be extracted, the resulting brew would have certain distinct qualities. For in it one might find the wholesome but slightly acid touch of Puritan New England, the mellow sweetness of the Old South, the substantial body of the Middle West, the wild raw tang of the Great Plains and Rocky Mountain Plateau, the peculiar spiciness of the Spanish Southwest, and the exotic flavor of the Pacific Coast all mingled in the peculiar blend that we call Americanism which, lacking any one of these elements would not be the same.

In addition to the regions named and some others, there existed for many generations in America another area in which conditions of life were in most cases essentially the same and whose people usually had a distinct regional consciousness. That area was the American frontier. The characteristics of the frontier did not vary much for at least two centuries and the people who occupied it, whether in the northern, middle, or southern zones of settlement, felt themselves bound together by common experiences, hardships, and dangers and by the necessity for solving the same problems. Remote from markets and from industrial and commercial centers, they usually felt themselves either neglected or exploited by the people of the more thickly settled regions farther east, and this too was a bond of union.

The purpose of this paper is to discuss very briefly the life of the people of two American frontiers—that of the log-cabin dwellers of the timbered regions east of the Mississippi, or largely speaking, of the first tier of states west of that stream, and the frontier of the early settlers of the prairie plains beginning as a rule some distance west of the great Father of Waters.

As agricultural settlement moved slowly westward from the Atlantic seaboard and passed the fall line of the rivers, there was always along its western rim a pioneer society composed of people who lived under frontier conditions and who looked to the West as an area of free land and economic opportunity rather than to Europe as the source of culture, as did the people of the coastal plain. On beyond the fall line to the foot of the mountains these settlements were gradually extended, then they jumped the first range of the Appalachian Highland into the great valley, poured westward through the Cumberland Gap or down the Ohio to occupy the Mississippi Valley, and eventually crossed the great river to settle Missouri, Arkansas, Louisiana, eastern Texas, and Iowa. Before 1840 Missouri and Arkansas had been admitted as states and half a dozen years later both Texas and Iowa had become members of the Federal Union.

By the time of the outbreak of the Civil War the edge of the great prairie plains had been reached and here this advancing agricultural population hesitated, reluctant to attempt to cope with a region so unlike any which it had known in the past. While certain portions of Ohio, Indiana, Illinois, Iowa, Kentucky, and some other states had fairly extensive areas of prairie, the life of the American pioneers had largely been that of forest dwellers and was shaped and conditioned by the wooded lands on which they lived or which lay in more or less close proximity to their homes. While generalizations are dangerous and can never be more than approximately correct, pioneer life in America up to this time had been a woodland life. The occupation of the vast stretches of level prairie plains lying to the west was still in the future.

Without too much logic we are always likely to judge the characteristics of any individual by the type of home which he occupies. By no means all of the people of the wooded regions of the frontier lived in log cabins and certainly less than half of those of the plains of Nebraska, Kansas, western Oklahoma or Texas resided in sod houses but log cabins seldom appeared on the prairie plains and the sod house was unknown east of the great prairies. In consequence, it is not without some reason that these two areas may be called the log-cabin and the sod-house frontiers.

Up until the middle 1840's many of the pioneers who migrated westward came down the Ohio by boat, thence to the mouth of either the Missouri or Arkansas and up those streams to a suitable spot from which they spread out into the interior. This ability to penetrate the West by means of rivers was largely responsible for the admission of Missouri and Arkansas to the Union in 1821 and 1836 respectively while that of Iowa was delayed until 1846. By no means all of these westward emigrants, however, came by water. Many came overland in covered wagons, some on horseback, some on foot with their possessions strapped on the backs of pack horses, and some on foot—period!

The story has been told of a family consisting of husband, wife, and two very small children who set out from eastern Missouri to reach free land in the western part of that state. Having no domestic animals, they had to carry all their household goods and utensils on their backs. Both husband and wife were so heavily burdened that the former could in addition carry only one child and the latter none at all.

This did not discourage them. The husband would pick up one child, carry it half a mile, and deposit it together with his axe, gun, and other impedimenta beside the trail. He would then walk back and carry the second youngster half a mile beyond the first, after which he would return for his property and the remaining junior member of the little group. In the meantime, the wife plodded steadily onward pausing occasionally to rest while the father did his own resting during the return trip for his offspring waiting more or less patiently beside the trail. In such intermittent fashion did the little family proceed toward the end of their own particular rainbow. Surely the lure of the West must have been well nigh irresistible to induce even the most courageous of pioneers to undertake a migration under such difficulties!

While this story was told in all seriousness and was abundantly vouched for, it must have been a very exceptional case. Most of the pioneers who removed overland to the wooded frontier region journeyed either by covered wagon or with their worldly goods on pack animals. Choosing a tract of land, they settled down, built a shelter from the weather, and set to work at the task of felling the forest trees in order to provide logs for the new home.

The first shelter occupied by the family was likely to be a "half-faced camp" such as the Lincolns are said to have occupied for a time. This was a rude shed open on one side except for quilts or blankets that might be hung there to keep out the rain and wind. This was only a temporary habitation, however, to be occupied while the log-cabin home was constructed.

Apparently the house built of logs notched at either end and slightly flattened on the sides, with any possible cracks plastered with clay, was first erected in America by the

Swedes of Delaware and was modeled on similar structures of the Scandinavian Peninsula. The log-cabin homes of the American pioneers were of several types. Perhaps the commonest was simply a square, or rectangular, structure of one room with a puncheon floor and a roof of rough, split shingles. Because timber was so abundant, however, many pioneers sought to provide a more commodious home by building the walls high enough to provide an attic bedroom, reached by a ladder, and by reducing the pitch of the rear roof and extending it back far enough to cover a "lean to" or second room, which might be used either as a kitchen or bedroom. A chimney, either of stone or sticks and clay, was built at one end of the main room—which usually served as a kitchen too unless the smaller rear room also boasted a fireplace. Cookstoves did not appear very much in the rural districts of Illinois or Missouri until the 1840's. Even then they were at first viewed somewhat askance by some conservative souls who had heard of boilers bursting on the river steamers and feared that the strange iron contraption might blow up and kill half the family.

The more enterprising settlers of a community frequently built a double log house with a fireplace and chimney at each end and a wide hallway, sometimes called "a dog trot," between the two rooms. In this hall were hung the tools, saddle, and harness. Here the dogs slept in winter and here the housewife sat on hot summer days to do her churning, sewing, or preparing vegetables for cooking, since this wide hall open at either end was the coolest part of the house. If in addition to the two rooms and open hallway the exterior walls were built high enough to provide attic bedrooms, and if a shady front porch were added, the family felt that the home was little short of luxurious.

The spot for the location of the home had been chosen with due regard both to the practical and the artistic. Sometimes it was in a sheltered glen where it would be protected from the cold winter winds. More often it stood on a low tree-crowned hill from which might be had a view of the surrounding country. If possible it was built near a spring which not only furnished a supply of water for domestic use but over which a springhouse might be built where milk, butter, and other perishable foods could be kept cool in summer.

Once the home had been erected, however, often with the help of kindly neighbors, the pioneer's task was only well begun. Unless he happened to be located at the edge of some small prairie the forest lay all about, so after building cribs, lots, and shelter for the domestic animals came the labor of clearing and fencing fields for planting. From dawn to dusk the settler toiled at the task of felling trees, splitting rails, and building the worm fences with stakes and riders to tie the panels together. All day long, in many cases, his axe sang a song of triumph over the forest, interrupted at times by the crash of a falling tree. Moreover, what the woodland pioneer could do with an axe would make the city dweller or one born and bred on the wide prairies gaze at him in goggle-eyed wonder. The curiously curved axe handle which is purely an American invention and is even yet virtually unknown to Europe was evolved quite early. In order the more quickly to provide a sizable area for planting, some of the larger trees were often merely "deadened" by girdling and left standing. Once the field had been cleared, it must be fenced, since the livestock usually ran at large. It seems useless to tell the people of the state which has produced the most famous rail splitter of all time anything about the labor of making rails!

The logs not to be used in building or for fencing were rolled together into great heaps at the neighborhood "log rollings" and burned, and the stumps and girdled trees were also burned as far as possible when they had become dry. The settler could not foresee a time when the American people would deplore the passing of the forests and need so desperately the vast store of timber thus so wantonly destroyed. Even if he had, it is doubtful if the possible wants of the future would have prevailed over the necessities of the present. Whether it was timber, game and fish, soil or mineral resources, the average frontier American has seldom thought much of conservation for the sake of future generations. "Have you no regard for posterity?" an old pioneer was once asked. "Regard for posterity?" was the answer. "No, I should say not. Why should I? What did posterity ever do for me?"

To the log-cabin settler the forest was a horrible impediment to progress and civilization—an enemy to be fought every day. Moreover, the forest fought back with a persistence and vigor that must at times have proved most discouraging. After a field had been cleared and the logs and slash burned, roots still remained deep in the soil and from these, each spring, sprouts shot up with an enthusiasm that must have made it appear that a giant hand had sown some strange variety of dragon's teeth on every hard-won acre. These must be cut down annually and, if possible, the roots from which they had grown, destroyed. The labor required to hold and utilize what had already been wrested from the forest made additional clearing proceed very slowly. In consequence, the area of cultivated land usually remained small for several years.

In most cases, however, there was little need that it should be large. Remote from markets, the settler sought only to provide for himself and family those fundamental needs of food, clothing, and shelter. Even this was not always easy and the ambitious man who sought each year to widen the clearing and so provide more land to produce more food for his family found his life one of unremitting toil. Corn was the staple breadstuff of most of the woodland pioneers and hominy, corn pone, griddle cakes and corn dodgers—sometimes known as "hush puppies"—were staple articles of diet.

At first, meat was largely obtained from hunting, and the long rifle and skill in its use furnished the best guarantee of an adequate meat supply for the family. It was not long until game began to grow scarce but by this time the first pigs brought in had increased to such numbers as to provide an ample supply of pork, ham, and bacon. Usually, hogs ran at large in the woods fattening on the mast, but were called up each evening to be fed a little corn—in the vernacular of the pioneers "just enough to ha'nt 'em home" so they would be at home at "hog killing time."

Two or three lean cows provided a somewhat inadequate supply of milk and butter while the only fruit during the early years consisted of wild blackberries, huckleberries, plums, grapes, persimmons, and pawpaws gathered in the woods. A few peach, apple, and pear trees were usually planted, however, and when these came into bearing the situation with respect to fruit was greatly improved. The garden supplied an abundance of fresh vegetables, and turnips, potatoes, sweet potatoes, and cabbage were stored in a cellar or buried in the ground for winter use.

Clothing was often homespun for there were at least a few sheep in almost every community, though they required considerable care due to the ravages of wolves and other predatory animals. Shoes were made at home from home-tanned leather and a warm coat was often made from the skins of animals while the buckskin shirt and coonskin cap were also common. Furniture for the cabin was likewise made at home. This consisted of bedsteads on which were placed feather beds, straw ticks, or shuck mattresses, hickory-bottomed chairs, tables of rough boards, or a bench on which the children sat at meals and which was usually placed behind the dining table next to the wall. Often two or three rag rugs were on the floor and one or two pictures on the walls. Light was furnished by tallow candles and in the later period by kerosene lamps.

With the passing years life grew a trifle easier. The log-cabin home was weathered by the elements. Gay morning-glories climbed over the windows or the front porch, and beds of old-fashioned flowers such as pinks, phlox, bachelor's buttons, and zinnias beside the front door or along the path leading to it added splashes of color to the scene. In time the humble home, which had at first appeared new and out of place, nestled into its setting and merged with the landscape as though placed there by the hand of God Himself.

The horizon of the woodland pioneer and his family was necessarily limited. Seldom did he know many people beyond walking distance from his own cabin though "walking distance" is a relative term and was greater than most people would regard it now. Yet, in spite of long hours of hard labor, time was found for social contact with neighbors. Often on Sunday morning the entire family would rise early, and with the numerous youngsters washed and scrubbed to within an inch of their lives, all were loaded into the wagon for a drive of two or three miles to spend the day with friends. Here they always received a warm welcome. When the horses were stabled and fed, the men sat in the shade of a tree and talked while the women went into the kitchen and prepared dinner and the children ran wild about the farm or played such games as marbles, town ball, or prisoner's base. Eventually dinner was announced and the older people went in and sat down at the long table, while the children were required to wait since there was no room at the table nor were there enough dishes for everyone to eat at the same time.

After grace had been said, the guests and hosts alike fell to with an enthusiasm that the abundance before them fully warranted. When they had finished, the dishes were washed, the second table was set, and the children attacked the food with appetites considerably sharpened by the delay. Those Sunday dinners in a frontier home, especially after the first two or three years of pioneering had passed, would make the modern housewife, accustomed to dealing with the problem of red points, blue points, and general shortages, turn green with envy. Chicken and dumplings, fried ham with red gravy, turnip greens and other fresh vegetables from the garden, blackberry cobbler, cool buttermilk, coffee, corn bread and golden butter were only a few of the items likely to grace the table in the early summer season. In winter, baked sweet potatoes, dried corn, and beans boiled with pork, turnips, or cabbage were substituted for the fresh vegetables, and nearly always there was chicken, or in some cases baked spareribs, country sausage, fried pork, or bacon and cream gravy. In fact many a person who can remember these earlier days will assert that he has eaten better meals in some log-cabin homes than he has ever been able to find in any fashionable New York restaurant where it costs a dollar or two to sit down and a great deal more to get up.

Such all-day visits were frequently almost the only form of social relaxation for many a busy housewife though there were occasional quilting or sewing parties, and sometimes an itinerant preacher held services in one of the homes or under a rude brush arbor.

The men, however, had more social contacts than did their wives. Eventually a gristmill would be erected beside some convenient stream which furnished the necessary water power, and men and boys bringing a "turn of corn" to mill would sit in the shade and gossip or swap stories while waiting for the grain to be ground, often commenting sarcastically but in good-humored fashion on the length of time required for that work. "Most persistent mill I ever saw," asserted Hank Johnson. "Just as soon as it gets one grain ground, it tackles the next one right off." "Yep," replied his companion, "my boy Sam says, sez he, 'Why, paw, I could eat that meal as fast as this mill grinds it.' 'Maybe you could, son,' sez I, 'but how long could you keep it up?' 'Well, paw,' sez he, 'I figger I could keep it up till I starved to death!' "

Soon some enterprising settler usually built a general merchandise store near the mill or at some crossroads and dispensed as much sugar, coffee, calico, and other commodities as the pioneer settlers could purchase, frequently bartering his merchandise for coonskins, buckskin, cowhides, tallow, and beeswax, or butter and eggs if not too remote from a larger market. The crossroads store also became something of a social center where people met their neighbors and exchanged neighborhood news while transacting business. A schoolhouse was soon built and this too became a center for social activities. Church services might be held there once or twice a month, a literary and debating society was organized, box suppers were held, and meetings for singing arranged on Sunday afternoons. The younger people also held parties, socials, play parties, and in some cases square dances at the more commodious homes. So the little community soon began to enjoy some social life.

As the years went by, the character of the log-cabin frontier began to change. The settler's family increased and he found it necessary to widen his fields by clearing additional acres in order to produce more food for so many hungry mouths. Families were, as a rule, large: half a dozen children being only an average number, ten or a dozen not unusual. With little hired labor available and money to pay for it very scarce even if it had been procurable, children were a distinct asset to people faced with the heavy task of clearing and improving a woodland farm. In consequence, the settler "raised his own help" just as he raised his own meat, fruit, and vegetables. Some months ago the writer and an elderly farmer from the wooded hills of northern Arkansas were walking along the streets of a small city with a huge Navy base located nearby, weaving their way in and out of an almost continuous procession of baby buggies pushed by young Navy wives. Presently the old farmer shifted his chew of tobacco to the other side of his mouth, spat generously over the curb, and remarked: "Well, it looks like that in eighteen or twenty years we're sure either agoin' to have to start another war or clear more land."

Here spoke a voice from the past—stating in succinct fashion the problem of the log-cabin pioneer of three-quarters of a century ago. With his family increasing so rapidly, he must clear more land, but the limits to which his fields might be extended were marked by the boundaries of his farm and before many years these had been reached. Except in certain parts of eastern Texas—a state always generous with land which was its most plentiful commodity—very few of the forest pioneers had originally acquired a large acreage. The famous advice given by Mrs. Means to her husband who sought land, "Git a plenty while you're a-gittin'," was seldom followed by the pioneer farmer. Few actual farmers had money enough to purchase a large tract and, moreover, there seemed little reason for it since years would be required to clear and put in cultivation even 40 acres. There seemed no point in holding title to extensive pasture lands which could hardly be enclosed at a time when the only fences must be made of rails or poles. Even if the settler owned as much as 80 to 160 acres a large part of it was likely to consist of hills or rocky land unfit for tillage.

As more and more settlers entered a new region, government land passed into the hands of individuals until none remained. Many of these individuals were the small subsistence farmers though naturally some large tracts were early acquired by speculators, in many cases nonresidents, who sold off their holdings at a generous profit in tracts of a size to suit the purchaser, and gradually increased their prices to "as much as the traffic would bear." Eventually some of these larger landholders came out to settle on their holdings bringing capital enough to build themselves large farmhouses and to develop their extensive acres. Other men, farther east where land was high, sold out their farms and came to this secondary frontier to purchase large tracts of relatively cheap land and establish themselves as prosperous farmers. Some of these rented a part of their holdings and the tenant farmer began to appear in a region where he had hitherto been unknown. Thus in time a differentiated society began to grow up in what had been the former log-cabin frontier. There were the original settlers on their small woodland farms, and on the one hand these larger and more prosperous landowners who were growing so called "money crops" of cotton and tobacco in the South or of wheat, corn, and hogs in the North, and on the other tenant farmers renting land from these large landowners.

Under such circumstances what was the log-cabin dweller with half a dozen boys fast growing up to do? Clearly his little farm would not support the entire family. Once these lads had reached manhood they must, if they continued farm life, either migrate or become tenant farmers, giving a large share of the fruits of their toil to the landlord. Prices of farm land were by this time too high for them to purchase farms in the community.

Of course from 1840 to 1865 events of nationwide importance came to confuse the picture. The migration to Oregon, the California Gold Rush, the Pike's Peak boom, and the Civil War took many thousands of young men from the log-cabin frontier, some of them permanently but in most cases only for a temporary absence. Those that returned came back only to find opportunities for them less promising than when they had left.

There were factors other than providing for the future of a growing family that caused many a log-cabin dweller to leave his hard-won clearing and seek his fortune on the western prairies. The fertility of the soil declined due to erosion and lack of crop rotation. The little farm, which now produced less than formerly, must provide a living for a larger number. Also on every frontier there have always been certain restless individuals who pioneer for the sheer love of pioneering. This applies not only to the hunters, mountain men, and other characters of the Great West but to settlers as well. It is in a sense the manifestation of the creative urge. Such men love the thrill that comes from building a home and carving a farm from the wilderness and helping to develop a new community. Once that has been done they are eager to push on and repeat the process.

All these factors and many more must be considered in determining the reasons for the rapid settlement of the prairie plains in the decades immediately following the close of the Civil War. Just to the west of the last log-cabin frontier lay the enormous stretch of level prairies. At their eastern edge settlement had hesitated for approximately a generation but, not long after Appomattox, the migration began and soon swelled to a flood covering all that part of the plains region suitable for crop growing and extending at times into other parts which we now realize were not suitable, due to lack of rainfall. In the two decades from 1870 to 1890 the population of the Dakotas grew, in round numbers, from 14,000 to 719,000; that of Nebraska from 122,000 to 1,058,000; Kansas from 364,000 to 1,427,000; and Texas from 818,000 to 2,235,000. Even in the next decade, from 1890 to 1900, there was a great increase in the population of some western states and territories, that of Oklahoma Territory rising from 61,000 to over 400,000. While a considerable part of this population, particularly in the North, was European born, much of it in the central and southern area came from the log-cabin frontier of the next tier of states to the east.

The log-cabin dweller who sought a new home on the prairies, like every other man who migrates to a new land, always did so despite the urgings and oft-expressed misgivings of his friends and neighbors. "Wild geese migrate—owls stay at home" declared the friends of Nathan Wyeth of Massachusetts when he expressed his intention of removing to Oregon. When Hiram Wick, a tenant farmer of the Texas Cross Timbers, who had a large family of girls and owned no property except a wagon and team, a few tools and household goods, and a number of "hound dogs" and a shotgun, announced his intention of going to Oklahoma, his old father-in-law was vociferous in his objections. Sitting at a neighbor's dinner table one day the old gentleman expressed himself in no uncertain terms. "Let me tell you, Mr. Smith," he exclaimed, pounding the table to give emphasis to his words, "whenever Hiram Wick goes out West with that big family of girls of his'n and no cattle—it'll break him—it'll break him—just as shore as I'm a-settin' here a-eatin' your grub." Yet Hiram had nothing to "break" except a pack of hounds and a shotgun.

Once he had acquired what was called the "Western fever," however, a man seldom gave much heed to the objections of his neighbors. The Homestead Law of 1862 gave 160 acres free of charge except for land office fees to every citizen twenty-one years old or the head of a family, or to those who had declared their intention of becoming citizens. Migration for the tenant farmer involved few preliminaries. Ordinarily he had only a wagon, team, and a few tools and household goods. Once his crops had been gathered, all movable property could be loaded into the wagon and a start made for the West. The same was true of a newly married couple who went west to establish their first home. Ordinarily the parents of the groom and bride each made some contributions toward providing the necessary outfit for the journey and the establishment of a new household.

Not much was required. Many a young couple set out for the Prairie West with high hopes for the future though their sole worldly possessions consisted of a pony team and an old wagon in which was stored a plow, hoe, spade, axe, and gun, together with a feather bed, half a dozen quilts, a couple of chairs, and a box containing a skillet, kettle, coffee pot, a very few dishes, and a meager supply of food for the journey. Often the young husband did not have $25 in real money tucked in the pocket of his faded jeans, and in some cases it was much less.

For the small landowner migration involved more complications since in most cases a buyer must be found for the farm. Seldom did the purchase price amount to more than a few hundred dollars, and not more than one-third of this was ordinarily paid in cash while the remainder was likely to be due in installments annually for three or four years. When the farm had been sold, with some misgivings and regrets, there remained the work of finishing the harvest of the crops, selling the livestock and such other property as could not be taken in the wagon, and a hundred other little chores and errands. The wife carefully packed her most treasured belongings and the junior members of the household went about swelling with importance while their young friends and playmates gazed at them with respectful admiration. They were going west—out into a land of romance and adventure—a region of wide plains traversed by mighty mysterious rivers and they already felt themselves "wild westerners." To any questions from the unfortunate youngsters that must remain in the drab and monotonous surroundings, they responded with imagination and enthusiasm. Yes, it would be a long and dangerous journey but their dad was a brave man and would see them all safely through to its end.

Once there, life was certain to be filled with adventure! Surely there were Indians out there and cowboys and wolves, bears and panthers! They themselves were going to learn to be great riders and hunters and perhaps scouts or ranchmen. Maybe some day they would come back mounted on dashing horses with silver-mounted saddles and dressed in buckskin with boots, and spurs, and all the regalia of real cowboys! It is little wonder that their youthful comrades were impressed by such flights of eloquence.

At last came the day of departure. Nearly everything had been packed into the wagon the day before. Old Rover could go West too, trotting along beside the wagon or beneath it, but sorrowfully the children carried the family cat to the house of a nearby neighbor who had promised her a good home because there was no way of taking her with them and besides "it is bad luck to move cats." Probably several friends came over early to see the emigrants off. The last box and bundle was packed in the wagon box and the children climbed to their seats on rolls of bedding beneath the canvas cover which had been looped up on either side so that they might view the landscape. Then the husband and wife climbed to the spring seat and, followed by the final goodbyes and good wishes of the assembled neighbors and with old Rover barking excitedly and capering about the wagon, out toward the mysterious West drove this family of pioneers.

Perhaps in most cases the husband kept his eyes steadfastly fixed on the road ahead and the children chattered excitedly, but we can believe that it was a very unusual wife who did not look back and wipe her eyes with her handkerchief as the old home which she had loved and helped so much to create faded into the distance. One who has himself journeyed west in a covered wagon and who has lived beside a road along which many migrating families have passed with the husband and wife sitting on the spring seat, and three or four children peeping out from beneath the brown, travel-stained cover, has never had any doubt as to which was the tragic figure in each such little family group. It was never the man, going out into a new region of free land and what he felt were great opportunities. It was not any of the children, for to all of them such a journey was one continuous picnic. Always the tragic figure was the woman sitting by her husband's side going away from home and church and old friends and all those little things which mean so much more to a woman than they can ever mean to a man—yet cheerfully and will-ingly going with those she loved to a far-off country. How many times had she packed away beneath the wagon cover, among the tools and household goods, two or three pictures, some lace curtains, a white tablecloth and napkins, a few choice pieces of glass, china, or silver, a few packages of flower seeds and some roots of the old rose bush by the window—packed away with tender loving hands in moist earth to be transplanted into the alien soil of a new home which as yet existed only in her dreams.

Probably the husband, knowing the desperate need for space, had urged that such useless things should be left be-hind. Perhaps he had asserted that they would be out of place in the crude frontier society of which they must for many years be a part, but the wife usually had her way and she was right. It was only the possession of a few such little treasures that sustained many a homesteader's wife through the cruel first years of life on a prairie claim, because these things represented to her at once a memory of her own old home, where she had a great pride in these possessions, and the hope of a time in the future when she would have a home into which these things would properly fit.

The journey westward might be long but as a rule it was a happy one. When the edge of the great prairies was reached the character of the farms and houses began to change. Log cabins gave place to structures of stone or lumber. Then the distance between houses lengthened as they entered the more thinly-peopled region. When they saw the first sod houses and dugouts they realized that they were truly in a new land and the sight of the first prairie dogs convinced the children that the real West had been reached at last. Finally, they came only to scattered settlements with long stretches of unoccupied land between, and here a tract of 160 acres was chosen and their long trek was at last ended.

Many factors were considered in choosing the land upon which to settle. Most important of all was fertile soil, but distance to railroad, the possible source of a supply of water, and of firewood and timber for framing a habitation all had to be considered. Also, it was desirable not to be too far from neighbors and to locate in an area where others were likely to settle in the near future so that it would be possible to have a school, church, and perhaps a store. More, perhaps, than the woodland pioneer, did the prairie settler hope for the rapid peopling of the region about him. This may have been due in part to the bigness and loneliness of the land. Or perhaps it was partially a hope for increased land values that were certain to come with more population, or merely the eager desire to see his own courage and faith justified and the region grow quickly to a thickly-peopled and prosperous region.

The preliminaries of visiting the land office and making entry of the tract chosen if it were a homestead, or of arranging with the railway land department for the purchase and first payment if it were railroad land, did not usually take long. Then came the building of a home and the task of creating a farm from a tract of virgin prairie.

As has been indicated, by no means all or even a majority of the prairie pioneers built and lived in sod houses. Only in localities where the soil is of firm texture with its particles firmly bound together by the roots of a thick coat of grass can a sod house be built. In areas of sandy soil covered by bunch grass, some other type of construction is necessary. Like the forest dweller, the prairie settler utilized for his house the material which he had available. In some cases it was stone, in others sod, in still others rough lumber. In many instances, the home was a dugout, or half dugout, partially underground but usually with the sides built up sufficiently to admit of two small windows.

Ordinarily, the cover was removed from the wagon and used as a tent while the first home was constructed. If it were a sod house, long ribbons of sod usually eight to ten inches wide were cut into blocks about eighteen inches long, walls were made of these with spaces left for a door in front and windows on either side. These spaces were framed with rough boards to hold the windows and door. A fireplace was usually put at one end of the structure with the chimney also built of sod. The earthen floor was beaten hard and smooth, and the roof, supported by the heavy ridgepole which extended the entire length of the building, was made of blocks of sod resting on willows or rushes placed on poles extending like rafters from the ridgepole to the side walls. Properly made, a sod house would last for several years, though some repairs might from time to time be necessary.

The dugout was often constructed by excavating a rectangular space in the side of a low hill and building up the front portion with sod, stones, or short logs. Its interior differed little from that of the sod house. In some instances stone was available to build the walls of the new home and in others the settlers had enough money to purchase lumber for a crude box dwelling of one or two rooms made of twelve-inch boards with the cracks between them covered by narrow strips of lumber. Such a house had a shingle roof and a floor but the great majority of people did not have sufficient funds for such a luxurious dwelling. The first home of the majority in many areas was either a sod house or dugout.

Once the home was finished and the scanty possessions moved inside and bestowed to the best advantage, the settler set to work at the task of improving the farm and at the same time providing a living for his family. Sod was broken and harrowed, a little crop and a few fruit trees planted, shelter provided for the livestock, and arrangements made for water and fuel.

From the very first the settler was acutely conscious of the wide differences between his present environment and his former one. The most impressive thing about the prairie was the prairie itself. A young man born and bred among the wooded hills of Arkansas once went out to western Oklahoma to visit his brother and reached his destination late at night. The next morning his brother conducted him outside and said: "Well, Bill, what do you think of the country?" Bill gazed for a full minute at the wide expanse of green prairie stretching out on every side to meet the purple horizon before he replied: "I don't rightly know, Sam, but it looks to me like the Lord or somebody else has done the best job of clearin' here I've ever seen!"

How to live in a region almost completely devoid of timber was a major problem. For the first time the settler realized the value of the forests and often yearned for just a few of the trees which he had so wantonly destroyed. Wood for fuel was scarce and must often be eked out by the use of cow chips or twisted hay. The few timbers required for framing the sod-house home must be hauled for many miles. The matter of enclosures was a problem. Locust or Osage orange seeds were planted about the fields and pasture lands but it would require some years for the young sprouts to grow sufficiently to form a hedge and in the meantime the horses and even the milk cows must be picketed out on the prairie or in some cases herded by one of the children throughout the day and driven up each night to a small corral made of poles often hauled from some distant ravine, or tract of land too rough for farming.

Securing water for domestic use and for the livestock was also likely to be difficult. Regretfully, the settler thought of the cold, flowing springs of his former homeland or of the shallow well near the log-cabin door from which an ample supply of cool water was drawn by means of a bucket and sweep or with rope and pulley. Springs on the prairie plains were few and far between and while, in some localities, good water might be had by digging a well to the depth of thirty feet or less, there were many other regions where it was necessary to drill for hundreds of feet before a supply of water was reached. Out on the high plains of western Texas a settler was encountered who was hauling water in barrels from a source nine miles from his home. Asked why he did not put down a well, he replied that he had tried it but had decided that it was just as near to water one way as another and he preferred to bring his horizontally rather than perpendicularly! Also in many large areas of the Southwest the water secured from wells was so impregnated with gypsum as to make it very distasteful and in some cases wholly unfit for household use.

The prairie pioneer also quickly discovered that he must adjust to new climatic conditions. Nature worked on a grand scale. Long periods of drought were followed by torrential rains. The summers seemed intensely hot and the winters were often very cold. Then, too, there was the wind which seemed to blow eternally and often proved most nerve-racking, especially to the women.

In addition, he found that he must revise his former conceptions as to distance. The nearest railroad town was likely to be forty or fifty miles away and from it must be transported most supplies. Even the little frontier store might be six to ten miles distant and the nearest neighbor at least a mile or more away. No longer was the settler's horizon bounded by the distance that he could easily walk. Trips to the railroad, to the store or little hamlet, or even to the homes of any but the nearest of neighbors must be made on horseback or by wagon. This ordinarily meant the acquiring of another horse or two, a better saddle, and far wider contacts than had been known in the past.

Even today the resident of the prairie plains has a conception of what constitutes distance that is puzzling to the rural or small town people of the East. Often he may drive forty to eighty miles to attend a show, for a few hours' shopping, or to have dinner with a friend. A traveler across western Texas suddenly remembered that he had a cousin living somewhere in that portion of the state and stopped at a ranchman's house on the remote chance of securing some information as to this relative. "Could you tell me where

Jim Blevins lives?" he inquired of the old cattlemen sitting on the front porch. "Sure can, stranger," was the reply, "he lives exactly ninety-five miles straight down this road and on the right hand side, in a two-story white house with a big cottonwood tree in the front yard. You can't miss it!"

Undoubtedly the prairie settlers were also affected by attitudes and viewpoints of those who made up the pastoral society which in many cases they came to displace. Unlike the woodland pioneer who found the region occupied only by an occasional Indian, the plains dweller came into contact with the ranchman and was doubtless influenced by the range rider's indifference to money and distance, as well as his buoyant cheerfulness, youthful spirit, and light-hearted attitude. This is another story, however, which has already been told and would require an exclusive monograph for any full discussion. At any rate the prairie pioneer felt at least that his viewpoint had been broadened by the bigness of the wide land in which he had settled. He felt that he was doing things worthwhile and was distinctly sorry for his old neighbors farther east. He believed that they were cramped by a narrow life and earnestly urged that they come out and join him in the development of a new country.

The sod-house dweller also soon found his food habits radically changed. His prairie land could easily be prepared for wheat and this rather than corn became his staple breadstuff. Bacon and pork were common but grass-fed beef appeared on his table far more often than formerly. Wild game was still an important addition to his food supply but instead of squirrels, pheasants, or venison, it was likely to be prairie chickens, plovers, curlews, or in some cases antelope. The garden supplied vegetables but the newly planted orchard would not come into bearing for years, and the mouths of the settler and his family often watered as they thought of the luscious blackberries and strawberries, or the succulent pawpaws and persimmons that grew so plentifully in the woods of the old homeland or of the apples, peaches, and pears produced by their trees planted in a sheltered spot near the log cabin which they had left behind.

Lack of fruit was one of the real hardships of the sod-house frontier but the ingenious pioneers sought substitutes so far as possible. Watermelons and cantaloupes often grew in astonishing fashion. Tomatoes, rhubarb, and several types of small melons known as pomegranates, or "poor man's apples" were common. Pies were made from pie melons and preserves from citron melons or watermelon rinds, and pumpkin butter or even a marmalade made from cantaloupes appeared on many tables. Trips were made to the sand hills bordering the nearest river to gather wild plums or grapes from which were made jelly and preserves, so far as the scanty supply of sugar permitted. On the whole, the sod-house pioneers seldom lacked food, though it might be coarse and lacking in variety. Yet with milk and butter, eggs, and fried chicken now and then—mostly then—they were reasonably well fed.

Perhaps the most significant change in the life of the man who migrated from the log-cabin frontier to that of the sod house was his enormous increase of leisure. In his old home he had a job three hundred and sixty-five days in the year and three hundred and sixty-six in leap year. Land had to be cleared, sprouts cut, stumps grubbed out, rails split, and new buildings erected from the abundance of material at hand. All such tasks were in addition to the ordinary labor of plowing, planting, cultivating, and harvesting plus the daily chores of living. Out on the wide prairie the first few months were busy ones while he was building a home, erecting a shelter for domestic animals, and plowing the prairie sod. When this had been done, however, long hours of labor every day were no longer necessary or profitable. If he were located forty to fifty miles from a railroad town there was little need to grow crops for sale. Even when wheat was a fair price at the market centers, it brought very little at the frontier railroad town due to the long haul by rail and the high freight rates. Any surplus grown yielded slight returns and besides, for the first few years, drought, hot winds, grasshoppers, green bugs, and the scanty yield of newly-turned sod kept the surplus down to a minimum. Under such circumstances it is not surprising that the settler merely practiced subsistence farming, seeking only to provide a living of sorts for his family while he "held down his claim" and waited hopefully for the coming of a railroad bringing nearer markets, more settlers, increased land values, and all the good things of civilization. Long, leisurely trips to the railroad or for wood might be necessary but of hard labor, to which he had once been accustomed, there was very little.

Unfortunately this did not apply to the mistress of the sod house. For her there were still the daily tasks of cooking, sweeping, washing clothes or dishes, mending, caring for the children, and all that work of women which it has been said "is never done." Life on the prairie frontier was hard for women and one can sympathize with the woman newly arrived in western Texas who wrote to her sister back in Tennessee: "Texas seems like a good country for men and dogs but a mighty hard place for oxen and women."

While the prairie wife did not have as much leisure as her husband, it seems probable that life in this new land was not without its advantages even for her. Back in the old home, particularly in the South, the average woman, recognizing the heavy toil of her husband, sought to relieve him of some of the labor often recognized as properly "a man's work" and took over most of the care of the garden, chickens, and cows. She felt with some reason that a man who had split rails all day should not be expected to milk three or four cows at night or feed and care for the chickens, and so cheerfully did this herself, only claiming as her reward the "butter and egg money" if there should happen to be any. With equal cheerfulness, she planted and cultivated the garden, only asking that her husband plow the land and make it ready for planting. Unless such habits had become too deeply ingrained, there was likely to be some readjustment on the sod-house frontier of this division of labor. Here the man of the house was likely to use some of his abundant spare time to do the milking, gardening, and at least helping with the poultry.

Also the clean pure air of the prairies promoted good health. Seldom was there any malaria, commonly known as "chills and fever" such as was all too common in portions of the woodland region, and strong healthy children, free to run wild on the open prairie, required comparatively little care. In addition the prairie settler's wife was largely relieved of such labor as making soap or hominy, grinding sausage, rendering lard, picking berries in the woods, or weaving rag rugs which had at times seemed all too common tasks of daily life in the old home. So, on the whole, she too perhaps did less hard work than formerly, though not to the same degree as her husband.

The effects of this more abundant leisure upon the cultural and social pattern of the sod-house frontier were soon apparent. Hard labor from dawn to dusk ceased to be regarded as a virtue and people no longer felt it necessary to apologize for taking time to go fishing or hunting or for spending long hours at the country store or tiny prairie town.

Social activities were promoted. There was much visiting of neighbors and friends and many picnics, parties, dances, fish fries, barbecues, and meetings for the purpose of singing. A little schoolhouse was built of sod or rough lumber and a teacher hired to conduct school for three or four months each year. This schoolhouse soon became a social center. Here were held box suppers, pie suppers, church and Sunday school. A literary and debating society was organized, usually giving a program twice a month. Every holiday was celebrated with enthusiasm—the Fourth of July with a picnic and Christmas with a community Christmas tree. New friendships were formed and among the young people romances began to blossom. Such social activities did not hinder work too much for apart from "holding down the claim" and watchfully waiting for the country to grow up, there was comparatively little useful work to be hindered.

That some years of virtually enforced leisure often affected the habits and outlook of the people was inevitable. Years later when, due to the coming of railroads and markets, some farmers had become prosperous enough to employ additional help, it was a common saying: "If you want a good farm hand, get you a young fellow from the woods of Arkansas or Missouri. He'll make you a fine hand for the first year or two but as soon as he's learned the ways of this prairie country, he'll get just like these boys that have grown up here." Undoubtedly, there was some element of truth in this.

While the prairie claim did not always afford the settler

steady profitable employment, there were such tasks as planting trees or building an addition to his sod-house home by which he could utilize some of his spare time. Then, too, since no labor could be found in his own community, he might in time of stress or distress leave the family at home for a month or so while he took the wagon and team and drove east to a more thickly settled region to pick cotton or work in the harvest fields, thereby earning enough money to provide shoes, clothing, and groceries for his little flock during the coming winter.

Enough has been said to make it apparent that the sod-house frontier was very different from that of the wooded region from which many of its people came. Topography, soil, climate, vegetation, remoteness from market, and the bigness of the land all combined to form a new economic and social pattern of life which America had formerly never known. It was a good life, on the whole, and not without its attractive features for these settlers were a great people. The humble home was, as a rule, always kept neat and clean. Flowers were planted in beds beside the sod-house door and the windows were framed with morning-glories or other vines. Family ties were close while hospitality and neighborly kindness were universal. On Sunday morning the children were washed and dressed in their pitifully poor best clothes and the day was one of rest and recreation. Lives were motivated by a simple but deep and sincere spiritual faith which to most people was literally "a rock in a wrong land, a shelter in the time of storm." In prosperity and adversity alike it led them on as a pillar of cloud by day and of fire by night. Remote from hospitals, doctors, or even medicines on those rare occasions when a child fell ill, what was the pioneer mother to do? She could only administer such home remedies as might be at hand and, if these failed, put her trust "in the Great Physician who can heal all diseases."

All of this applies to the typical settler of the better class. There were trashy people and even near-degenerates on both the log-cabin and the sod-house frontiers and of these a few authors have written books in the the name of realism that have attracted wide attention. Such writers have mistaken facts for truth. The conditions and the people they have described may have existed but they were very exceptional and their descriptions are untrue in the larger sense of the word.

The period of the sod-house frontier was of short duration. Railroads were rapidly penetrating the western prairies, their builders encouraged by the level nature of the land and the comparatively cheap cost of construction. Towns sprang up mushroomlike along their lines, to which flocked men eager to erect elevators, and mills, or to establish stores, banks, and other business enterprises. More settlers poured in and the ranchmen either turned to stock farming or drifted farther west to lands too arid or rough for successful crop growing. With markets close at hand, the settler sowed a larger acreage of wheat and a bounteous crop enabled him to erect a two or three-room house of lumber to replace the crude structure that had been his first prairie home. Successful farmers of the Middle West came out on excursions promoted by the railroads and were so much impressed that they promptly sold their high-priced lands and returned with money to buy these cheaper ones and to erect commodious homes and barns.

The original settler sought to follow their example. With the proceeds of two or three more good crops and all too often with the aid of a mortgage, he too built a big white house and red barn and purchased more farm machinery which the mechanical and industrial pioneers so soon made available. Barbed wire came into universal use, deep-well drilling machines and windmills provided an adequate water supply. The old "sod buster" was replaced by a gangplow, drills, binders, headers, and eventually combines came into general use. The internal combustion engine brought in cheap automobiles and tractors. Rural mail delivery and telephones became common. Some of the busy small towns grew to the stature of little cities, the road over which the covered wagon jolted westward was widened to a broad highway and the old-time pioneer life passed into the realm of things that used to be.

Just as a well-built log cabin will endure almost indefinitely while the life span of any sod house is but a few years, so did the log-cabin frontier, together with all that it represents, persist for many generations while that of the sod house quickly disappeared. Even today one may find in certain remote districts of the Appalachian highlands or in the hill regions of Oklahoma, Arkansas, or Missouri, families living in log houses and little communities in which conditions are strangely reminiscent of the woodland frontier of nearly a century ago. On the western prairies, however, one is likely to search in vain for a sod house or dugout or for a social and economic order resembling that of this same region in the latter part of the nineteenth century.

Though the frontiers of the log cabin and the sod house are largely gone and the pattern of life which each produced is only a memory, their influence still lingers and is of real significance to this new America of ours. For it takes no great stretch of imagination to make us believe that some of the qualities shown by our men all over the world in the bloody conflict that has just closed may be in part due to that heritage of courage, resourcefulness, stamina, hardihood, and spirit developed on these frontiers of other days. It may be urged that a majority of the men in our armed forces were born and bred in towns and cities. Yet it is certain that the forebears of a large part of our urban population were rural people lured to the city by what seemed greater opportunities and not a few of these came from one of these two frontiers.

Whether or not one accepts the idea that frontier characteristics persist as a cultural heritage long after the conditions which produced them are gone forever, few will deny that these pioneers had certain qualities or characteristics that America will need in the crucial years that lie ahead. Very much shall we need the courage, patience, persistence, energy, and industry of the log-cabin dwellers, the buoyant optimism, breadth of vision, and belief in the future of the prairie settlers, and the tolerance, kindness of heart, and deep spiritual faith of both. In the words of your state's greatest son, "fondly do we hope, fervently do we pray" that the ideals and qualities of heart and mind of these pioneer peoples may be ours as we face the future and the problems of a stormy and unstable world.

The Speech of the Pioneers[*]

"Out of the abundance of the heart," says the Word of God, "the mouth speaketh." The adventurous pioneer who, from the time of the planting of the first English colonies along the Atlantic seaboard down to the near present, and who settled that ever-changing geographic region known as the American frontier, was no diplomat. He used words to reveal rather than to conceal his thoughts. His speech, moreover, was a reflection of this life which he lived. Through it he expressed the thoughts which had to do with his work and play and all the experiences and incidents of daily life and from it may be gleaned an understanding of the heart and mind of the individual himself.

Our first pioneers were those hardy souls who sailed three thousand miles west to plant the seed of European culture in the American wilderness of Virginia or New England. Here they built their crude little homes, cut down the forest trees, planted little crops, and began the task of the conquest of a continent. They had come here English in speech, manners, customs, and traditions, but in this new environment all of these began slowly at first to be modified. When later groups of settlers came over a generation or more later they discovered that the language of these earlier pioneers, like their food, dress, homes, manners and customs had undergone

* Published in *The Arkansas Historical Quarterly*, VI (Spring, 1947), 117–31.

what might be called a "sea change." Many new words and expressions had crept into their language which must at first have proved puzzling to the newcomers.

The earliest immigrants had found themselves faced by the task of giving names to the new lands occupied as well as to the capes, bays, gulfs, rivers, lakes, and mountains and in addition to the new towns and settlements which they had established. With true British loyalty to king and country, members of the royal family and the towns or subdivisions of the old homeland were given first honors. Capes Charles and Henry; the James, Charles, and York Rivers; Carolina, Charleston, New York, New Jersey, New Hampshire, New London, Salem, Dover, Williamsburg, and Jamestown, as well as a host of other names, all bear witness to this tendency of the early colonists. Also discoverers and early explorers, with true frontier modesty, often gave their own names to rivers and lakes, as Lake Champlain, or the Hudson River. As settlements steadily advanced westward, these same general principles were applied except as the mother country became more remote and memories of royalty faded, the names of our own early leaders, of more recent discoverers, or the homeland or towns of the first settlers, were used instead of these earlier English terms. Washington, Franklin, Jefferson City, Jackson, Lincoln, Vermontville in Michigan, Salem and Portland, both in Oregon; Pike's Peak, Long's Peak, or Fremonts Peak are all familiar examples.

At the very first, however, and throughout the entire period of the settling of America, the pioneers were in close contact with the aboriginal inhabitants of the country and from the Indians were derived a very large proportion of our place names. These include those of more than half of the states extending from Massachusetts to Utah or from Minnesota to Alabama as well as of a large number of the most important rivers as the Mississippi, Ohio, Missouri, Arkansas, and Illinois.

In addition to providing numerous place names, the Indians also added many new words and expressions to our language. From them came such words as potato, tomato, tobacco, calumet, squaw, papoose, hominy, succotash, wampum, tomahawk, moccasin, and tepee, as well as many phrases still in common use, though their origin is often almost forgotten. Many persons who have almost never seen an Indian "put on their war paint," "do a war dance," or give the "war whoop," and "go on the warpath" use these expressions. Later they may decide to "hold a powwow," "make medicine," "smoke the peace pipe," and "bury the hatchet."

It is not the contributions of these native inhabitants, however, that have made the speech of the pioneers so expressive and colorful so much as have been those words, phrases, and expressions which they themselves coined and which grew out of the incidents and experience of their daily lives. Obviously they must be given as they were spoken since any attempt to put them into correct English would destroy their flavor and make them meaningless or in some cases even ludicrous. They are highly condensed, without a superfluous word and are characterized by their vivid imagery. The pioneer, like the Indian, was a close observer. He noted every detail and in speaking of something, did not seek to describe it but with a few bold strokes to paint a word picture. He did not *tell* the listener but preferred to *show* him and show him he did in one apt and sometimes salty phrase that meant more than could any lengthy description. "Well, parson," said Tom Smith of East Texas to the Reverend Johnson, who has just concluded a morning sermon couched in such simple language that even the unlettered old cowman could not fail to understand its every word, "you shore did put the fodder down where the calves could reach it." The words might have been meaningless to a city-bred person but to the minister familiar with farm and ranch life, they could be considered only as the highest possible praise. "Yes, I know Old Man Winters," said Buck Jones speaking of an elderly, narrow-minded individual in the community. "He's one of these fellers that looks through a knot hole with both eyes!" "And do you know his Cousin Jake?" he continued, referring to a pompous but busy, bustling little man of the neighborhood. "Jake allus reminds me of a little dog in high oats."

Every pioneer settler and all of his sons above the age of ten or twelve years had considerable skill in the use of firearms. This was in some cases due to the danger of Indian attack or the necessity of self protection in a region remote from law enforcing agencies and courts but it was primarily because much of the meat consumed by the family must be obtained by hunting. The commonest type of gun in earlier days was the flintlock rifle loaded from the muzzle or the smooth bore fowling piece or shotgun. The rifle bullet was placed on a small circular bit of cloth called the "patching" and pushed by means of a long straight ramrod down against the charge of powder that had been poured into the muzzle. In the case of the shotgun a wad of tow or paper was hammered down on top of the powder with the ramrod and a charge of shot poured in and held in place by a second wad pounded lightly down on top of it. A small circular receptacle called the "pan" was affixed to the barrel near the breech and connected with its interior by a small hole. Into this "pan" a few grains of powder were poured and these were ignited when the gun was fired by a spark struck by the falling hammer from a flint just above them.

This mechanism and the universal use of firearms gave rise to a number of pioneer expressions. If the tiny hole leading from the pan to the interior of the gun barrel was clogged, there was merely a flash of powder in the pan when the hammer was snapped but the weapon did not fire. In consequence any abortive action was "only a flash in the pan." A person ready to act was said to be "all cocked and primed to go" while one who stood very erect was said to "look like he had swallered a ramrod." The patching which held the bullet in place was, of course, lighted by the burning powder when the gun was fired. Certainty of a battle or skirmish was indicated by the statement: "We shore will smell th' patchin' before mornin'." A worthless individual was "not worth th' powder and lead it 'ud take to kill him" and one whose life work was ended was declared to "have shot his wad." "To give 'em both barrels" meant your best efforts and a man who disposed of all his property was alleged to have "sold out lock, stock, and barrel" "Wouldn't that cock yer pistol?" meant would it not startle you. Any guarantee of safety in government or business was "a gun behind the door," while a scantily clad girl was declared not "to have on enough clothes to wad a shotgun."

There were many other expressions with respect to guns. A favorite one was sometimes given a name. "Whenever Old Betsy speaks," remarked an old hunter, "you can be shore there'll be meat in th' pot." A lone revolver was called a "hog leg," and buckshot were referred to as "blue whizzers." When an eastern tenderfoot displayed a small nickel plated thirty-two caliber pistol to Ranch Foreman Hank Blevins, the latter snorted contemptuously: "Bud, if you'd ever shoot me with that thing and I ever found it out, I'd beat you half to death!" "Don't worry about my pullin' a gun on you," said a young cowhand, "any time my gun comes out, it'll come out a-smokin'." When Sam Thompson was told he'd better not quarrel with Mike O'Donnell, who was six and a half feet tall and weighed two hundred and fifty pounds, Sam only said: "I don't care how big he is. Colts make all men equal." "But suppose he catches you some time when you don't have your Colts?" someone asked. "Well, in that case," said Sam, "I'll just out with my old knife and whittle him down to my size."

Hunting and its logical partner, fishing, were responsible for a large number of the expressions of the American pioneers. The frontier settler hunted and fished not for sport, as most men do today, but for food. Meat, which was quite rare on the tables of most of the poorer people of Europe, was the staple article of diet of the frontier settler and during the first few years after he had established his home in a new western region, much of it was "wild meat" secured by hunting in the forest. In fact, meat was often easier to obtain than bread until sufficient time had elapsed to enable the settler to clear ground and plant and harvest a crop. One who provided an ample supply of food for his family was said to be "a good provider." "I'll admit ain't been too good a provider," said Old Man Hunt, who lived most of his life on the frontier of Texas, always remaining in the vanguard of settlement. "But in th' whole thirty years I've been married, I hain't let my family git plumb out of bread but twice."

Common similes related to hunting were "gentle as a fawn," "wild as a buck," "squall like a catamount," and "he fit like a pant'er." A "fightin' fool" was said to be able to "lick his weight in wildcats," a drunken boaster sometimes asserted that he was "a wild wolf and it was his night to howl," a speedy penman was able to "write like a deer in a walk," and an individual who was too hasty was warned "not to get ahead of the hounds." A man who was in error was alleged to be "barkin' up the wrong tree," while one who hesitated over a decision was urged "either to fish or cut bait," and one who had "been played for a sucker" was declared to "have swallered it, hook, line, and sinker." "Wouldn't that set yer cork to bobbin'?" meant would it not make you nervous and a man ready for an important event or emergency was said to be "loaded for bear." This latter expression came from the pioneer's habit of loading his gun with a heavy charge of powder and eight to twelve buckshot if he thought there was a possibility of his seeing a bear.

The life of the pioneer, however, was by no means all hunting, fishing, and fighting Indians. Fields must be cleared and plowed, crops tilled, water and wood brought for household use, domestic animals cared for, corn taken to the mill to be ground into meal, and the country store visited to barter butter and eggs or coonskins for "store tea," sugar, coffee, dry goods, or notions. The system of barter probably gave rise to the expression, "I've got a little tradin' to do at the store" which was used even when only cash purchases were to be made. There were, moreover, all the daily chores of cooking, sweeping, housecleaning, washing, ironing, feeding, milking, and all the other little tasks of daily life. The children must be fed, clothed, taught, and disciplined, and some attention given to the church, school, recreation, social life, and local government. All of these things affected the speech of the people creating many colorful and expressive phrases.

Many of these were connected with food since it is the

most fundamental of all human needs. White sauce or cream gravy was a staple article of diet and the pioneer's children were sometimes literally brought up on it. Any left over was fed to the dogs which probably was the reason why it was commonly called "hush puppy gravy." The term, "hush puppies," was also applied in the South to "corn dodgers" made of corn meal which had been scalded and made into round cakes which were fried in deep fat. "Calico gravy" was made by adding a little water to the skillet in which ham had been fryed. A plate of large, tough biscuits was said to "look like a gang of terrapins a-comin' " while a bachelor who was a good cook was able to "make biscuits with woman tracks on 'em." "Open face pie with pumpkin movement" is self explanatory and frosted layer cake was crudely referred to as "stair steps cake with calf slobbers on it." Sauce to be poured over pudding was "whippem-whoppem," eggs "hen berries," and rice "moonshine." Syrup and sugar were sometimes referred to respectively as "long sweetenin' " and "short sweetenin'," while in the Cow Country syrup was "lick," gravy "sop," and stew, or in some areas a type of bread pudding, was known as "slumgullion."

"That's th' best pie I ever flopped my lip over," said an old Texan noted for his love of good food, "but I've allus been a great eater; guess I'll just dig my grave with my teeth." "But you don't get fat," someone remarked. "Get fat? No, of course I don't." was the reply. "Guess I just eat so much it makes me pore to carry it." A particularly delicious dish was said to be "so good I nearly swallered my tongue," or "it 'ud make a mule colt kick its mammy," or "make a boy push his daddy in the creek."

"Does Mrs. Barker feed pretty well?" someone asked one of a rich widow's hired hands. "No, not too good," was the answer, "generally we has apologies for breakfast, promises for dinner, and disappointments for supper." "Why don't you come to see us?" asked Farmer Taylor, "the latch string always hangs outside th' door and if you'll come, we shore will put th' big pot in th' little one and make soup out of th' skillet."

Other expressions with respect to food were common. Coffee was "so strong it could git up and walk," a certain bachelor always made "good firm biscuits," and steak was "so tough you couldn't stick a fork in th' gravy." "Can you manage to eat th' biscuits, Uncle Billy?" sarcastically asked the cook of a threshing crew, when an old teamster complained that the beans were not done and the meat tough, "or had I better throw 'em out and bake another batch?" "They ain't so bad," was the reply, "if you spread lots of this butter on 'em, you can't taste 'em so much. Course you kin taste th' butter but I'm purty strong too as th' feller said and anyhow yer coffee's weak enough to bring up th' gineral average." "Speakin' of coffee," another one of the crew remarked, "lots of people don't know how little water it takes to make good coffee." "Anyhow," he continued, "there ain't no such thing as strong coffee; only weak people!"

One of the most pronounced characteristics of the pioneer's speech, as is also true of his humor, was exaggeration. The tendency to tell tall tales was common on every frontier and this same quality appears in the language of the pioneer. Many of his expressions were neither classical nor elegant but they were vivid and highly descriptive. The average person today might say that a man's "eyes widened and he turned ashy pale with fright" but Bill Jones used more colorful phraseology. "Old Sam shore wuz skeered," he declared; "why, his eyes looked like fried eggs in a slop bucket." "I seen him," chuckled one of Bill's comrades, "his eyes stuck out till you could have roped them with a grapevine and he run so fast that when he finally stopped, it took his shadder twenty minutes to ketch up with him."

"How are you today?" an old freighter was once asked. "Oh, fat as a match and straight as a fishhook," was the prompt reply. Other inquiries as to a neighbor's health were likely to bring the answer, "All so's to be up," "all so's to be about," "all able to eat our daily allowance," or "all gaily." "How's yer fat" was likely to bring the response, "Just a little bit streaked." Other highly exaggerated expressions were common. A knife was "so dull you could ride to mill on it." A girl's hair hung down her face until "she looked like a steer a-peekin' through a brush fence," and she was "so pore she had to stand twice in th' same place to make a shadder." The ground was "so muddy it'd bog th' shadder of a buzzard," while a man with projecting front teeth "looked like he could bite a pun'kin through th' fence," and one convalescing from a serious illness "looked like he had been pulled through a knot hole" or "had been chewed up and spit out." A tall, lean individual was "tall as a telegraph pole but not quite so heavy set" and a horse was "so pore you had to tie a knot in his tail to keep him from slippin' through th' collar."

There was an alliterative quality about many pioneer phrases and in some a rhythm that was almost poetic. A dejected appearing individual "looked like he'd supped sorrow out of a big spoon." An unfortunate one "had th' luck of a lousy calf—live all winter and die in th' spring." A man was so ignorant that "he didn't know B from a bull's foot," and determination to accomplish something was expressed by saying, "I'll make a spoon or spile a horn." It was said that

143

"he took to tall timber" or "come out of there like a bat out of a burnin' stump." Mary White's beau was very small and slender but when twitted about it, Mary only remarked, "Well, maw, I've allus heerd that precious goods is put up in small packages."

The homespun philosophy of the pioneer settler was responsible for some phrases that were almost proverbs. "Even a blind sow will find an acorn once in a while;" "it seems that th' world is gettin' weaker and wiser;" and "it's a mighty dry year when th' crabgrass fails" are all familiar examples. The chagrin or embarrassment of an individual were sometimes expressed in apt terms. "Old Wes looked down his nose like a pore sow." He "took th' dry grins," or "Sam wuz like th' little boy th' calf run over—he didn't have much to say." A man "stumbled around like a blind dog in a meat house" or "like a blind horse in a pawpaw patch."

Sneers and jeers or terms of reproach were often expressed in curious fashion as in the following expressions: "He's so contrary that if he ever gets drowned, I'll shore hunt upstream for him;" "if I could buy him for what he's worth and sell him for what he thinks he's worth, I shore would git mighty rich;" "I wouldn't trust that feller as fur as I could throw a steer by th' tail—why he'd ruther lie on ninety days time than tell th' truth fer cash." All these are self-explanatory as is the saying: "Why, I could lick a whole cow pen full like you and mind th' gate." To say that a man who would do that "would pull up young corn," or that "he ort to be shot, hung, and snake bit" was to refer to the activity of the crows that were often a pest and to the three most common causes of sudden death in some frontier communities. The pioneer usually chose his words carefully. When Old Man Carter, who was notoriously stingy and disagreeable, died, a group of neighbors came in "to sit up with the corpse." Under the time honored rule that no evil must be spoken of the dead, conversation with respect to the deceased languished until Ab Walker suddenly spoke up with considerable enthusiasm. "Well, there's one thing you kin say fer Mr. Carter; he wuzn't as mean *all* of th' time as he wuz *some* of th' time."

Words were often used in curious fashion as they still are in certain remote hill regions where the customs and traditions of a century ago still exist as "fossil remains" of a way of life that elsewhere has gone forever. It often became "hit," whip "whup," fire "fahr," James "Jeems," and the plural you became "you-uns." A bag was a "poke" and in alliterative fashion, one was warned not to "buy a pig in a poke." People were likely to "pack in some wood" or "tote a bucket of water from the spring" or "carry the cow to the pasture." Nouns were doubled as "ham meat," "hound dog," "man person," or "biscuit bread." Nouns were turned into verbs. A man "neighbored his meals" and did not mind work but "hated to be muled around." Hospitable and generous persons were "mighty clever people" and an irritable one was said to be "ill as a cat." The frontiersman, moreover, defended his use of words quite ably at times. "Why do you say that you 'are satisfied' that this corn will make forty bushels to the acre?" an old Arkansas farmer was once asked. "Satisfied means the same as contented." "No such thing," was the prompt response, "I'm satisfied that Nigger Sam over here is stealin' my chickens but I shore ain't contented about it." The questioner made no answer. Like the little boy the calf ran over, he didn't have much to say!

Social life and especially courtship and marriage brought out a great number of interesting expressions. A young girl who seemed to be interested in a certain young man was said to have "set her cap for him," while a young chap diligently wooing a girl was said to be "waitin' on her," surely a very apt phrase! A man who had evidently made up his mind to get married was alleged to have "set out" and a young woman who has just married was reported to "have jumped the broom." "I saw Henry and Ruth settin' on a bench and you just couldn't see daylight between 'em," an old lady once remarked. Boys were said to have "gone a gallin'," and a bunch of flowers "smelled like girls a-goin' to meetin'." Frank and Ed called so frequently on the Armstrong sisters that "Miz Armstrong says she cain't throw out a pan o' water without throwin' it on one of them boys." "Why didn't you come to the party Saturday night?" someone asked Besse Blevins. "Just couldn't make it," was the reply, "it 'uz too fur and snaky." "I told my wife I'd be home by five o'clock," remarked Tom Burton to his cronies sitting around the country store, "and here it is after six." "Well, when you do git there," one of his friends remarked, "you'll probably git all beat up and have yer tobaccer took away from you."

There were many smart sayings of children or adolescents and a host of miscellaneous phrases and expressions which require little or no explanation. "Don't let that take up with you," a boy was warned when he picked up his friend's knife or some other bit of property to examine it. To "carry water on both shoulders" meant to refuse to take a stand on any question, while "he's any man's dog that will hunt with him" had about the same connotation. A coat or other garment too small for the wearer looked like it "had been pulled too soon" and a balky horse "wouldn't pull th' hat off yer head." "If Jenny likes that feller, she shore must have a taste for roughness," an elderly livestock man once remarked when his niece had manifested an interest in an uncouth and disreputable young fellow in the community. "That's right," said his companion, "believe me, if she marries him, she shore will drive her ducks to a pore market." The phrase, "take a turn of corn to mill," probably originated with someone who had to wait his turn to have the corn ground. "If he wuz my boy, I'd tie him up and whup him till he broke loose," said Old Man Richey referring to a bad boy in the community. "Yes, sirree," said a backwoods school teacher, "there's a whole lot of new ideas bobbin' up these days about education and any time one comes out, it ain't three days till most all of the teachers in our county are whuppin' theirselves with their hats to git in on it."

"You'd better let me alone," said a boy to a bullying companion, "if you don't, in about three minutes you'll be goin' around with yer hand on yer head and a knot under it." "If I win that prize, I'll cut my galluses and go straight up," needs no comment, nor does the saying that "if you bored a hole in that feller's head, you wouldn't find brains enough to grease the gimlet." To become angry was to "fly off the handle," evidently referring to an axe which was likely to hurt someone if it flew off the handle. "If it had been a snake, it would a-bit me" meant that the sought-for object had at last been discovered within easy reach of the hand, while "polite as a whipped nigger" was a common phrase on the Southwestern frontier. Similes had to do with objects or incidents common to daily life. An individual was "tall as a tree," "big as a barn," "thin as a rail," "dirty as a pig," "pretty as a spotted pup," "fat as a bog," "bright as a dollar," "sharp as a briar," or "ugly as a mud fence." One who fiercely attacked an antagonist "went after him like a bitin' shoat," and another who fled in terror was alleged to have "run like a skeered Injun."

Some pioneer settlers had a real flair for language and used words that were meaningless or absurd with studied deliberation. "I'd shore like to sell you that cow," said Walt Maxwell. "She's a good cow and she's been sold lots of times and always with a good many extrys. A pitchfork, a log chain, and shotgun always goes with her. She never had a calf. Her mother before her never had one. She was raised by her grandmother." "What luck did you have fishin'?" a settler once asked his neighbor. "Oh, I caught a good many," was the response, "some of 'em wuz all of three inches long and the rest of 'em little bitty fellers." The term "suffer" was often used. People "suffered" from heat or cold and crops "suffered" from lack of rain. "I just got in last night after dark," said a man who had been away from home for a month, "and it seems pretty dry to me. I guess th' corn ain't re'ly a-sufferin', though, is it, Jim?" "Law no," Jim replied, "mine ain't. It did suffer a great deal, though, before it died."

The extension of settlement to the prairie plains and the development of the Cow Country brought in many new phrases and expressions, but the older ones brought from the hills and woods of the East still persisted in spite of the new environment. "I hope you don't churndasher the calves," said an old ranchman to a homesteader to whom he had loaned some cows to milk. A man was so poor a marksman that "he couldn't hit a barn door" and moreover "couldn't rope a pile of buckhorns." Spurs were "flesh diggers," a saddle a "kack" or "hull" and cartridges were universally called "catteridges." "Slim," an ill featured cowhand who slept in a shed room of the ranchhouse with an old man hired to build fence remarked the second day: 'No, th' old man don't kick none but he allus seems to want to take his hundred and sixty right in the middle of the bed and give me eighty acres on each side." There were other exaggerated and quaint phrases and sayings. "She nearly shook th' bark off th' trees with chills;" "shut th' door—Arkansas!" "He'll do to tie to;" or "He'll do to throw in with;" "he had th' gall of a government mule," or "was all swelled up like a pizened pup," are typical. Shakespeare's "something rotten in Denmark" had its frontier equivalent of "there's something dead up the creek," or "there's a bug under the chip." "Well, this ain't buyin' th' baby a new dress nor payin' for th' one it's already wore out" meant that it was time to get to work as did also the phrase, "We're burnin' daylight, boys." "You can't find that between th' lids of th' Bible," an old fellow well versed in the Scriptures would sometimes exclaim. Or "that must be either on th' left hand side of Genesis or th' right hand side of Revelation." Before matches were in common use, a neighbor sometimes hurried over to borrow a shovel full of coals which was the origin of the query: "Did you come to borry fire?" when someone stopped in for only a minute or two.

A drunken man walked "like he'd lost his rudder." Liquor was variously referred to as "squirrel whiskey," "tanglefoot," "busthead," "red eye," or "kill devil." Old English words appeared at times. Help became "holp" and a man could not move a boulder or a log because "a fellow just can't get no purchase on it." Visitors were asked to "alight and tarry awhile," to pet a dog was to "much" him. A half sick individual was likely to remark that he felt like he "had been sent for and couldn't go;" a man who was so carried away by delusions of grandeur as to seek to exceed his limitations was "too big for his britches," while a fervent kiss "sounded like a cow a-pullin' her foot out of th' mud."

Such phrases and expressions of the American pioneers might be continued indefinitely but enough and more than enough have been given to reveal that the speech of long ago was vivid, colorful, and filled with meaning. It is plain, too, that it was a reflection of a life now gone forever except in a few remote localities where something close kin to the customs of past generations still survives. Yet the quaint phrases are still sometimes used by a people who never knew the conditions out of which they have grown. Persons born and bred in a great city still refer to the "grapevine telegraph" or hospitably remark that "the latchstring always hangs outside the door" though they know nothing of rural life in the wooded hills and have never occupied a log cabin. For, though the frontier has gone, it still exists as a "state of mind" to give flavor to the words of those who never stop to think of the origin of the phrases they use or of the history which they might reveal.

In recent years there has been a revival, amounting almost to a renaissance, of many of those things which grew in pioneer soil. One who travels through the Appalachian Mountains, or the Ozark Mountains, may frequently find offered for sale beside the road the old fashioned hooked rugs and hand woven coverlets, as well as the ladder backed chairs, and other articles that belong to the handicrafts of a century ago. One can tune in on the radio any evening and get hillbilly orchestras, old fiddlers' contests, and quartets that sing the songs of long ago. Wealthy men often build log cabins far back in the hills to which they retire at times for a few days to live again the life of their great grandfathers. We have developed almost a mania for cowboy songs, dude ranches, rodeos, square dances, and pioneer celebrations. College students wear overalls, cowboy boots, plaid shirts, and sombreros, and there is some indication that the styles of half a century ago may be coming back even in more formal clothing. Collectors comb the hills seeking for old glass, furniture, china, and cooking utensils, and once they are found, bear them home in triumph to be proudly displayed to their envious friends who may be financially able to buy the finest articles of modern manufacture.

It may be that all this is merely a passing fad but some talented artists and able scholars believe that the old time arts and crafts, music, and even the earlier ways of life have something to contribute to the culture and civilization of modern society that will be not only permanent in its nature but will serve to make that society richer and more attractive. If this is true, may it not also be true that the salty, picturesque phraseology of our early pioneer settlers has something to contribute to our language which will make it stronger, richer, and more expressive? Is it not possible that teachers of English or of speech may learn by a study of the apt, condensed expressions of the frontier settlers, which reveal so much in so few words and bring to the mind such vivid pictures, something which they can use to develop more forceful and colorful writing and speaking by their students? May it not also be possible that students and teachers of history will gain from a study of the language of the American pioneers a better understanding of the life, manners, and customs, which that language must unquestionably reflect? Perhaps no one can say, but these questions may be worthy of consideration.

The Frontier Literary Society*

The pioneer settlers who poured westward in the decades following the Civil War to occupy homesteads on the prairies of Nebraska, the Dakotas, Kansas, and western Oklahoma were in their own language a "sociable" people. It had been with deep regret that they left old friends and neighbors of their former homeland. Once established in new homes on the western prairies these settlers eagerly sought to form new ties with the people about them.

The first social contacts usually took the form of visiting with the families on the adjoining or nearby homesteads. Often an entire family would rise early in the morning, scrub the children within an inch of their lives, dress them in their Sunday best, and drive three or four miles to the home of a congenial neighbor to "spend the day." Most people were so poor that they had little else to spend so could only spend the day! Such visits, together with shorter ones for an evening or afternoon were for a time almost the only social diversion of the older people of the new community.

It was not long, however, until the young unmarried people began to demand something a trifle more exciting than friendly visits. What they wanted was "something to go to." This may seem strange to many of us today who must live in the midst of the bustle and hurry of a more sophisticated society. What we prefer is "something to stay

* Published in *Nebraska History*, XXI (September, 1950), 167–82.

away from!" Life on a prairie homestead, however, doubtless seemed a trifle drab and monotonous to active young people, especially in a land which afforded far more leisure than the pioneer settlers of the wooded regions farther east had ever known. In that time and region entertainment and recreation were not purchasable commodities as they are today. There were no picture shows, ball games, carnivals, night clubs, or amusement parks. Entertainment, like most of the clothing, must be homemade. In consequence these Victorian youths and bobby soxers soon began to arrange and attend numerous socials, dances, play parties, picnics, candy breakings, and similar affairs, designated by the more Puritanical adults as "frolics." The erection of a little school house and the establishment of a four or five months school afforded opportunities for additional activities. The school building eventually became something of a social center. Here were held not only church services, Sunday school, and prayer meetings, but singings, box suppers, pie suppers, and church dinners.

In virtually every community, however, there were at least a few persons of scholarly tastes and literary leanings who felt that while parties, taffy pullings, hayrides, and similar frivolous activities were harmless enough they should not be allowed to absorb the entire social activity of the neighborhood. What they felt was needed was some organization of an educational nature which would provide intellectual stimulus for the entire community. Obviously, it should be something with activities in which both young and old could participate and which would not only furnish entertainment but promote the cultural growth of all who attended its meetings. The formation of a literary society seemed the ideal way to meet this need.

The origin of the literary society in America seems lost in the mists of antiquity. Certainly it appears very early in our nation's history and in some instances may have been formed as a sort of artificial substitute for the New England town meeting. In the prairie West the organization of such a society appears, in some instances, to have been suggested by the Friday afternoon exercises of the rural school.

The country school teacher was usually keenly alive to the fact that his salary was paid by the people he served. In consequence, with grave forebodings in his heart and fingers discreetly crossed, he hospitably invited his patrons to visit the school at any time they might feel so inclined. A people starved for entertainment usually accepted his invitation in considerable numbers. Almost invariably they chose the worst possible time for such a visit, which was Friday following the afternoon recess. At that particular hour the youngsters, eagerly looking forward to the two whole days of freedom, seemed possessed of the devil while the teacher, with nerves worn to a frazzle by a hard week's work, always appeared at his worst.[1]

To get past this "grave yard shift," the period was often given over to exercises by the children. These might take the form of a spelling match or "ciphering match," but more often consisted of the "speaking of pieces." Then it was that *Mary Had a Little Lamb, Twinkle, Twinkle, Little Star, The Boy Stood on the Burning Deck, The Widder Spriggins Daughter*, and all the other old time favorites were given. Sometimes they were presented haltingly and at others with express train speed apparently with the objective of getting

---

[1] E. E. Dale, "Teaching on the Prairie Plains, 1890–1900," *Mississippi Valley Historical Review*, XXXIII (September, 1946), 293–307.

it over with as soon as possible, making a bow, and getting back to the safe haven of a seat.

To the "frontier intellectuals" these Friday afternoon exercises suggested the formation of a literary society in which children and adults alike could share. Some had belonged to such an organization in the region from which they had come and so had acquired a body of experience that would prove useful in the establishment of another. Once the suggestion was made it was received with enthusiasm. In typical American fashion, a meeting was held at the schoolhouse, a constitution and by-laws framed and adopted, officers elected, and committees appointed.

The most important of these was the program committee of which the school teacher, as the educational leader of the community, was usually a member. With commendable zeal this committee set to work to canvass the neighborhood for persons willing to give a reading, sing a song, or take part in a debate. Talent, like gold, is where you find it, and the diligent committee members often found it in most unexpected places. Sometimes a near illiterate would be discovered who could play the banjo or guitar like a real artist, or who had an excellent voice and a large repertoire of popular songs. A shy young girl might be revealed as a surprisingly good reader, or as having great ability in playing the leading role in a dialogue or short play. Men never suspected of any knowledge of public speaking sometimes proved to be clever debaters, delivering speeches that were wise, witty, and convincing. It was the task of the program committee to seek out all this talent and put it to work and at the same time to encourage the backward and help the inexperienced to improve and gain greater confidence.[2]

2 *Ibid.*

In addition it was necessary to make a diligent search for materials that might be presented. Poems suitable for reading might be found in old school books or magazines. One or two "speech books" or collections of dialogues were likely to be unearthed, and in some instances others were ordered from publishers in the East. A small library was often assembled by securing donations of books and occasionally by purchasing a few volumes. These were kept at the school house and checked out by the librarian at the close of each meeting.

Meetings were usually held twice a month, though in some cases they might be weekly—usually on Friday night. If the school room did not have a stage one was constructed of rough lumber. Wire was stretched from wall to wall in front of this stage from which curtains of dark calico were hung by small rings so that they could be slid back and forth by two willing volunteers from the ranks of the older boys of the school. Since people often came three or four miles to attend the meetings, the school house was usually filled to overflowing by a little after dark. The program consisted of recitations, or readings, interspersed with drills, musical numbers, and dialogues. Readings included such ancient classics as *Spartacus to the Gladiators*, *Rienzi to the Romans*, *Curfew Must Not Ring Tonight*, *The Face on the Barroom Floor*, *Whistling in Heaven*, and many more of a dramatic nature. Some in a lighter vein were *How Ruby Played*, *Little Orphan Annie*, *Darius Green and His Flying Machine*, *How We Tried to Lick the Teacher*, and many others chosen with due regard to the age and ability of the reader.

The dialogues were as varied as the readings. Popular ones, to be given by three or four persons, were *Arabella's Poor Relations*, *Sam and the Postman*, and *The Train to Mauro*. Usually they were of a humorous nature but as was to be expected of a generation brought up in the tradition of *McGuffey's Readers* most of them sought to point a moral or teach a good lesson. Drills by school children were often held since a large number could take part. This was good psychology on the part of the officials of the society for the larger the number that participated in the program, the greater would be the interest of the community. A favorite drill was called the "Choice of Trades." Each child was given a tool or other object typical of a trade or profession. Carrying it with him he came out and gave a few lines of verse describing how he expected to carry on his life work. After each had spoken they all marched about the stage each reciting his verse. For example a lad with the medicine case of a doctor would appear and deliver the following:

> When I am a man a man I'll be
> I'll be a doctor if I can and I can
> My pills and powders will be nice and sweet
> And you can have just what you want to eat
> When I am a man.

Others would express in verse their preference for the role of a farmer, carpenter, blacksmith, cowboy, lawyer, or teacher. A dozen youngsters presenting such a number was nearly certain to mean the presence at the program of a dozen fond fathers and mothers to view the whole proceeding with beaming approbation.

After the recitations, dialogues, drills, and musical numbers had been presented it was customary to have a brief recess followed by a debate. Subjects were frequently of an abstract or philosophical nature as: "Resolved, that fear of punishment has a greater influence over human conduct than does the hope of reward." Other subjects dealt with historical questions or current political issues. Sometimes, but not often, the subject chosen would be of a humorous or frivolous type, as: "Resolved, that a clean cross woman makes a better wife than a dirty good natured woman."[3] Such a subject was unusual, for the debate was in most cases a serious affair. Those participating planned their speeches with great care, practiced them diligently, and delivered them with as much fire and vigor as though the destiny of nations hung upon their words.

The organization and carrying on of a successful literary society might become a major activity for a large number of people. Children must be drilled on their speeches and songs, reluctant individuals persuaded to share in the programs, and rehearsals held by the characters in the dialogues. This was all preliminary to the actual presentation of the program. Yet the latter also had its problems. Stage properties had to be brought in and arranged. The curtain sometimes stuck at most inopportune times or youngsters forgot their speeches and had to be prompted. Characters in dialogues might easily forget their lines or garble them in fantastic fashion.

Slips of the tongue were sometimes made with tragic results. At a literary society meeting in a rural schoolhouse in central Kansas a young woman gave the favorite old reading, *Curfew Must Not Ring Tonight*. She moved along beautifully and had the audience almost in tears as she described how Bessie climbed to the belfry and clung to the clapper of the swinging bell the tolling of which was to be the signal for the execution of her lover. When she came to the final lines, however, detailing the maiden's appeal to Cromwell and his promise of pardon for the young man,

[3] *Minutes of Mt. Gilead (Texas) Literary Society*, November 20, 1891.

158

disaster struck. She meant to say: " 'Go, your lover lives,' cried Cromwell, 'curfew shall not ring tonight.' " Frightened and nervous, she said: "Go, your liver loves,' " which nearly broke up the meeting and caused the girl to flee from the stage weeping bitter tears of humiliation.

Scarcity of suitable materials also sometimes caused the selection of a reading not suited to the appearance and personality of the one who gave it. Joe Williams, a former Oklahoma cowhand, has related that he once rode ten miles to attend a literary society at Valley View Schoolhouse. The third number was a reading given by a girl about seventeen years old. He described her as tall, lean, and crosseyed, with stringy red hair, freckled face, and projecting front teeth. But the subject of her reading and the refrain closing each stanza was this: "The Lips that Touch Liquor Can Never Touch Mine." Joe said it was a good speech but not temperance argument at all![4]

No doubt literary societies flourished in many rural communities of Nebraska during the last quarter of the nineteenth century but most of them kept no records. The minutes of one very interesting one, however, have been preserved. These are significant, not only for what they say, but for what can be read between the lines. The organization was established in the Rock Creek community, about sixteen miles northeast of Lincoln, sometime prior to 1880. It was first known as the *Mutual Improvement Society* and as such met every Friday evening during the autumn and winter months for nearly three years. It seems to have lapsed for a time after 1882 but was reorganized in October, 1884, as the *Rock Creek Literary Society*. Under this name it was carried

[4] Joe Williams, *Statement*, March 10, 1948.

on, with some lapses and reorganizations, until 1895.[5] Possibly it was continued after that date, but if so the minutes have not been found, the last entry being for March 8, 1895. The change of name made in 1884 is apparently meaningless for the membership rolls show that the same persons were officials and members, in some cases for the entire period of fifteen years.[6] The objectives of the Rock Creek Literary Society are revealed by the following constitution and by-laws:

CONSTITUTION AND BY-LAWS OF THE ROCK CREEK LITERARY SOCIETY

I

This society shall be known as the Rock Creek Literary Society.

II

The object of this society is to promote the intellectual and social interests of its members; to encourage the study of subjects literary, scientific, philosophical, amusing, musical.

III

This society shall be governed by Cushing's Manual and the following by-laws, which may be amended as the occasion demands.

I

A membership fee of five cents for each person over fifteen years of age shall be charged to defray incidental expenses.

II

The officers of this society shall consist of a President, Vice-president, Secretary, Treasurer and Sergeant-at-Arms.

III

The duties of the officers shall be as follows:

The President shall preside at all meetings of the society,

[5] Minutes of the Mutual Improvement Society and of the Rock Creek Literary Society. Original in possession of Lloyd Jeffrey, Waverly, Nebraska. (Hereafter referred to as *Minutes*.)

[6] *Minutes*, Lists of members for 1880, 1881, 1882, 1884, 1886, 1887, 1888, 1894.

call extra meetings, decide points of order, appoint committees, levy all fines, and with the assistance of the sergeant-at-arms, preserve order.

The Vice-President shall preside in the absence of the president and perform all the duties of that office upon such occasions.

The Secretary shall keep an accurate record of all meetings of this society, call the roll, read the program.

The Treasurer shall collect all fines and dues, keep an exact account of all moneys received and paid out, and report each month to the society.

The Sergeant-at-arms shall clean the lamps, build the fires, sweep the floor, cut a dog-wood club and preserve order in the hindermost parts of the house and such other parts as may require his services; he shall also perform all other duties not herein mentioned that may arise from time to time.

IV

The members of this society shall be cheerfully governed by the officers, and respond promptly to duties assigned them, and work first, last, and all the time for the best interests of this society.

V

All members failing to respond or to furnish an acceptable substitute shall be fined five cents (cases of sickness only excused) for every failure.

VI

The regular meetings of this society shall be held on Friday evening of each week.

VII

The officers of this society shall be elected every fourth meeting.

VIII

Nine members shall constitute a quorum for the transaction of business.

IX

The order of business shall be as follows:

1. Call to order.

2. Reading of the minutes of the last meeting.
3. Roll call.
4. Reports of committees.
5. Unfinished business.
6. New business.
7. Exercises of the evening.
8. Reading of program for next meeting.
9. Adjournment.[7]

The society could hardly be called a wealthy one. The minutes of the meeting for November 12, 1880, show the following entry: "The question of making the sergeant-at-arms a saleried [sic] office was brought before the house and it was voted to pay the holder of that office 40 cts. a month." On March 10, 1882, it was voted "to pay the Sergeant 20 cts for building fires and 10 cts. for lamp chimney." On November 5, 1884, the treasurer rendered a report showing "total on hand $1.94. Expended as follows: Lamp .60, paper .25, lamp wick .05, coal oil .25. Total $1.15. Remainder on hand $0.79." Clearly the duties of the treasurer were not too onerous and it is plain that there was no reason for bonding that official.

The unusual provisions for electing officers every fourth meeting was probably designed to stimulate interest in the society by giving a large number of members an opportunity to serve as officials. Also it gave many persons experience in presiding over meetings and conducting the work of the organization. In view of the duties outlined for him it is not surprising that the office of sergeant-at-arms should have been made a "saleried" office or that one member should have protested that he had not been legally elected since the individual nominating him "had failed to rise and address the chair before making the nomination."[8]

[7] *Minutes.*
[8] *Minutes,* Feb. 18, 1881.

The society had a library of nearly forty volumes. These were probably largely donated and were constantly checked out by the members of the organization, probably to be used in many cases in assembling information for the debates.[9] Such debates were a regular feature of nearly every program, the first part of which consisted of readings, songs and dialogues. A short recess was then held and the debate, with two speakers on each side, was the concluding feature of the evening. Occasionally there were three speakers for each side and in some instances only one. Since the decision of most judges is unconsciously influenced by their own views the results of the discussion of current questions may give some index as to the political opinions of the people of this part of Nebraska during these years.

After the reorganization of the society in 1884 the debate does not seem to have formed so prominent a part of the programs as formerly. Yet it was by no means abandoned and various new questions were discussed and some of the older ones brought up again. In the case of the latter, however, the decision of the judges seldom varied from the one given before. On November 12, 1884, the society voted to have a "paper" prepared and read at the meeting on November 26 instead of holding a debate. An editor and assistant were appointed and until the organization closed its year's work the following March the "paper," called *The Rock Creek Astonisher*, seems to have been a regular feature of nearly every meeting.

It is unfortunate that no copy of *The Rock Creek Aston-*

[9] Some of the volumes most used were *Dictionary of American Politics*, Macaulay's *History of England*, 5 vols., *Our Republican Monarchy*, *Seven Financial Conspiracies*, *Rise and Progress of Human Slavery*, *Thirty Years of Labor*, *A Short History of the French Revolution*, *The Money Monopoly*, *Protection of Free Trade*, and various others.

isher seems to have been preserved. Probably it was not unlike most other literary society papers, which have come down to us, or that can be largely restored from the memories of a few older people who in their youth edited them. These "community organs" usually gave news items of the neighborhood but this was only preliminary to the main feature which was the good natured "ribbing" of the local belles and beaux. Special attention was always given to budding romances of the young people. Typical gibes and quips might be as follows:

"No, that is not the rising sun you see in the east. It is Hank Smith's new red-wheeled buggy headed in the direction of Mary Johnson's house." "Mrs. Simson says that Ed Adams and Sam Williams come so often that she 'can't throw out a pan of water without throwing it on one of them boys.'" "When Bill Jones told Bessie Jenkins that he was going to hang himself if she wouldn't marry him Bessie said: 'Well my dad says you'll sure have to do it at home because he's not going to have you hanging around here!'" "Bonnie Phillips says that Earl Wilson's new mustache reminds her of a base ball game—nine on a side."

Such joking always brought a laugh and resulted in the persons whose names were mentioned receiving a good deal of chaffing from their friends in the community.

The Rock Creek Literary Society was a type. Similar organizations existed not only all over Nebraska in the pioneer era but in virtually every other western state, and their influence upon the cultural development of the communities in which they were held must have been very great. Members read widely in seeking materials for the programs or in preparing speeches for the debates. Poems and dialogues were memorized and current questions to be discussed studied.

The historical or philosophical subjects debated also required wide reading and diligent study by the speakers. The information which they had thus acquired was then passed on to an eager audience. Confidence as well as skill in public speaking was gained by all who participated in the programs. No doubt many lawyers, legislators, members of Congress, and other public officials received their first training in public speaking in the frontier literaries and debating societies.

The educational influence of such an organization also must have been very important for the children of a community. Youngsters not old enough to participate in the activities of the Rock Creek Literary Society when it was first formed grew to young manhood and womanhood during the fifteen years of its existence. From observing the work of their elders in the organization they were stimulated to participate in its programs themselves as soon as they were old enough. In consequence they literally grew up with the institution having an important influence upon their lives. The literary society created and sustained an interest in history, literature, and public speaking. It affected the cultural growth of children in the same fashion that the church and Sunday school influenced spiritual development.[10]

In a newly settled region the literary society was also a powerful factor in bringing people more closely together, in the creation of friendships, and the establishment of a community consciousness. In 1897 the people of the Timber Creek community in western Oklahoma established a literary

[10] The Literary Society also must have been an important factor in promoting romances. I. F. Dale was elected president and Emma Core secretary of the Rock Creek Society in October, 1882. They were later married and reared a family of seven sons and two daughters. Of the sons three still live (1950) in Nebraska, where one is a county farm agent. Of the other four one is a physician, one a college professor, one a chemist for the federal government and the fourth a farmer in Virginia.

society. The settlers had come from many states of the Union and most of them had occupied their homesteads in the past twelve months. At the conclusion of the first meeting of the society the newly elected president who was from a northeastern state made a brief speech. In closing he said:

"I am very proud of the honor you have bestowed upon me by electing me President of the Timber Creek Literary Society. We have all come here within the past year to settle and make our homes in this new country. We have come from many regions. I happen to be from the Northeast while many of you are from the South or the West. But we must not let this influence our feeling toward one another. In the future we want no North, South, East, or West in our thoughts, but only Timber Creek. Let us forget everything except that we are all friends and neighbors working together in this society to advance the cultural and educational development of the Timber Creek Community."

Medical Practices on the Frontier*

Many persons now past, or approaching, the age of the three score and ten years traditionally allotted to man and who grew up on the American frontier will assert that in the old days sickness was quite rare. They seem to remember that in their youth they had no aches or pains but were always strong and healthy and even declare that all other people in their home communities were the same.

Such people must either be afflicted with acute amnesia or have what the late Professor Edward Channing once referred to as "a constructive memory." While it is quite true that the American pioneers were a vigorous and hardy breed partly because the weaklings did not live long under the conditions of frontier life, they were, nevertheless, human animals and as such were subject to most diseases and ailments which afflict people today plus some additional ones that were the result of their manner of living and their lack of knowledge of the most elementary principles of hygiene and sanitation.

The practices herein described were as common in such states as Indiana, Illinois, Kentucky, and Tennessee between 1840 and 1870 as they were in the trans-Mississippi states during a later period and prevailed to a considerable extent throughout the rural districts of the entire Mississippi Valley down to the end of the nineteenth century. In fact, traces of

* Published in *The Indiana Magazine of History*, XLIII (December, 1947), 307–328.

them may still be found in the more remote and backward communities of the southern and central portions of the United States.

In the pioneer West an entire family lived in a log cabin, sod house, dugout, or structure of rough lumber usually consisting of not more than three rooms and often of one or two. Even though the great majority of these frontiersmen were comparatively young people, there were often three or four children and in some cases as many as six or seven or even more. Such a small house meant crowded quarters for five to eight or nine people. In winter it was cold and draughty and yet ventilation was often poor. The family slept two or three in a bed with the windows tightly closed just as they had been throughout the day. It has been said that "the air is pure in the country because country people always sleep with the windows closed!" Certainly that was the custom in the frontier communities because in the prairie region fuel was scarce and even in the wooded areas the pioneer found it easier to close the windows than to chop more wood.

Screens for the doors and windows were unknown and flies were a perpetual plague in summer by day and in many places mosquitoes a great source of annoyance by night. A child was frequently given a leafy branch and assigned the task of "minding flies off the table" when company was present, but the guests usually felt that it was only courteous to assert that this was unnecessary and that everyone should be expected to "mind his own flies." That disease germs were frequently carried to food by flies was of course certain. A sheet of mosquito bar was frequently spread over a cradle to keep flies off a sleeping baby but many were likely to find their way beneath it. The same material was also used to prevent the entrance of mosquitoes, but few householders had a sufficient quantity to cover all windows and a "smudge" was sometimes kindled to discourage these pestiferous insects.

The water for household use came, in most cases, from a near-by spring or stream or was drawn from a shallow well. It was not always pure and in many instances must have been contaminated by the presence of colon bacilli or other germs of disease. The whole family drank from a common cup, gourd, or tin dipper, washed in a single pan, and dried their hands and faces on the same towel. The crossroads store always had a shelf in the rear equipped with a pail of water with a tin cup hanging on a near-by nail from which thirsty customers drank freely, undisturbed by any thought of the unsanitary nature of such a practice. The country school had a single water pail to accommodate thirty or forty youngsters who seemed to the teacher perpetually thirsty. The little hotel or tavern had similar drinking arrangements and guests, after washing their hands and faces in a common basin, dried them on a "roller towel," the most fastidious ones rolling it up or down often in a vain effort to find a reasonably clean and dry spot.

Visitors to a home drank from the common dipper and used the same washbasin as did the family with the hostess making no concession except to put out a clean towel. The small son of the household filled a basin half full of water, and he and his little playmate alternately snorted into it a couple of times, dabbing a little water on the more central portion of their faces, and sometimes chanting the little couplet: "Wash together, Friends forever."

Bathing facilities were extremely meager. In summer the settler and his sons swam in the creek or pond, and in winter a washtub was filled with water every Saturday night and the children placed in it by strong-arm methods and scrubbed within an inch of their lives. If water had to be hauled or carried a long distance, the "rinse water" of the family washing was sometimes saved until evening and the youngsters bathed in it before they were put to bed.

Every family had a single comb and brush which was used by all of its members. Toothbrushes were unknown unless a hackberry root with one end chewed sufficiently to form a small mop could be so designated. It was dipped in salt and used to rub the teeth lightly or they might be polished a bit with one corner of the towel. Some men carried a gold-plated toothpick, or one made of deer bone and used it to remove particles of food from between the teeth after every meal. Chewing gum, commonly called "wax" in the South, was scarce and a single chew was passed about from mouth to mouth of three or four children sometimes for days.

When a number of boys had assembled to play ball one hot Sunday afternoon at the edge of the Cross Timbers of North Texas, one of the four Dye brothers eagerly besought his younger brother to go to the nearest well a quarter of a mile away and bring a pail of water for the benefit of the sweating, thirsty players. "Now, Walter," he pleaded earnestly, "if you'll take the bucket and bring us a bucket of nice cool water from Mr. Clark's well, I'll let you chew the wax! Monroe is chewin' it now but his hour is about up and it's my time to chew it next. Now you do that, Walter, like a good boy, and I'll skip my turn and let you chew the wax!" Unable to resist the promise of such a reward, Walter seized the water pail and started in a lope for Mr. Clark's well.

It was not only in the home, school, store, or tavern, however, that such unsanitary practices prevailed. The idea of individual cups to be used in partaking of the Lord's Supper, had never entered the head of any churchgoer. When the time came for the sacrament, a glass of wine and a cake of unleavened bread were placed on a tray and passed up and down the rows of benches on which members of the congregation sat. Each held the bread with one hand while he broke off a fragment with the other and put it into his mouth. He then took a sip from the glass. If the little church boasted a cottage organ, the worshippers could at least get their disease germs to the strains of soft music and in a spiritual atmosphere!

Under such conditions, it is not strange that when any person acquired a communicable disease, it was not only likely to be transmitted to all other members of the family but to sweep through the entire community. Colds, flu, measles, mumps, whooping cough, scabies, sore eyes, and other contagious or infectious diseases were very common among the American pioneers. Smallpox was usually regarded as serious enough to demand the isolation of the patient though it too might occasionally reach epidemic proportions. Venereal disease was uncommon among rural settlers but by no means unknown, and tuberculosis must have taken a considerable toll of lives. Trachoma undoubtedly existed but was not known by that name but as "granulated lids." The treatment of any of the diseases named was, moreover, usually crude and quite unscientific.

The food of the average pioneer settler was abundant and substantial and of a type calculated to enable him to swing a heavy ax, hoe, or maul for hours but the character of the meals in most frontier homes would be viewed with horror by the modern dietitian. They leaned heavily towards fats and starches. Meat was plentiful, but, except in the early years of the settlement of a region where game was abundant, it was usually salt pork, bacon, or ham. Fresh meat was rare in summer or, in fact at any other season except "hog killing time" in the late autumn, or upon those occasions when a neighbor killed a beef. At such times, children, who had subsisted largely on strong "side meat" for many months, ate "not wisely but too well," often with disastrous results. Refrigeration and ice were of course unknown and food frequently spoiled in warm weather. If the family had a spring house, milk, butter, and other perishable foods were kept in it. Otherwise milk was strained into large shallow stone "crocks" and placed on a table in the cellar, along with butter wrapped in a wet cloth. A jug of buttermilk was often tied to the end of a long rope and "hung in the well" in much the same fashion as was "the moss covered bucket." Nearly every kitchen had a cupboard with sides made of wire screen or perforated tin to allow a free circulation of air without admitting flies. Dishes and food were kept in this cabinet which was commonly known as a "safe" but with a number of perpetually hungry children about, the term was something of a misnomer so far as food was concerned.

During the winter months there was a lamentable lack of fresh fruits and green vegetables. As a result many impatient youngsters could not wait for fruit to ripen but often ate green apples or watermelons. Even later when fruit was ripe they stuffed themselves to repletion with plums, peaches, berries, and grapes, as well as green corn and various types of vegetables. The result was often grave disturbance of the digestive system commonly referred to as "summer complaint." Milk was abundant in some areas but very scarce in others where even small children drank strong, black coffee.

Knowledge of what constitutes a proper diet for young children was almost wholly lacking. Babes in arms were fed mashed potatoes, cabbage, spinach, squash, pie, cake, and cookies. While so young that they had only their natural food, they usually remained reasonably healthy, but once they began to be fed such things as would tax the digestion of an adult laborer, it frequently became another story. The type of solid food given to them was probably largely responsible for the widely prevailing belief that the most dangerous period for every baby was "the second summer." In the light of modern medical science it is not surprising that infant mortality was shockingly high, but that any child lived to maturity. As a matter of fact while only the strong and healthy survived, one who lived to the sixth or seventh year was likely not only to reach manhood or womanhood but to achieve a ripe old age.

Since hospitals were unknown all babies were brought into the world in the primitive homes often without the benefit of any further medical skill or attention than such as could be furnished by some ancient midwife commonly known as a "granny woman." Under such circumstances childbearing was a frightful ordeal accompanied by much suffering and grave danger. The cemeteries scattered about the region that was frontier half a century or more ago have many grave stones inscribed "mother and infant" which tell a tragic story.

The manner of life of the pioneer settler was such that he and the members of his family suffered many minor injuries as cuts, burns, bruises, and abrasions. The children cut their fingers or stepped on nails, thorns, or bits of broken glass. They were stung by bees, wasps, or scorpions, bitten by spiders, or occasionally by a snake, or developed boils and felons, or acquired stone bruises. A foot was sometimes cut open by an ax. Children were hurt at play and there is the old story of the small boy who came running in to tell his mother that: "Oscar got hit in the back of the head by the ball and the bawl came out of his mouth!"

Such injuries were usually of minor importance but there were some that were serious and proper methods of treating them were seldom employed. Common baking soda was put on a sting or bite of an insect while the turpentine bottle was to be found in every household and was brought out upon numerous occasions. Turpentine was applied to bruises or aching joints and sometimes was mixed with lard and rubbed on a sore throat or chest. Other common remedies for bruises, abrasions, or to reduce swelling and inflammation were goose grease, mutton tallow, gizzard oil, or snake oil. Some of these were mixed with turpentine or camphor to insure greater potency.

In addition there were poultices of infinite variety. These were made of bread and milk, onions, flaxseed, scraped beef-steak, hot salt, mustard, poke root, and a host of other substances. They were applied to a boil or "felon" to "draw it to a head" or to any wound, bruise, or sore spot. Mustard plasters were designed to relieve a soreness in the chest. A small chicken was split in halves and one-half of the warm, quivering flesh applied to a spider bite to "draw out the poison." A snake bite was usually treated by administering a stiff drink of whisky and cutting the wound to make it bleed freely. It was then sometimes cauterized with a hot iron or by pouring a little gunpowder on it which was then ignited with a match or flaming splinter. If a child were bitten on the foot, the entire member was sometimes placed in a pail filled with kerosene.[1]

[1] Indian-Pioneer Papers, University of Oklahoma, III, 340. These Papers contain 116 volumes and an index. They consist of the reminiscences of

In addition to these home remedies, there were various types of liniments and salves purchased at the local drug store. These were of great variety and included many preparations known by the name of their manufacturer and recommended as "good for man or beast and a sure cure for aches, pains, cuts, bruises, old sores, or burns." Also there were eye salves, eye water, "red precipity," used as a cure for itch, arnica salve, and ointments of many kinds.[2] Axle grease or tar was sometimes applied to cracked hands, and glycerine to chapped lips, while sweet cream was used to relieve sunburn or skin eruptions due to poison ivy.

Most pioneers had a marked fear of hydrophobia and every community sooner or later had its "mad dog scare." Rumors that a rabid dog had appeared in the community

old-time Indians and early pioneer settlers of Oklahoma. The volumes average about 450 pages each of double-spaced typed material. The collection was made in 1937 and 1938 under the terms of a W.P.A. project sponsored jointly by the Oklahoma Historical Society and the Department of History of the University of Oklahoma, with Dr. Grant Foreman from Muskogee as director. Nearly 100 W.P.A. workers were employed to visit and interview old Indians and early pioneer white settlers and to secure from them statements as to their early experiences in Oklahoma. While some of the statements are quite brief, consisting of not more than three or four pages, many of them are lengthy and may run fifteen to twenty pages or even more. As fast as they were collected, the interviews were transmitted to a central office where a staff of typists under the direction of Dr. Foreman typed them and prepared them for binding, making one carbon. There are but two sets of the Indian-Pioneer Papers in existence. One is in the files of the Oklahoma Historical Society, Oklahoma City, Oklahoma, and the other in the Frank Phillips Collection of the University of Oklahoma, Norman, Oklahoma. The interviews were arranged alphabetically under the name of the person interviewed throughout the set and the post-office address of each contributor is given. The collection is a mine of information with respect to early life in Oklahoma but must be used with care with respect to dates and events.

[2] Fort Smith, Arkansas, *Elevator*, September 13, 1889, advertised Hunt's Cure for Itch, and *ibid.*, January 11, 1895, contains advertisements of S.S.S. for Eczema, Bucklen's Arnica Salve, Bond's Cream Eye Salve, and Ballard's Snow Liniment.

created intensive excitement and were carried by the "grapevine telegraph" to everyone in the neighborhood. The men promptly armed themselves with rifles and shotguns loaded with buckshot and tramped the fields and woods in search of the animal, their steps guided by reports of its having been seen at various places in the community. Most of the searchers declared that they would be less alarmed by the knowledge that a ferocious lion was loose in the neighborhood. In the meantime, the women remained close at home and tried to keep the children indoors, regaling one another with horrid tales of someone of whom they had once heard who had been bitten and some days later had gone raving mad. The victim was alleged to have had convulsions, accompanied by foaming at the mouth and an insane desire to bite anyone who came near. In his lucid moments, he was said to have earnestly begged to be put out of his misery but nobody caring to accommodate him, the unfortunate person had suffered frightfully for two or three days and at last died in great agony. The popeyed children who listened to such frightful stories were usually not difficult to keep inside the house. Few of them could have been induced to step outside even for a moment.

When the animal had at last been tracked down and dispatched, the entire community heaved a sigh of relief. Even then, however, the incident was not closed. There still remained the task of slaughtering all dogs that had been bitten or that were even suspected of having been bitten. In consequence faithful old Rover was likely to be sent to the happy hunting ground by a charge of buckshot, secretly if possible to avoid the tears and lamentations of the younger members of the household.

If by chance some person had been bitten by the rabid

animal, which was seldom the case, he was immediately rushed to a "madstone" if one could be found in a radius of twenty or thirty miles. The stone which was said to have been taken from the body of a white deer was applied to the wound and if it refused to stick, it meant that there was no poison in the wound and so no cause for worry. On the other hand, if it stuck, there was no doubt but that the deadly germs of hydrophobia were present. When the faithful madstone had decided to call it a day and refused to cling longer to the wound despite repeated applications, it was regarded as *prima facie* evidence that a complete cure had been effected. The madstone was then placed in a bowl of sweet milk and lurid stories were related of how the milk curdled and became green in color from the poison that it had drawn from the wound. In any case, the patient felt safe and returned home relieved of any further concern.

Other animals than dogs were alleged to have hydrophobia in some instances and there were hair-raising stories of experiences with rabid wolves and "hydrophobia cows."[3] The bite of the small striped skunk, sometimes known as a "hydrophobia cat," was alleged always to produce hydrophobia. They were dreaded even more than rattlesnakes and any person bitten by one must rush to a madstone immediately. If such a cure was not available, it was commonly believed that he might as well make his will, arrange his worldly affairs, and, in the words of the old story, start making a preferential list of those he expected to bite when he became mad!

The superstition with respect to the madstone was common on the frontier but was only one of many that related to the prevention or cure of ailments. A man sometimes

[3] Statement of J. M. Ferris, Navajoe, Oklahoma.

carried a buckeye in his pocket to ward off rheumatism. A mole's foot was attached to a string and tied about a baby's neck to make cutting teeth easier. Also a small bag of asafetida was worn on a string around the neck of a child to keep away disease germs. Probably there was some justification for this practice since no one cared to go close enough to a child so equipped to transmit any germs to him! The same reasoning may have been responsible for the idea that eating large quantities of onions would prevent taking a cold.

On the frontier the use of internal medicine was quite as prevalent as was the application of salves, ointments, liniments, and plasters to relieve pain or heal minor injuries. There were some attempts to practice preventive medicine, though most of the many concoctions taken to ward off disease apparently had little or no value. In the early months of spring, children were given a mixture of sulphur, molasses, and cream of tartar to purify the blood. Also they were dosed with sassafras tea to thin the blood and to make them fit to face the heat of summer. Tonics were of infinite variety. A quart of whisky would be put into a jug and some wild cherry bark, prickly ash berries, and sarsaparilla roots added, and the mixture allowed to stand for several days or until the medicinal properties of the various other elements had become merged with the whisky. A swallow of this taken night and morning was said to prevent malaria, tone up the system, and improve the appetite. Other forms of bitters were made of a brew of sarsaparilla roots, bitter apple, and various additional roots and herbs in order to stimulate the appetite and improve digestion. Rusty nails were put into a bottle of water and a sip of the liquid taken every day to insure plenty of iron in the blood.

As already suggested, digestive disturbances due to improper food or excessive eating were very common especially among children. A tea made of boiling the roots of a plant known as "red root," which grew abundantly in the Southwest, was often given as a remedy for diarrhea, dysentery, or "summer complaint." In fact "teas" were of as wide variety as poultices. In addition to those already named there were sage tea, pennyroyal tea, ginger tea, sarsaparilla tea, beef tea, rhubarb tea, horehound tea, and teas made from blackberry roots, oak bark, or sheep droppings. They were ladled out to children not only for digestive disorders, but also for colds, fever, or general "puniness" and a "run down condition." Commercial tea called "store tea" was widely used in some parts of the North as a beverage but on the Southern frontier it seldom appeared except in cases of sickness. The same was true of lemons, rice, and oranges which in many pioneer communities were seldom purchased unless some member of the household was ill.

On the frontier, as today, children attacked by colic due to overloading the stomach with more or less indigestible foods were liberally dosed with castor oil. Appendicitis must have been fairly common but the name was unknown, and it was commonly called "inflammation of the bowels." Typhoid fever, usually known as "slow fever," was also prevalent in most cases being acquired from drinking contaminated water from shallow wells. It was treated by giving the patient calomel or "blue mass" and sometimes quinine and limiting his diet to soup and soft foods.

In winter, coughs, colds, bronchitis, sore throat, and pleurisy were widespread and pneumonia was by no means uncommon. Every person had his own remedy for a cold which is not too different from the situation today. Soaking the patient's feet in hot water and requiring him to drink a hot lemonade or a large cup of hot ginger tea before going to bed was almost universally regarded as the proper treatment. The masculine members of a household usually regarded a "hot whisky stew" as more effective than either the lemonade or ginger tea but in any case the patient must retire immediately and be covered with heavy blankets so that he might perspire profusely and so "sweat the cold out of his system." A favorite remedy for coughs and colds was whisky in which had been dissolved a considerable quantity of rock candy. In addition there were cough syrups of various types, but the most common was made by making a strong tea of horehound leaves, adding sugar and boiling it until a thick syrup was formed. A teaspoonful of this three or four times a day was regarded as a sure cure for a cough.

Malaria was common on nearly every part of the frontier except the high arid plains. This is not surprising with no screens on the doors and windows of the homes which were often near a stream or pond that produced myriads of mosquitoes. The cause of malaria, commonly called "chills and fever," was, however, quite unknown. Some asserted that "chills" were due to eating green watermelons, excessive swimming in the creek, or merely to "being out in the night air." Just what air you were expected to be out in after dark if not "night air" nobody took the trouble to explain. The term malaria obviously means "bad air" but tradition rather than the word was responsible for the pioneer's fear. The remedy was quinine but since gelatine capsules had not yet been invented, it was hard to get it down the youngsters. Sometimes it was dissolved in coffee, or more often wrapped in a piece of soft stewed fruit and gulped down with the hope that the wrapping did not slip while it was still in the mouth. Often a quantity would be added to a quart of whisky and the mixture shaken up and a swallow taken night and morning in chill season as "preventive medicine."

In some sections of the Southern frontier chills were accepted almost as an inevitable part of life and the man who was virtually "shaking the bark off the trees" with a chill in the late afternoon would be going about his work the following morning singing, whistling, and apparently in the best of health and spirits. In fact one individual, with that trend toward exaggeration characteristic of most pioneers, declared that in his community a man who did not have a chill every other day and an addition to his family every year would hurry to a doctor to find out what was wrong with him!

In addition to quinine, there were on the market numerous "chill tonics" some allged to be "tasteless" which was usually another example of exaggeration. As a matter of fact, the average pioneer settler, in addition to the use of home remedies, spent an astonishingly large percentage of his meager income for medicines both for external and internal use. The local drug store sold huge quantities of "liver regulator," "black draught," liver pills, or "bile beans" all advertised as a sure cure for "biliousness." Of the so-called "patent medicines" there was an infinite variety, some of which are still sold. They included: Peruna; Swamp Root; Golden Medical Discovery; Vegetable Compound; Stomach Bitters; Wine of Cardui; Beef, Iron and Wine; Ozomulsion, and a host of others. Some were recommended for a single disease while others were real "omnibus remedies" alleged to be a sure cure for any or all of a dozen ailments. For infants and young children there was a wide assortment of soothing syrups, cordials, and of course, paregoric, and Castoria.

Makers of patent medicines advertised their wares widely

in the weekly papers and especially in the monthly or semi-monthly household journals. Such advertisements sometimes showed the picture of a dejected-looking individual labeled "before taking" and a stalwart physical specimen tagged "after taking." Testimonials from grateful users of the remedy were often printed as: "I was run down and life was a burden but after taking only five bottles of your wonderful medicine, I am now entirely recovered."[4] Occasionally an advertisement writer essayed verse asserting that:

> Used outward or inward it never does harm
> As sure as you're faithful it works like a charm

One knowing the virtue, or lack of it, of most charms and amulets worn by primitive peoples to ward off disease would probably agree that the statement was correct. Another widely circulated bit of blank verse designed to promote the sale of a popular child remedy was as follows:

> When baby was sick, we gave her Castoria,
> When she was a Child, she cried for Castoria,
> When she became Miss, she clung to Castoria,
> When she had Children, she gave them Castoria.[5]

The constant repetition of the name could hardly fail to impress it upon the reader and fix in his mind the perennial value of the medicine though on one occasion an over particular Victorian was heard to remark that some mention of a change in "Baby's" marital status should have been indicated prior to the last line!

Other makers of patent medicines also essayed verse in

---

[4] Fort Smith, Arkansas, *Elevator*, July 15, 1887.
[5] *Harper's Weekly* (62 vols., New York, 1857-1916), XXXII, 838 (November 3, 1888). Also Fort Smith, Arkansas, *Elevator*, January 15, 1895, and many other periodicals of this time.

bringing their wares to the attention of the ailing public as the following:

> Little spells of fever
> Little chills so bland
> Make the mighty graveyard
> And the angel band.
> A little Cheatham's Chill Tonic
> Taken now and then
> Makes the handsome women
> And the healthy men.[6]

There is some evidence that manufacturers of so-called "patent medicines" made an earnest and concerted effort in the eighties and nineties to induce people to substitute such preparations for the old time home remedies of earlier years. Certainly the volume of advertising increased enormously, no doubt, in part due to the fact that the number of newspaper readers grew rapidly as many additional periodicals were established and the older ones greatly increased their circulation. Makers of numerous proprietary medicines advertised in virtually all of these local newspapers so almost any one of them is typical of a hundred others all of which carried the same advertising matter. The Fort Smith *Elevator*, a four-page weekly periodical, in its issue of July 15, 1887, carried nineteen advertisements for as many different remedies including two on the front page. Among these medicines were Castoria, Ague Busters, Ayers Sarsaparilla, Prickly Ash Bitters, Dr. King's New Discovery (for consumption), Botanic Blood Balm, Dromgoole's English Female Bitters, Merrell's Penetrating Oil, Tansy Capsules, Shiloh's Vitalizer, and Spark's Blackberry Balsam.

Several of these had disappeared from the pages of this

[6] Fort Smith, Arkansas, *Elevator*, September 13, 1889.

newspaper two years later but there were many new ones including "Malarion," "Arkansaw's Own Famous Liver Remedy," Morley's T-X-S Ague Tonic, Dr. Haine's Golden Specific to cure the liquor habit, Hunt's Cure for Itch, Clarke's Flax Salve, Syrup of Figs, and some others.[7] Some six years later the names of most of these had vanished from the pages of the *Elevator* and had been replaced by a whole crop of new ones.

The issues of 1895 each usually carried about twenty-five patent medicine advertisements including those for Dr. Pierce's Golden Medical Discovery, Brown's Iron Bitters, Ozmantis Oriental Pills, Mother's Friend, Plantation Chill Cure, Dr. Green's Onion Syrup, Herbine, Nerve Seeds, Dr. Miles Heart Cure, Karl's Clover Root, Shiloh's Catarrh Remedy, Electric Bitters, Ballard's Horehound Syrup, and Solalium Carolinense for the cure of fits.[8] These ads together with those of doctors and dentists occupy approximately one-fourth of some pages of the paper.

It was not only in the small town weeklies, however, that vendors of remedies and medical appliances advertised their wares. The St. Louis *Globe Democrat* carried on its front page advertisements of Nerve Beans, Swayne's Ointment, Bile Beans, and Dr. Owen's Electric Belt and Suspensory.[9] The last named was a contraption consisting of a number of metal disks strung on a leather strap. It was worn about the waist next to the skin and was alleged to "cure rheumatic complaints, lumbago, general and nervous debility, kidney disease, nervousness, trembling, wasting of the body, etc." The electric belt proved so popular that an enterprising

---

[7] *Ibid.*

[8] *Ibid.*, January 11, 1895. The last named was made by a doctor in Indianapolis.

[9] St. Louis, Missouri, *Globe Democrat*, November 29, 1890.

manufacturer designed and placed on sale an "electric ring" which when worn on the finger was guaranteed to have the same curative properties as did the cumbersome and uncomfortable belt, which was probably true. *Harper's Weekly* also advertised proprietary medicines including Dr. Scott's Electric Plaster described as "combining electro-magnetism with all of the best features of standard porous and other plasters." It was said to cure colds, coughs, chest pains; nervous, muscular and rheumatic pains; stomach, kidney, and liver pains; dyspeptic, malaria and other pains; rheumatism, gout, and inflammation, and the advertiser asserted that:

"They who suffer ache and pain,
Need suffer never more again."[10]

Even trade and technical journals of the 1890's carried advertisements of proprietary medicines. The monthly *National Detective and Police Review* published at Indianapolis advertised Carter's Relief for Women, Cancer Cure, and Rupture Cure.[11] Many of the medical preparations so widely advertised were made in New York but others were manufactured in Indianapolis, Buffalo, St. Louis, Chattanooga, and various other cities and a few were made in smaller cities and had a considerable local sale.

Most manufacturers of the patent medicines most widely distributed realized that a large part of the frontier population did not in their own language "take a paper." This was especially true of the less literate people to whom the pur-

[10] *Harper's Weekly*, XXXII, 740 (September 29, 1888).
[11] *National Detective and Police Review* (Indianapolis, Indiana), VI, August, 1897. Presumably the publication began in 1892. It was listed in the *Indianapolis City Directory* for 1894 and 1895 as the *National Detective* and from 1897 to 1907 as the *National Detective and Police Review*, but does not appear after 1907. It is not listed in the *Union List of Serials in Libraries of the United States and Canada* edited by Winifred Gregory.

veyors of such preparations looked for a large part of their customers. In consequence, many such manufacturers published an almanac for distribution through the mails or local drug stores. These were of the type of the old *Farmer's Almanac* established in 1793 by Robert B. Thomas and published in recent years by Little, Brown and Company of Boston.[12] Like their ancestor, these almanacs contained a calendar, astronomical calculations, the names and characters of the signs of the Zodiac, the dates of holidays, and much miscellaneous material including household hints, weather forecasts, recipes, advice to farmers, and jokes and anecdotes. On every page, however, the virtues of the remedy were proclaimed in type that could hardly fail to catch the reader's eye. Advertising was yet in its infancy and modern techniques of making the product offered only incidental to the picture of a dizzy blonde in abbreviated costume had not been discovered. The cover of the almanac carried a picture but it was always one designed to fix the attention of the reader upon the remedy. Sometimes it depicted St. George plainly labeled as the medicine, slaying the dragon of disease. Among the pioneers the belief was common that the Indians had much medical lore especially with respect to the curative properties of certain roots and herbs. The cover of one popular almanac pictured an Indian woman pointing to a growing plant and exclaiming to her white sister bowed down with suffering, "The Great Spirit planted it!"

Doctors, except in the towns, were few and far between and most of them had little to recommend them except imposing whiskers and an impressive bedside manner. Yet they made up for their lack of medical skill and scientific knowl-

12 See George L. Kittredge, *The Old Farmer and His Almanack* (Cambridge, Massachusetts, 1920).

edge by an enormous energy and conscientious devotion to duty. In sub-zero weather, often through sleet and snow, they traveled many miles in open buggies or on horseback to relieve suffering and minister to those in need of help. They brought to many a household comfort and hope and uncomplainingly made enormous sacrifices and endured frightful hardships to give their poor best to suffering humanity. To them the people of America owe a heavy debt of gratitude.

This scarcity of physicians was obviously responsible for the rapid increase in the sale of proprietary remedies or "mail order" medical treatment. It was also responsible for the early appearance of the traveling doctor with his "medicine show," an institution which was continued well down into the twentieth century. Usually he was a somewhat corpulent individual in striped trousers, a Prince Albert coat, white shirt, and black string tie who appeared on the streets of a western village just after sundown in a large flat truck drawn by two white horses with silver mounted harness. Sitting in chairs on the truck were two or three black-faced comedians vigorously playing a violin and a banjo, guitar, or accordion. Stopping at the most prominent street corner, these black-faced boys would burst into song and continue until a considerable crowd had gathered. Then the "Doctor" would stand and in a deep, sonorous voice begin his speech:

"Ladies and Gentlemen: I am traveling about over the country trying to bring aid to suffering humanity. We have not come out here this evening to try to sell you anything but only that we may all have a good time—" "Yum, yum," would interpose one of the comedians, "Ain't we a-gwine hab a *good time!*" "Shut up, Sam," the doctor would exclaim. "Now, folks, we are not interested in making money or selling you something but only in helping you to feel better and in curing any ailments you may have. I look at you men standing there and I can see that some of you have a dull ache in the back, and twinges of pain in your shoulders and legs." The villager who had worked at a forge all day sharpening plows, or shoeing horses, and the farmers who had hoed corn since sunrise and then dropped over to town to do an errand would look at one another and nod knowingly. It took no great stretch of imagination to make them feel the dull aches and twinges so aptly described by the wise doctor. Having planted the seed, the doctor proceeded to cultivate the crop certain of a reasonably bountiful harvest. "Now, men," he would continue, "In my laboratories at home I've worked for years hoping to find a preparation that would cure cases just like yours and at last I found it. Here it is, gentlemen, Dr. X's Marvelous Elixir. Take one tablespoonful and that dull ache will vanish as if by magic and if you'll take a dose night and morning for three weeks, I'll guarantee that it will never come back. You'll have a better appetite, feel better than ever before in your life, and be able to do a full day's work without that run-down, wornout feeling you now have. Only a dollar a bottle for anybody that wants one and you'll say it's the biggest dollar's worth you ever saw in your lives. Step right up, gentlemen, who'll be first?"

After one or two had stepped forward and rather sheepishly tendered a dollar, the contagion grew and there was likely to be a rush to exchange dollars for bottles of the Elixir. When sales began to fall off, a brief recess was held and the black-face boys played again and sang more songs while others joined the little crowd. Then sales were resumed and continued until all customers had been supplied after which one of the boys mounted to the driver's seat and, with the others gaily singing and playing, the truck was driven to the camping place that had been selected just beyond the edge of town.

There were of course many variations. Some proprietors of medicine shows dispensed several remedies including liniments, salves, an "inhaler" for catarrh and colds in the head, or soap "made from the roots of the Mexican yucca." There were also traveling "corn doctors" who usually displayed a large box of corns and calluses taken from the feet of former customers. It is doubtful if the preparations sold by these itinerant shows had any curative effects but they at least gave to those who "enjoyed poor health" a new remedy to try and the entertainment features brought a little color and excitement to drab and monotonous lives.

Dentists were even more rare on the frontier than were general practitioners, though one or two could usually be found at the more important towns. They advertised extensively in the local newspapers offering their services at prices that would shock present day members of the profession. "A fine set of false teeth" was offered for eight dollars, and teeth would be extracted "without pain" at twenty-five cents each.[13] Outside the larger towns, however, people paid virtually no attention to their teeth unless one began to ache. Then a hot poultice would be applied to the jaw or a cavity stuffed with a bit of cotton soaked in laudanum or some form of "toothache drops." The loose milk tooth of a child was pulled by the father or mother with the fingers or yanked out by looping a bit of thread about it and giving a quick jerk or tying one end of the thread to the open door and suddenly closing it. The youngster was always told that if he did not put his tongue into the vacant space a gold tooth would grow there but never found it possible to test the truth of this assertion.

[13] Fort Smith, Arkansas, *Elevator*, January 11, 1895.

If an adult's aching tooth could not be eased by poultices or medicated cotton, it was sometimes knocked out with a chisel or screwdriver and hammer, or pulled by means of a pair of bullet molds in the hands of a husky neighbor.[14]

A traveling dentist equipped with a small case of tools of his craft would sometimes appear in a community but he seldom did more than pull bad teeth and give some advice as to the care of those left. When an individual had very few teeth left, eating became a serious problem but many managed to struggle along with surprisingly few. There is an ancient story to the effect that one old lady at an experience meeting expressed her thanks to the Lord that she still had "two teeth left and they hit."

When false teeth became absolutely necessary, a trip was made to the nearest dentist which sometimes required a journey of two or three days. Once there, impressions were made and the patient returned home to receive his teeth two or three weeks later by mail. Naturally they seldom fit well and were usually worn in a pocket most of the time and placed in the mouth only when required for eating or when visitors appeared.

In addition to traveling doctors and dentists, spectacle salesmen also peddled their wares throughout many frontier areas and persons with failing eyesight fitted themselves with glasses by the simple method of trying on a number of pairs and choosing the one with which they could see best. There is an old story to the effect that one such salesman stopped at a country store in the Ozark Mountain region on a Saturday afternoon and, observing that nearly every man of the considerable number of loafers assembled there had a red mark across the bridge of his nose, was very hopeful of doing

[14] Statement of J. M. Ferris, Navajoe, Oklahoma.

a big business. To his disappointment, however, he was solemnly informed that none of these men had ever worn glasses but had acquired these marks in drinking corn whisky out of a fruit jar!

While physicians and dentists were very few on the frontier, it was usually possible to obtain the services of either if the emergency were sufficiently grave but often only after considerable delay. Trained nurses, however, were unknown. Sometimes there might be found in a community a woman who would care for sick people for hire but this was unusual. Such a woman would today be called a "practical nurse" but it must be admitted that if one of these could be found on the frontier, she was as a rule, to paraphrase Voltaire, "neither practical nor a nurse." At best she was only a person with considerable experience in the sick room who was willing to come into a home and work on a twenty-four hour shift for the duration of the emergency getting what sleep or recreation she could when relieved by relatives or friends of the patient.

Of professional nursing, however, there was virtually none. A sick person was cared for by members of his family and kindly neighbors who were always ready and willing to lend assistance. "Sitting up with the sick," was regarded as the plain duty of everyone if the need arose and some persons achieved a local reputation as humanitarians by virtue of being "so good to wait on the sick." If anyone in the community became seriously ill, it was expected that his family would notify the neighbors, and any failure to do so was regarded almost as an affront. It was only necessary to pass on the word of illness in a family to a very few. The grapevine functioned with amazing efficiency and kindly persons hastened to call to bring special dainties to tempt the patient's appetite and to offer their services to "sit up" or to aid in any other possible fashion. Usually two or three would come in each evening and do some quiet visiting as they watched from an adjoining room. During the day there were likely to be many visitors to inquire about the situation and to sit and talk with the patient unless the latter were so ill that it was deemed inadvisable to admit any "company" to the sick room.

It must be confessed that an occasional visitor to the sick might be characterized as a "Job's comforter" whose influence was far from salutary. Such a person would come in on tiptoe, seat himself by the bed, and after a long survey of the patient would shake his head sorrowfully and remark: "You must be pretty bad, Bill; I don't like your color. You look a lot like my Uncle Joe did just before he passed on." If the patient protested that he felt much better than he had the day before, the visitor would again shake his head and continue: "Yes, Uncle Joe did, too. He rallied a little right at the last and then all at once went out just like a light." By the time the pessimistic individual had at last departed, the patient was likely to be in a cold sweat of fear and to feel that at any minute he might begin "picking at the cover," which among pioneer peoples was regarded as a sure sign of impending death.

Fortunately such gloomy visitors were very few. Most persons who came to call upon the sick brought not only food and flowers, and help to the overburdened family but something even more important—cheerfulness and sunshine and a breath of the pure air of the world outside. Among a people who lacked all modern facilities for the care of the suffering the kindly helpfulness of friends and neighbors robbed illness of much of its terror for the patient and his family alike. Many a person at last rose from a sick bed with a heart filled with gratitude for many favors and a spirit humbled and chastened by the knowledge that so many whom he had formerly regarded with indifference had, in his hour of need, proved themselves true and devoted friends. Undoubtedly illness often served to strengthen the bonds of friendship and helped to promote that neighborly feeling and community consciousness so characteristic of the American pioneers.

With the passing of the years, the old frontier days and ways began to disappear. Manners and customs were changing and this was as apparent in medical practices as in everything else. The coming of railroads brought in a larger population, towns grew up, and with economic advancement more physicians came in to open offices and begin a medical practice. They were, moreover, men of far more training and skill, in most cases, than had been the old-time frontier doctors. Hospitals supplied with modern equipment were established. Graduate nurses became available. The old-home remedies gave way to the prescriptions of physicians and even the rage for patent medicines began to abate as scientific investigations were made proving many of them worthless. Some standard remedies are still sold but many preparations disappeared from the market and the sale of others was far less than formerly, though weekly and daily newspapers still advertise some proprietary medicines. New remedies appeared on the shelves of the pharmacies and new treatments of disease were evolved. In addition many of the ailments that had formerly afflicted the pioneers have largely disappeared.

Only in a few backward communities do the old medical practices still persist in the nature of "fossil remains" of customs that half a century or more ago were virtually universal, at least in the rural districts of most states west of the Mississippi River and in many east of that stream. A long and intensive study of the medical practices of the American people in the West during the past three-quarters of a century and of how they have changed would undoubtedly produce a worthwhile contribution to the field of social history.

Old Navajoe*

About ten miles east and three miles north of the little city of Altus some seven steep mountain peaks rise abruptly from the level plain to a maximum height of about a thousand feet above the surrounding prairie. They extend north and south across the open end of a horseshoe bend made by the North Fork of Red River as it sweeps eastward and then back in a great loop some four or five miles in diameter. These peaks were formerly called the Navajo Mountains because of the tradition that about the middle of the last century, a great battle was fought at their base between a war party of Navajo, who had come east to prey upon the horse herds of the Comanches, and a band of warriors of the latter tribe, in which the Navajo had been completely destroyed.

Perhaps a mile west and slightly north of the highest peak of these mountains, on a low sandy hill, is a little wind-swept cemetery enclosed by a wire fence. No human habitation is near and this grass-grown "God's acre" contains only a hundred or so graves, most of them marked by very modest stones on which are usually carved only the names and dates of the birth and death of those buried there. Here lie the bodies of more than one man who died "with his boots on" before the blazing six gun of an opponent and of others who died peacefully in bed. Here also lie all that is mortal of little children, and of tired pioneer women who came west with

* Published in *Chronicles of Oklahoma*, XXIV (Summer, 1946), 128–45.

their husbands seeking a home on the prairie only to find in its bosom that rest which they had so seldom known in life.

Half a mile south of this small cemetery are cultivated fields where the plowman often turns up bits of glass and broken china or scraps of rusty and corroded metal and, if he is new to the community, he may be deeply puzzled as to their presence here so remote from any dwelling. In such cases inquiry of some old settler may reveal to the curious individual that these fields were once the site of the thriving little town of Navajoe. Nothing remains of Navajoe today. It is one with Nineveh and Tyre, flintlock guns, side saddles, baby golf, and all those other things that lie within the boundaries of the land of Used to Be. Yet, in its time Navajoe was a flourishing center of commerce with half a dozen stores and other business establishments and the dwellings of a score or more of families.

Since the nearest railroad point was Vernon, Texas, nearly fifty miles to the south and there was none to the north, east or west for from eighty to a hundred and twenty-five miles, Navajoe had a vast trade territory and was the southern gateway to a huge though thinly peopled empire. In consequence, it was to some extent both a business and social center for an enormous area. To it came settlers from their prairie claims often many miles away to barter butter and eggs for sugar and coffee or to purchase with their few hard-earned dollars shoes, dry goods, or clothing. Here also at times came the boss of a herd of cattle to the trail running a few miles west of town bringing the chuck wagon to replenish his stock of provisions before entering upon the long stretch of unsettled lands extending north to Kansas.

In addition there often came a band of Comanche or Kiowa Indians to pitch their round tepees near the north edge of town. Here they remained for two or three days strolling about from store to store clad in their bright blankets or shawls and moccasins, spending their "grass money" for groceries or red calico, selling in contravention of law their annuity issue blankets, coats, trousers, and coarse "squaw shoes" for a price determined by their own needs or wants rather than by the value of the articles sold. Above all the men spent many hours playing monte with the three or four professional gamblers who were permanent residents of the town, dealing out the cards on a blanket spread on the ground inside the tepee while the women looked on or pottered about camp cooking, bringing water from the public well, or busying themselves with other chores.

To Navajoe also came at times young people to attend a dance or party given by some citizen of the little town or a box supper or literary society held at the small unpainted school house. Among these would-be merrymakers might be included a long haired, unshaven cowhand from some remote line camp on the nearby Indian reservation. Riding in with his "good clothes" in a sack strapped behind his saddle, he usually put up his horse at the little wagon yard and surreptitiously made his way to the store to buy a white shirt and thence to the barber shop hoping against hope that he might not meet one of the girls of town until he had been able to make considerable improvement in his personal appearance. Once in the barber shop, he demanded "the works" and emerged an hour later clad in his best raiment with his hair cut, shampooed and "toniced" and his face shaved, bayrummed, and powdered. In fact, he was so transformed that his partner who had remained in the camp on Sandy, East Otter, or Deep Red, sometimes because of a reluctance to come within easy reach of the long arm of the law, would hardly have been able to recognize him either by sight or smell!

The foundations of Navajoe were laid about 1886 when two brothers-in-law, W. H. Acers and H. P. Dale, established the first general store, no doubt hoping to get some Indian trade, as well as to provision the outfits of trail herds on the way north, and also to supply the needs of settlers that were by this time beginning to come into the area in considerable numbers. Eventually Acers and Dale applied for the establishment of a post office under the name of "Navajo" but the Post Office Department insisted on adding an "e" to the name to avoid possible confusion with another Navajo post office in Arizona so it was officially recorded as *Navajoe.*

Undoubtedly, the spot for this store was selected largely because of the proximity of the great Kiowa-Comanche Indian reservation whose border was only three miles away and of the cattle trail which passed four miles to the west. In addition it was in the midst of fertile lands and the high mountains furnished a picturesque and convenient landmark for the embryo town. There were in addition the promotional activities of the man who was in some respects the father of Navajoe—the professional booster, J. S. Works.

Navajoe lay within the limits of the area bounded by the two Red rivers and the hundredth meridian which was claimed by Texas and had been organized by that state as a county as early as 1860. This claim the government of the United States disputed asserting that the real Red River was the South Fork of that stream and in consequence Greer County was really outside the limits of Texas and so part of the public domain of the United States.

Joseph S. Works was a typical pioneer of the promoter type. He was a tall, spare individual who always wore a buckskin shirt and his hair in long curls reaching to his shoulders. Because of his peculiar dress he was commonly known as "Buckskin Joe." Apparently he became interested in the Greer County lands about 1887 or possibly earlier. At any rate he came to the site of Navajoe about that time and erected for himself and family a small house of the "half dugout type" which he asserted cost only thirty-five dollars to build. In addition he built a hotel to accommodate land seekers. He was energetic and ambitious, with wide contacts and ample experience in land promotion. His enthusiasm for Greer County, particularly that part of it lying about Navajoe, was boundless. The recently completed Fort Worth and Denver Railroad extending northwest across Texas was only twelve or fifteen miles south of the Red River. It was plain that settlers of Greer County must purchase supplies from merchants of the little towns along the line sold to the latter by jobbers in Fort Worth. Works accordingly visited that city and told such an alluring tale of the future of Greer County that Texas business supplied him with funds for the printing of many thousands of copies of his little publication, *Buckskin Joe's Emigrants' Guide*, which was issued monthly for about a year. In this he extolled the beauty and fertility of Greer County in general and the area about Navajoe in particular.[1]

[1] The following item appeared in *The Emigrant Guide*, Navajoe, Greer County, for June 1888 (bound volume in Newspaper Files, Oklahoma Historical Society) under the heading "Buckskin Joe's Texas Oklahoma Colony," p. 2, col. 3:

"Founded in December, 1885, located at Navajoe Mountain, Greer Co., in 1887. Membership 400 families, no assessments.

"Terms of membership in full, $5.00 including lot in Navajoe. One dollar paid on application for membership, with guide and full instructions and rates for coming to Navajoe. The balance due when lot is selected. Some of the best lots in Navajoe can be secured by joining the colony and building."

Perhaps Works had considerable influence in attracting settlers to the region but though he remained at Navajoe for a year or more, he was too restless to stay long in any one place or to devote himself exclusively to any one project. In addition to booming the settlement of Greer County, he also engaged in townsite promotion and diligently sought to develop the town of Oklaunion a few miles east of Vernon, with the object of making it the chief supply point for the Greer County settlers. Doomed to disappointment here, "Buckskin Joe" after the construction of the Rock Island Railroad across Oklahoma in 1891, turned his attention to booming the town of Comanche near the western border of the Chickasaw country and to urging the opening of the Kiowa-Comanche Indian reservation to settlement. While his promotional activities never proved too successful, they seem to have netted him a living until 1908 when he was granted a pension by the United States Government for his services in the Civil War.

The store built and operated by Acers and Dale was quickly followed by other business establishments. Settlers were coming in, probably stimulated by the activities of Works, and taking claims in the community which they held by squatter's rights despite the warning of the President of the United States that the title to lands in Greer County was clouded and in consequence they might lose their lands. In addition the leasing of the lands of the Kiowa-Comanche Indian reservation to cattlemen gave those Indians considerable sums of "grass money" which they were eager to spend

---

The location of Navajoe was shown in T. 3 N., R. 19 W., on map of Oklahoma Territory, 1891, Department of Interior, General Land Office, in Volume 2, p. 952, Supreme Court of the United States, October term, 1894, No. 2, Original, *The United States vs. The State of Texas.*—Ed.

and Navajoe was their nearest trading point. Also the ranch-men purchased supplies for their men as did the foremen of herds on the trail. It was not long until the little town became a considerable center of business as judged by fron-tier standards.

The creation of the post office helped very considerably. Mail service from Vernon, Texas, was at first tri-weekly which the periodic rises of Red River caused many local wits to assert only meant that the carrier went to Vernon one week and "tried to get back the next." Eventually, how-ever, a daily service was maintained, the carrier driving only to Red River where he met and exchanged mail bags with another coming out from Vernon.

One corner of the establishment of Acers and Dale was partitioned off for the post office and the arrival of the mail about eight o'clock in the evening usually found most of the male population of the village, together with a number of near-by settlers, and a few cowpunchers, assembled and patiently waiting in the store. Here they sat on the counter, smoked cigarettes, chewed tobacco, and told yarns or in-dulged in practical jokes while waiting for "the mail to be put up." Once this was accomplished and the window opened each and every one walked up to it and solemnly inquired: "Anything for me?" Few of them ever got any mail; most of them would have been utterly astonished if they ever *had* got any mail but asking for it was a part of a regular ritual and missing the experience was a near tragedy. All of which seems strange and a little pathetic too. In few cases did any-one in the world care enough for one of these men to write him a letter but they refused to admit it even to themselves!

North of this pioneer store another was soon built by Bennight Brothers, John and Lum. It was a long, red building housing a stock of general merchandise but it did not attract nearly as many of either customers or loafers as did the establishment of Acers and Dale. In addition to his activities as a merchant, John Bennight also served for a time as deputy sheriff.

Beyond this second store was Ed Clark's saloon. It had a long shiny bar extending along the south side complete with brass rail in front and a good sized mirror on the wall behind it. On this wall also hung a large sign with this legend:

Since man to man has bin so unjust
I scarsely know in hoom to trust
I've trusted meny to my sorrow
So pay today, I'll trust tomorrow.

In addition to the bar, the room had two or three tables where the town's loafers and visiting cowhands sat and played poker, seven-up, or dominoes. The saloon received considerable patronage but the church-going element among the settlers regarded it as a den of iniquity and under the local option laws eventually voted it out and the town became dry except for individual importations and such patent medicines, as Peruna, lemon and ginger, "electric bitters," and other so-called patent medicines purchased at the drug store.

This last named business establishment stood a short distance north of the saloon and was owned and operated by W. H. H. Cranford, who sold drugs, compounded prescriptions, and did a considerable business in notions, cosmetics, and toilet articles. Among other things he sold considerable patent medicine of high alcoholic content to Indians since under the federal laws they could not be supplied with liquor. At the holiday season, he always laid in a considerable stock of Christmas goods consisting of dressing cases, manicure sets, shaving mugs, mustache cups, autograph and photo-

graph albums, and toys. Cranford was in Navajoe but not of
it! He was a slightly corpulent individual who always wore a
neatly pressed suit, white celluloid collar and four-in-hand
tie and was entirely lacking in any sense of humor or interest
in what passed for social or civic affairs. In short he was in
no sense a frontiersman. He was cold, dignified, and unre-
sponsive, and was alleged to have poisoned marauding cats
which was probably untrue.

At the extreme opposite end of the street from the drug
store was the little grocery store of John Brown and his wife.
It did little business and Brown spent most of his time in
warm weather sitting in a chair in front of his place of
business taking his ease, his bright red socks revealing a
brilliant splash of color between the bottoms of his trouser
legs and his shoes. Some of the town's loafers offered three
boys a pound of candy each if they would go down there,
one by one at twenty minute intervals, call Brown aside and
gravely ask what he would take for his red socks but, though
the lads talked about it enthusiastically and planned it again
and again, they were never able to get up enough courage to
carry it through.

All of the buildings named were in a row running north
and south, and all faced the east. Most of them had a porch
in front with a roof supported by wooden columns and
between these pillars was usually placed a long seat made of
two-inch lumber where "gentlemen of leisure" could sit
during the long summer afternoons and whittle to their
hearts' content. In cold weather they assembled inside about
a pot bellied stove fed with wood hauled contrary to law
from the near-by Indian reservation. Here they told stories,
played checkers, rolled and smoked cigarettes, or chewed
tobacco and spat in the general direction of a flat box half

filled with sand. Here practical jokes were planned and sometimes executed and the news and gossip of the little community exchanged.

Across the street from the drug store was the home of Dr. H. C. Redding which also contained his office. Redding was for a time the only doctor of the village and its surrounding country. He was an elderly man with long whiskers, who hated Cranford with an intense hatred because the latter often prescribed and sold medicine when so requested by an ailing settler thus depriving the doctor of a patient and a fee which he felt should rightly be his.

South of the doctor's house and directly across from the saloon was a small unpainted church of rough lumber originally a dance hall and skating rink but bought and transformed through the efforts of the more spiritual members of the community. Church and saloon faced one another like two duellists each battling for a cause as indeed they were. Here services were held every Sunday when a minister was available and a revival meeting was usually held each summer. Sunday afternoons people also met at the church sometimes to sing and Christmas festivities with a community tree were usually held there.

With the exception of a little barber shop north of John Brown's store, these were the only buildings on Navajoe's main street during the earlier years of the town's history. Some two hundred yards southeast of a central point in this row of business houses was the City Hotel, originally built by Buckskin Joe. This was a large unpainted building displaying a big sign which read: "Meals 25 cents." Near one corner was a tall post crowned by a large bell. Around noon and about six in the evening Aunt Matilda Smith or her husband Uncle Tom who were proprietors of the establishment came out and pulled the bell rope vigorously to call their hungry boarders up town to "come and get it."

Just as pigs leisurely rooting in the woods will at the call of their owner's voice suddenly stop to listen and then with flapping ears race madly for the barn lot, so did every un-attached man in town at the first sound of the bell drop whatever he was doing and start in a sort of lope down the path leading to the hotel gathering speed at every jump until he came to a skidding halt before Aunt Matilda's well-spread table. Despite her low rates, Aunt Matilda always "set a good table" and in a community where beef sold at five or six cents a pound, frying chickens at fifteen cents each, eggs at five or ten cents a dozen, and butter at "a bit" a pound, some profits were derived from meals even at twenty-five cents each. Prices were ridiculously low and money almost un-believably scarce.

Flour could be purchased at from a dollar to a dollar and a half a hundred pounds and settlers hauled sweet potatoes forty-five miles to the railroad and peddled them out among the residents of Vernon at fifty cents a bushel. As for actual cash, it is doubtful if some men holding down a claim ever saw fifteen dollars in real money at any one time throughout an entire year.

The ranchmen, as the Herrings, Stinson and Waggoner, all of whom leased lands for grazing on the Indian reservation, were of course well to do and their cowboys who drew wages of twenty to thirty dollars a month usually had a little money but most settlers were extremely poor. Occasionally one would get a few days work building fence or plowing fire guards for some cattlemen or would sell a rancher a little feed but sums derived from such sources were small. Some raised a small crop of wheat but it must be hauled forty-five miles to the railroad where it usually brought only fifty to sixty cents a bushel and since teams were usually small and there was the wide sandy river to cross, it was seldom possible to haul more than twenty to twenty-five bushels in a load and the trip consumed three to four days.

In the winter, a few men eked out a small income by poisoning and skinning wolves or from hunting prairie chickens and quail but coyote skins sold for only fifty cents and prairie chickens and quail only twenty-five and ten cents respectively at the railroad. Two or three young fellows broke horses for the Indians usually at a price of one dollar for each year of the animal's age which was anything but easy money.

Even though most people were very poor, however, life at Navajoe and in the surrounding community was colorful and varied. As a rule it was characterized by abundant leisure. Merchants, so called, were seldom kept busy waiting on customers and in consequence had ample time to talk, exchange gossip, and philosophize with one another or with the visitors who frequented their places of business usually only for purely social purposes. The three or four professional gamblers who specialized in playing monte with the Indians, or with an occasional easterner with money who might be passing through, had long periods of inaction during which they played cards with one another merely for pleasure and to keep in practice or with the local residents, or two or three cowhands. Every winter three or four cowboys laid off until spring would come to Navajoe and loaf for two or three months visiting with their friends, playing poker or dominoes in the saloon, "getting up" and attending dances as often as possible and in general enjoying a little vacation until time for spring work to start and the boss called them back to riding again. All of these men together with a few bachelor claim holders spent a large share of time sitting around in the stores or saloon, telling jokes or stories, or devoted themselves to arranging dances and candy breakings, courting the few girls, and as a rule enjoyed life hugely.

While in some respects the summer season may have been a bit more dull, it too was not without attractions. Picnic parties to climb the mountain and enjoy the magnificent view from its summit with dinner at some beauty spot at the foot was a favorite diversion. Groups would also make all day trips to the sand hills along the river to gather wild plums or to Otter or Elk Creek for a fish fry. All day singings with dinner on the ground were common and a two-weeks revival meeting was welcomed by many people quite as much for its social as for its spiritual significance.

Like every other frontier town, Navajoe had its share of unusual and picturesque characters. Among these was Uncle Billy Warren, a small, dried up old fellow who had been a scout for the United States Army in earlier days. He spoke the Comanche and Kiowa languages and was regarded as a man of substance since he drew a pension of thirty dollars a month as he said "just as regular as a goose goes to water." Another interesting character was a gambler known as "eat 'em up Jake" because he was alleged to have once found himself with five aces, and when his eagle-eyed opponent demanded a showdown, Jake crumpled and ate the extra card to avoid being caught redhanded.

For a considerable time an elderly remittance man named Harlan lived at Navajoe boarding at the hotel and spending a good deal of time around the saloon. He seemed to have considerable education and when drunk would talk elo-quently using numerous legal terms which caused him to be commonly called "Judge." One day the postmaster was much surprised to receive a letter from Justice John Marshall Harlan of the United States Supreme Court inquiring about the welfare of his brother whom the Justice had learned was now living at Navajoe. The postmaster promptly answered the letter assuring Justice Harlan that his brother seemed to be in good health, was comfortably situated, and that he was highly respected when sober and well cared for when drunk so it was not necessary to feel any uneasiness about him. No reply was ever received and eventually "Judge" Harlan left Navajoe and drifted away no doubt to some other little frontier town that also had saloons and congenial company.[2]

Still another interesting character was a young man commonly called "Diamond Dick" because he reached Navajoe wearing numerous large diamonds set in rings, shirt studs, cuff links, and a tie pin. Apparently he was the wayward son of a wealthy father somewhere in the East though he was quite reticent about his family and former house. He did not drink anything like as much as did the old "Judge" but played poker for modest stakes, rode about with the cowpunchers, attended dances, and seemed to have a good time for several months after which he too departed for some unknown destination.

One day a young man came up on the mail hack from

---

[2] The following news item appeared in *The Emigrant Guide* for June, 1888, *op. cit.*, under the heading "Our New Secretary," p. 2, col. 4:

"Judge James Harlan, of Kentucky, has cast his lot with the settlers of Navajoe, and as secretary and treasurer of the colony will devote his time to the up-building of Greer. Judge Harlan's high character as a citizen, his ability as a lawyer, and long experience as a judge is strong assurance that any movement with which he is connected will command the confidence of the public and government authorities. He is about the same age of his brother, who is justice in the United States Supreme Court, and esteemed equal in his knowledge of law. We welcome the judge to Navajoe."—Ed.

Vernon who said that he came from New York City and
so was promptly nicknamed "New York." He established
a little store stocked with men's clothing but was active in
local sporting circles and frankly stated that he had come to
the West for the sole purpose of "catching suckers."

Looking about for some means of turning a more or less
honest dollar, he thought he had found it when two drifting
cowpunchers visited him and explained that they wanted to
go to New Mexico but had a considerable number of horses
which they would sell cheap as they needed money for the
trip. They added that the animals were ranging on the Indian
reservation across the river but they would be glad to show
them to him. "New York" gladly accompanied the two
young fellows who showed him some fifty head of excellent
saddle horses all bearing what they said was their brand.
When a price was named which was clearly only a fraction
of their real value, "New York" jumped at the chance of
making some easy money and quickly closed the deal. The
cowhands gave him a bill of sale, received their money and
departed, but when their new owner rounded up the horses
and started for Vernon to sell them, he met a keen-eyed cowboy working for one of the ranchmen grazing cattle on the
reservation who noted that every horse bore the well-known
brand of his employer. This cowhand notified the deputy
sheriff and "New York" was promptly arrested and lodged
in jail where he died a few weeks before the date set for
his trial.

Another very interesting character was J. M. Ferris, commonly known as Jim who lived with his wife and some nine
children in a three-room house three-quarters of a mile south
of town. Ferris had been a Texas Ranger, secret service man,
and deputy sheriff, and so was a professional peace officer

trained in that hardest of all schools, the Texas-Mexican border. He became deputy sheriff in that part of the county after the departure of the Bennights and served as the representative of law and order in a wide region. He was a spare, blue-eyed man of medium height with a gentle, kindly voice and who always walked, Indian-like, with a soft, cat-like tread. Those who knew him best said that when his blue eyes began to shine and his voice fairly dripped sweetness it was time to climb a tree and ask the reason later!

When Tom Anderson, a wild nineteen year old boy, shot his employer through the shoulder and fled on foot for the Indian reservation carrying his Winchester with him, Deputy Jim set out on horseback in pursuit armed with a long shotgun strapped to his saddle. Ferris overtook the young chap about noon but Tom had his own ideas about submitting to arrest. At two hundred and fifty yards he shot Jim through the thigh inflicting a bad flesh wound and would have killed him with the second shot if the deputy had not swung over behind his horse. The lad then took refuge in a thicket and Ferris leaving a cowpuncher to keep watch at a safe distance rode home, dressed his wound and then rode up town to gather a posse.

It was Saturday afternoon and almost the entire population of the community, masculine, feminine, and canine, had assembled as usual in Navajoe. Every man and boy who could find a horse and any kind of shooting iron followed Jim and to the number of something like a hundred they bombarded the young outlaw for three hours without scoring a hit. It was not a one-sided battle, however. From a shallow pit he had scooped out in the thicket, the youngster returned the fire with an uncanny skill, putting a bullet through the hat of one of his too inquisitive besiegers and missing two or three more by such a narrow margin as to make them decidedly uncomfortable. Finally, running short of ammunition, he tied a handkerchief to the stock of his rifle and lifting it above the tops of the bushes, came out and surrendered. He was promptly lodged in jail from which he escaped a month later and disappeared to parts unknown.

The people of the county seat town of Mangum, thirty-five miles away, took up a collection for the benefit of Deputy Ferris and sent him thirty-five dollars. Jim returned the money the same day, accompanied by a brief note thanking these people for their kindness but asserting that the only expense incurred as a result of his wound had been fifteen cents for a bar of Castile soap and ten cents for a bottle of turpentine. He added that he had been able to pay this himself but if he had not, he was quite sure that some of his near-by neighbors would have been glad to make him a loan. Of such independent stuff were the early Oklahoma pioneers made!

It is impossible to name any considerable number of the many picturesque and colorful individuals who lived for a time in or near Old Navajoe. Among them were two brothers—both physicians—Doctors Joe and Dee Reynolds who settled in the little town and became for a time competitors of Doctor Redding. None of the three had much practice for the people of the community were unusually strong and healthy. Any who were not had long before been weeded out. Doctor Joe added to his income by hunting prairie chickens, hanging the birds up on the north side of his house until he had what his wife called: "a real good chance of them" when he sent them to Vernon by some passing freight wagon.

In addition there were the elderly Mr. Rusler who because

of his age was always Santa Claus at the community Christmas tree, and Yeakley Brothers who grazed seven or eight hundred sheep on the mountains and were the only shepherds in the entire region. There were also John Passmore and Joe Lee Jackson who eked out a precarious living playing monte or poker with the Indians, Dave Davis, bronc buster extraordinary, Old Man Fink who lived for music, was always present when people met to sing, and who had been known to leave his team standing in the field while he hurried to the house and wrote the words of a new song to be sung to the tune of *When the Roses Come Again!* Some were good, Christian men and others worthless men but all were generous, unselfish, and kind in their dealings with others. Almost without exception they were hospitable, deeply respectful toward all women, and every man of them would have gladly given the shirt off his back to someone in need, though it must be admitted that no person in his right mind would, as a rule, have wanted the shirt of any one of them!

Tragedy occasionally stalked the town's one street as when George Gordon shot and killed W. N. Howard. The latter was a one-armed man from the hills of Kentucky who had brought his family to Greer County and settled on a claim about three miles north of Navajoe. The basis of the quarrel between the two men has long been forgotten but both were hot tempered and dangerous. One afternoon they met on the street and Howard reached for his gun only to discover that he had left it at home, and Gordon shot him. Despite the fact that his opponent was unarmed, Gordon was acquitted, on the grounds of self defense, the jury probably reasoning that a man who sees his adversary reach for his hip is justified in assuming that the latter has a gun and cannot be expected to wait long enough to discover his mistake.

The town had periods of excitement, too. One of these was in 1891 when Chief Polant of the Kiowa tribe was killed a few miles north of Navajoe by a young cowpuncher. The belligerent old chief had left the reservation and crossed the river into Greer County to demand an explanation of why some of his people had been refused a gift of beeves. He emphasized his remarks by drawing his Winchester from its scabbard whereupon the young cowhand promptly shot him through the head and then made his way to Navajoe to relate what he had done and ask for protection. A large number of Kiowas quickly armed themselves and demanded that the young man be surrendered to them. This was, of course, refused but an Indian war seemed imminent and the near-by settlers hastily brought their wives and children to Navajoe for safety. All the men in the community gathered at town armed to the teeth and prepared to defend themselves and their families from the threatened attack. News of the affair reached Colonel Hugh L. Scott, the Commanding Officer at Fort Sill who led his cavalry in a forced march to the Kiowa camp on Elk Creek and at last persuaded the angry Kiowas that it would be folly to start a war which could only result in their own destruction.

Within a few years considerable changes came to the town of Navajoe. "Buckskin Joe" had departed in search of a more profitable venture in promotion. The opening of the Cheyenne-Arapaho reservation to settlement on April 19, 1892, took several citizens of Navajoe to that region. Among these were Tom and Aunt Matilda Smith who pulled down the hotel, hauled the lumber to Cordell, and rebuilt it in that newly opened town, and H. P. Dale who sold his interest in the store to his partner and took up a homestead in the "Cheyenne Country." W. H. Acers operated the store for more than a year but with the opening of the Cherokee Outlet on September 16, 1893, he sold it and drifted up to that region.

The Post Office was transferred to W. H. H. Cranford who enlarged his store, and put in a stock of dry goods and clothing on one side, retaining the shelves on the other side for drugs, medicines, and notions. He also added a room for the post office and its lobby and finished up an attic room above the store where he kept surplus merchandise, empty packing cases, and a stock of coffins of assorted sizes.

About the middle nineties a wave of outlawry swept over Greer County and the surrounding region when Red Buck Weightman, Joe Beckham, and two or three of their comrades appeared in that area and turned their attention to robbing stores, stealing horses, and other forms of deviltry. Cranford as postmaster often had considerable sums of money in his safe since there was no bank nearer than Vernon and remittances were usually made by money order. In consequence he eventually developed an almost morbid fear of being robbed. In anticipation of this he not only buckled on a heavy Colts revolver the latter part of every afternoon but also installed a bed in the attic and hired a young man as assistant in the store and post office with the provision that he should go armed and sleep in the attic at night among the coffins! In addition he often talked of installing a wood vise behind the counter beside the opening leading to the rest of the store and clamping a cocked pistol in it when he locked up at night with a string attached to its trigger, looped around a nail behind it, and stretched across this opening. With such a device prepared, he declared that anyone breaking in who started to go behind the counter would shoot himself through the legs.

Evidently he considered any such protection unnecessary so long as he had a clerk sleeping in the attic but in 1895 Cranford lost the post office and decided to remove to Cloud Chief in the Cheyenne Country and open a drugstore there. Here he fitted up his long-talked-of booby trap for malefactors but unfortunately his wife became suddenly ill one night and he ran hastily down to the store to get some medicine for her and in his excitement completely forgot the product of his own ingenuity. It worked all too well! Cranford shot a leg off and like Peter Stuyvesant of historic fame, was doomed to stump through the remaining years of his life on a wooden leg! Moreover, he lacked even the consolation of the sympathy of his neighbors since no one who knew his story ever felt particularly sorry for him.

As more and more of the first business men and residents of Navajoe departed, others came in to take their places. In 1896 the Supreme Court in the case of the *U. S. vs. Texas* held that the South Fork of Red River was the principal stream and therefore Greer County was not a part of Texas. This was followed by a special act of Congress attaching the region to Oklahoma Territory. With the cloud removed from land titles, many more settlers came in to take up homesteads and the little town grew in importance as a business center. Bennight Brothers sold their store and returned to Indian Territory. The church-going part of the population voted out the saloon under local option laws and Ed Clarke returned to his old home state of Kentucky.

George Blalock came from Texas with his family, purchased the claim joining the town on the south and opened a general merchandise store in the building formerly occupied by the establishment of Acers and Dale. W. Z. Peters replaced Cranford as postmaster, and a new hotel was built on the main street of town. John Brown's wife died and he sold his little stock of groceries and drifted away to parts unknown.

Blalock's store remained the chief business enterprise for some years but he was eventually elected County Sheriff and removed to Mangum which was the county seat. Other business establishments with new owners followed one another in rapid succession, though a few old timers remained. Conn and Higgins opened a general merchandise store in the former Cranford building. A hardware store was established by the Martin Brothers which eventually came to be operated by the two Ricks Brothers. Conn and Higgins sold their business and Blackwell and Akin came in and opened a dry goods and clothing store followed by Bailey Brothers with a stock of general merchandise. An elderly individual named White operated a small grocery store. A little wagon yard was built, a meat market, a pool hall, and a new barber shop were established. The little box-like school house made of twelve inch boards with knot holes which the older tobacco chewing boys, endowed with a spirit of daring and a sure aim, felt had been placed there by Divine Providence, was torn down and a new one of two rooms erected at the western edge of town. Ben Hawkins continued for years to operate his blacksmith shop at the same old stand with Old Man Chivers who sang hymns to the accompaniment of his ringing anvil as his chief competitor. Several new residences were erected where the business men lived with their families and a few settlers removed to town in the winter in order to send their children to school.

Life in Navajoe was still varied and colorful and was not without its frontier characteristics but gradually changes were creeping in. Cowhands and ranchmen were less in evidence and most of the men who came in to "do a little trading" or merely for the social stimulus derived from "going to town" were homesteaders or their grown up sons. More farming was carried on in the surrounding country and a little more sophistication became apparent. Men remained largely in the majority in the community and an attractive young woman still had plenty of suitors but not to the extent apparent in earlier years when the appearance of a new girl in town or anywhere near it was an event of major importance.

In the late nineties, Navajoe was struck by a mining boom which brought in a considerable number of new people most of them entirely unlike any of the earlier inhabitants of the town. The Navajo mountains were the most southwestern group of the Wichitas which extend east some forty miles or nearly to Fort Sill. For many years old timers had solemnly asserted that: "Thar's gold in them thar hills." There were legends of lost Spanish mines and it was even declared that the Indians knew where vast stores of gold could be found, a rumor which gained credence by the average Indian's tendency to make sport of the white man.

About 1896 there appeared in the little town a lean bewhiskered individual about forty years old named Edson L. Hewes. He came from Nevada where he had been a prospector and could see a color of gold in any pan of dirt regardless of its source that he decided to wash out. Hewes was a remittance man receiving every week a money order for two dollars from the New Orleans post office since he had once lived in that city and apparently still had relatives there. He had studied law, had been a journalist, and apparently a good many other things but for years had followed the open road more or less as a hobo. From Nevada he had marched on

Washington with the state's contingent of Coxey's army and was an ardent champion of democracy, and the under dog and the bitter foe of the "interests" and of all aristocrats. He had dreams of writing a book called *The Wandering American*, but apparently could never get around to it. Hewes was certain that there were rich deposits of gold in the Wichitas so staked some claims in the Navajo mountains, found a worthless young fellow as partner, and fitted up a shallow cave among the giant rocks of his favorite claim as a dwelling place. He and his partner worked diligently at panning the mountain dirt, carried their groceries on their backs from the Navajoe stores and, while dining on cheese and crackers, talked of the great wealth to be theirs in the near future!

Other so-called miners came in—some with wives as worn and faded as the dresses they wore—and a troop of ragged children. More were single men, most of them old and virtually all shabby and unkempt and without money, property, or ambition to work at anything except digging for gold. They included such men as Lige Williams, Robert Rayel, the Petersons, father and son, and a number of others.

Some of these told colorful tales of their profitable mining experiences in the past. One asserted that in a remote canyon of the Rocky Mountains he had once turned over a rock with a crowbar and found thirty-three thousand dollars in gold nuggets beneath it. One such experience would doubtless keep the average man busy turning over rocks for the rest of his life! Another shabby, long-whiskered old man who, now that the saloon had been closed, spent most of his scanty, occasional funds at the drug store for Peruna at a dollar a bottle was alleged to have once sold a mining claim in Colorado for two hundred thousand dollars. What he had done with the money no one knew but some one was heard to remark that it probably went for two hundred thousand bottles of Peruna!

The Navajo Mountains not offering sufficient field for their activities, the miners began to cross the river and operate in the rough mountains on the Indian reservation along the headwaters of Otter Creek. Here they staked mining claims, built little shacks and, regardless of the fact that United States law prohibited such occupation of Indian lands, eventually secured the establishment of a post office. It was called Wildman in honor of a prosperous citizen of one of the near-by Greer County towns who had given some aid and encouragement to mining ventures. Since the miners frequently shifted the center of their activities the post office was placed on wheels and so resembled a field kitchen or the cook shack of a threshing crew. It followed its patrons about over a considerable area and in consequence, the mail carrier coming out from Navajoe two or three times a week always started without knowing his exact destination. In the early summer of 1901 a troop of cavalry was sent out from Fort Sill to destroy the miners' shacks and escort their owners to the reservation line where they were left with a warning not to return.

The mining boom collapsed and was succeeded by something of much greater importance—the opening of the Kiowa-Comanche Indian lands to white settlement. This occurred late in the summer of 1901 by a lottery. All persons desirous of securing a homestead in that region were required to register their names either at Fort Sill or El Reno. Cards bearing their names were then placed in great hollow wheels, thoroughly mixed and drawn out and the 160 acre tracts, to the number of 13,000, were selected by the lucky registrants in the order that their names were drawn.

Virtually every young man about Navajoe who was twenty-one or more years of age hastened to Fort Sill to register since there was no longer any government land of value left unclaimed in Greer County. They were accompanied by many older men who had come into the Navajoe community too late to secure land there. It seemed that the opening of these Kiowa-Comanche lands to settlement should have greatly aided the growth and prosperity of Navajoe located so close to their border by rounding out the town's trade territory and bringing in much new business.

As a matter of fact it was the beginning of the end. Not a few of the citizens of the town or the surrounding country secured land in the newly opened region to which they promptly removed. Far more important the settlement of this large territory brought in railroads and the establishment of new and prosperous towns. Even before registration for lands began, the Rock Island Railway Company was constructing a line south through Lawton and trains reached that city early in the autumn of 1901. The Blackwell, Enid, and Southwestern was also building a line south to Vernon on which were located Hobart, Snyder, and Frederick. Soon after the construction of these railroads, the Frisco extended a branch from Oklahoma City southwest to Quanah, Texas, on which its officials laid out a town called Headrick only seven or eight miles southeast of Navajoe. This marked the end of the little town which had flourished for more than fifteen years. Every business establishment was promptly removed to Headrick. The smaller buildings whether residences or shops and stores, were jacked up, placed on wheels and hauled to the new town. Larger ones were wrecked and the lumber either transferred to Headrick to be used in building there or sold to some settler for the construction of a farm house or barn. The church and school house, both growing old and dilapidated, were torn down and a new school building erected on the road half a mile west. The town site was acquired by a farmer who plowed and planted the land in cotton and kaffir corn and Navajoe was no more. Even the school house did not remain long. The consolidated school movement was sweeping the country so the district was merged with four or five others and a new, modern building called Friendship Consolidated School was erected a few miles away. Only the little cemetery on its low, sandy hill and the bits of broken glass and china occasionally turned up by the farmer's plow remain today as mute reminders of the thriving little town which was for so many years the commercial and social center of a large region.

Navajoe was never a large town as Oklahoma regards size now but for many years it was the largest and most important one which a traveler would pass near in a journey north over the Western Cattle Trail from Vernon, Texas, to Woodward, a distance of some two hundred miles. Moreover, it was the trading center for the people of an area far larger than is the so-called trade territory of almost any Oklahoma town today with a population of upwards of ten thousand.

Importance, however, does not depend entirely upon size. Except for the fact that it was located near the border of the Kiowa-Comanche reservation and in consequence had much trade from these Indians as well as that of the ranchmen who leased their lands, Navajoe was typical of hundreds of other little prairie towns of its time, not alone in Western Oklahoma but throughout the length and breadth of a great region extending north to the Canadian border. Therein lies the justification for telling its story.

Yet, in some respects Navajoe was almost unique. Not so

much because of the picturesque and colorful character of many of its inhabitants, for every town has its interesting and colorful individuals, but because Navajoe, like Peter Pan, never grew up. Always it was young, lusty, and vigorous with hopes and dreams for a future that were never to be realized. Like the gay young soldier cut down by the enemy's bullet, the little town never knew either the comforts and responsibilities of middle life or the pains and infirmities of old age. Some other towns secured a railroad, a county seat, and industrial or commercial enterprises which caused them to grow to the stature of thriving little cities with paved streets, water works, chambers of commerce, and civic clubs. Others, less fortunate found their trade and population drained away by improved roads and automobiles to some local metropolis, leaving them only as decadent, sleepy little villages, where a few elderly people still cling to a spot hallowed by memories and live in a past now gone forever. Navajoe met neither of these fates. In the full vigor of youth it simply vanished from the earth.

Few strangers ever visit the site of Old Navajoe now. Once in a great while an automobile, perhaps bearing the license tag of another state, will stop at the little grass-grown cemetery and a gray-haired man alight to spend a few hours in cutting weeds or planting some rose bushes about the grave of one who nurtured and cared for him in his childhood of more than half a century ago. Sometimes he may linger at his task until the sun has gone down in a radiant glory of crimson and gold and twilight begins to wrap the wide prairie in an ever darkening mantle. Then as he returns to his car and pauses for a moment to watch the first stars peep over the dark bulk of the Navajo Mountains he may almost imagine that he can hear the ring of ghostly spurs as some lean, brown cowhand rides in to visit his old familiar haunts where these pioneer people lived and loved, and dreamed of the future in the ruddy dawn of Western Oklahoma's history.

Wood and Water: Twin Problems of the Prairie Plains*

There is a venerable story of many variations to the effect that an old gentleman from the wooded hills of Tennessee once paid a visit to his two nephews who were ranching on the plains of western Texas. The two young men met him at the nearest railroad point with a spring wagon and camping outfit and the trio set out in the early afternoon for the ranch some seventy miles distant. A little before sundown they stopped to make camp near a windmill that stood not far from the banks of a dry, sandy arroyo which meandered across the level prairie. One of the young men took a pick axe from the wagon and began digging in the dry earth nearby from which grew a few mesquite sprouts.

Soon he had unearthed an armful of large mesquite roots, brought them to the wagon and kindled a fire. In the meantime his brother had unharnessed the horses, watered them at the big circular metal stock tank beside the windmill and staked them out to graze on the thick buffalo grass. He then seized an iron pail and hung it over the end of the iron pipe leading from the windmill to the stock tank. There was not a breath of air stirring but the young man climbed the steel ladder leading to the top of the windmill tower and turned the great wheel with his hands until a stream of fresh, clear water poured from the pipe and filled the pail. Returning to

* Published in *Nebraska History*, XXIX (June, 1948), 87–104.

the campfire, he filled the coffee pot and began to prepare supper.

The old uncle who had been sitting on the wagon tongue watching these proceedings with a jaundiced eye but considerable interest suddenly inquired: "Is there ever any water in that creek?" "Oh, yes," was the answer, "when it rains and for a few days or weeks afterward." "What's the name of it anyhow?" continued the old man. "Jose Creek," answered the nephew, "J-o-s-e, pronounced hosay." The old man snorted indignantly: "I don't know why you boys want to stay out here. I wouldn't live in any country where you have to climb for water and dig for wood and spell hell with a J!"

While it was only in the Southwest that the Anglo-American pioneers had to struggle with the vagaries of Spanish spelling and pronunciation, it must be confessed that the early settlers of all the prairie states from the Dakotas south to western Oklahoma and Texas found that their twin problems were always the securing of an adequate supply of wood and water. Many settlers on the Southwestern Plains for a time depended largely upon mesquite roots grubbed from the hard earth to cook their food while, unless a handle had been attached to the pump rod of a windmill, it was always necessary to climb the tower and turn the wheel by hand to pump fresh water when the wind was not blowing, though it must be admitted that this was not often.

Explorers of this region as well as the "mountain men," Indian traders, Mormons en route to Utah, gold seekers headed for California, and the emigrants to Oregon have commented upon the difficulties encountered due to the arid nature of the area and the almost complete absence of timber. W. A. Ferris journeying west for the American

Fur Company in 1830 complained of the shortage of fuel as had many before him.[1] James Akin who went with a party from Iowa to Oregon in 1853 kept a diary in which a short entry of three or four lines was made each day. Of the thirty entries made in June when they were crossing Nebraska, twenty-four refer to fuel or water or both, indicating that these two necessities held a most important place in the minds of the emigrants.[2]

To these early explorers and travelers, however, the vast prairie plains formed only a barrier to be crossed as quickly as possible to reach some predetermined destination beyond. The thought of establishing permanent homes there had never entered their heads. In fact, it was not until much later that any considerable number of people began to believe that these wide prairies would ever support a great population of agricultural settlers. For the American people who had pushed relentlessly westward ever since the early years of the seventeenth century, hesitated, for approximately a generation at the edge of the dry, treeless plains reluctant to attempt to cope with a land so unlike any which they had known in the past. It is true that there were fairly extensive prairies in portions of Ohio, Illinois, and many other states east of the Mississippi.[3] These, however, were comparatively small. Timber for fuel and building purposes was usually available within a few miles. Moreover, the rainfall was sufficient to mature crops virtually every year and numerous streams, springs, and ponds, together with wells, which in

[1] W. A. Ferris, *Life in the Rocky Mountains*, Edited by Paul C. Phillips (Denver, 1940), p. 26.

[2] E. E. Dale, Editor, *The Journal of James Akin, Jr.* (Norman, Oklahoma, 1919), pp. 11-15.

[3] Illinois was said to be seventy per cent prairie. E. M. Poggs, *The Prairie Provinces of Illinois* (Urbana, 1934), p. 70.

most cases were comparatively shallow, insured a bountiful supply of water.

This western land was very different. The level prairies stretched away for scores of miles unbroken by a single tree. Streams were few and far between and many of them were only broad strips of sand for a large part of the year even though heavy rains occasionally turned them into raging, muddy torrents. Springs were even fewer than streams and in large areas non-existent while whether or not pure water could be had by digging or drilling wells was a question that in many cases seemed likely to demand a negative answer.

It was not a reluctance to face hardships or the fear of hostile Indians which caused would-be settlers to pause at the edge of these western prairies, largely, until after the close of the war between the states. The American pioneers had never shrunk from the hardships of frontier life in the past and the early settlers of the eastern portion of the Mississippi Valley had been confronted by forest Indians quite as warlike and dangerous as were the plains tribes west of that stream. Primarily it was the lack of timber for fuel, buildings, and fences, and of water for domestic use and livestock which halted the pioneer settlers at the edge of the prairie plains for so long a period.

Eventually, however, the increasing scarcity of agricultural land which could be purchased at what was considered a reasonable price and the eager desire for homes caused some of the more hardy souls to venture out into a land where most of what they had learned of pioneering in the past was of no value and where new methods must be devised to solve new problems.

Certainly, from 1866 to 1900 there was an enormous outpouring of settlers to the Prairie West. Obviously, this movement was greatly accelerated by the Homestead Act of 1862[4] but there were other factors that were almost as important. These were the westward advance of railroads promoted by huge grants of land from the Federal government, which the railway companies offered for sale at comparatively low prices. Still others were the taming of the Plains Indians and their concentration upon reservations, the influx of immigrants from Europe, and increased travel back and forth across the region due to the settlement of the Pacific Coast and the development of mining operations in the Rocky Mountains.

Along the eastern edge of the prairies there were in some places a few groves or islands of timber and a considerable fringe of trees along the streams but as settlers advanced westward into a land which ever grew higher, dryer, and more nearly level, the dual problem of securing wood and water became increasingly acute. Most of the lands east of the Mississippi and of the first tier of states west of it were wooded and the people who first occupied them were faced with the immediate task of clearing fields for cultivation. To these settlers the forest had seemed largely an unmixed evil. It appeared to them only an impediment to progress. With enormous energy they set to work to fell or girdle the trees in order to provide a clearing for the growing of crops. The first logs cut were utilized for building a home, barn, and outbuilding, or split into rails for fencing the fields. The surplus ones were burned after being rolled into great heaps with the assistance of kindly neighbors who gladly came to participate in these "log rollings" at which a jug of corn whiskey often stimulated the efforts of the participants.

In time the clearing became a symbol of economic and,

[4] *U.S. Stats. at Large*, 12, pp. 392–393.

to some extent, cultural progress. To widen the clearing in order to provide more tillable land for growing crops to feed his family and to sell in order to get money for clothing and other necessities became the settler's chief task. After the trees had been felled, the stumps must be pulled or grubbed out, or in some cases burned or blasted out with gunpowder. To the average pioneer in the densely wooded regions life must have seemed an almost endless conflict with the forest. Moreover, the forest was no passive enemy. It fought back with a stubborn persistence that at times made its complete subjugation seem well nigh impossible. Even after all stumps had been removed from the cleared land, there were many roots left in the soil from which sprouts grew with astonishing rapidity and vigor. These must be dug up or cut down with a mattock or grubbing hoe and they often seemed to have more than the nine lives usually credited to a cat.

The forest trees which bordered the clearing not only shaded and drew sustenance from a wide strip of soil but also sent out long roots which when broken by the plow sent up shoots which if not promptly destroyed seriously threatened again to "let in the jungle."

One who migrated from the wooded regions to the wide prairies at first viewed his new homestead with pride and admiration. Here he need no longer wrestle with the tasks of clearing land, grubbing out stumps, and cutting sprouts. Furrows entirely across his land could be plowed without encountering a root or stone. He soon discovered, however, that he had fled from ills which he had formerly borne only to encounter others that he had hitherto "known not of." For the first time the American pioneer began to realize the value of those forests which in the past he had striven so hard to destroy. His entire pattern of life was changed and much of that change was due to the great scarcity of the two commodities which in the past he had accepted as a matter of course because they were so abundant—timber and water.

His first task was to provide housing for himself and family. In the old homeland the pioneer settler had found it necessary only to hew and notch logs and lay them up to form the walls of a comfortable log house which was covered with rough shingles split with an axe and smoothed down a bit with the axe or a plane. In a prairie region he must utilize for constructing a home such material as was available and this was in most cases sod or earth. Moreover, to decrease the height of the walls it was sometimes advisable to build it partly underground. Even a sod house or dugout required some timber for its construction, however, since it was necessary to provide a ridge pole, corner posts, and stringers along either side to support the roof made of narrow poles covered with hay on which were placed sods or a thick layer of closely packed earth.

The settler accordingly erected a small tent from his wagon cover as a temporary shelter and then set out in search of the required timbers to frame the new home. This often required a journey of ten to thirty miles to reach a stream bordered with a thin line of cottonwood, elm and hackberry trees or some ravine or canyon in the bottom of which there usually grew at least a little timber. Such ravines were usually in a hilly region where there was little land suitable for cultivation. In consequence these lands were not occupied by homesteaders until all of the level, fertile prairies had been settled and so remained for some years a part of the public domain. Eventually Congress enacted a law permitting settlers to take timber from unoccupied government lands "for domestic use." This, however, was largely a meaningless gesture since the pioneer settler had never hesitated to take timber anywhere he could find it except from the land of another settler. This might be the public domain, state or territorial school lands, railroad land, some ranchman's range, or an Indian reservation.[5] Cutting and removing timber from Indian lands was contrary to law and deputy United States Marshals sometimes derived a considerable revenue from arresting "wood haulers" on the great reservations of Oklahoma, South Dakota, and some other western states, since they received not only a fee for making the arrest but mileage for the distance traveled in taking the luckless timber cutter to the nearest United States Court.[6] The lands of the Cherokee Outlet in northern Oklahoma before they were opened to settlement in 1893 had been largely denuded of timber for many miles south of the border of Kansas by the pioneer settlers of that state as were those of the Kiowa-Comanche reservation by settlers of Greer County, Texas. The Indians, seeing that the activities of the wood cutters could not be stopped, sometimes patrolled the border of their reservations and collected twenty-five to fifty cents a load for wood taken from their lands. In the middle 1890's the author paid fifty cents for a load of wood to an old Comanche Indian who had displayed an official looking paper which he apparently thought was his authorization from the Department of the Interior to demand such payment. The document, however, was only a circular letter

[5] Julie Stelle Bellows, *Indian Pioneer Papers*, VII, 112. These papers in 116 volumes of typed sheets consist of statements made by early settlers of the West now living in Oklahoma. Of the two sets made, one is in the Frank Phillips Library of the University of Oklahoma and the other in the collections of the Oklahoma Historical Society.

[6] Thomas Arthur Banks, *Indian Pioneer Papers*, V, 124; and Allie Wilson, *Ibid.*, XCIX, 96.

signed by the Secretary of the Interior warning white persons not to purchase wood from Indians since the latter were not permitted to sell timber from their lands!

Regardless of their source enough timbers were eventually secured to frame the proposed dwelling and the homesteader set to work to construct it. If the soil happened to be firm in texture and thickly interlaced with the roots of a thick coat of grass, a sod house wholly above ground might be built. In areas of sandy soil, however, it was necessary to construct a dugout or half-dugout though its walls were usually built sufficiently high above the level of the ground to allow the insertion of from two to four half windows. For window frames, a little lumber was required, though in a pinch they might be made from three or four wooden boxes or packing crates. No boards were required for a floor since it was in most cases only the hard beaten earth while the roof was also of earth or sod. From this plants often sprouted and the new-comer from the East was sometimes astonished to see a house on the roof of which were growing weeds or sunflowers.[7]

After the house had been completed and the family moved in and the furniture arranged, there still remained the task of providing shelter for the livestock. This usually took the form of a hay-covered shed but this also required some timber and in addition, enough poles must be secured to build a small enclosure about it, variously called a lot, pen, or corral. All of this construction necessitated several more trips to the all too distant source of timber.

In the meantime the problem of fuel for cooking the food and heating the home was an acute one. The majority of people who migrated to the prairie plains did so in the early autumn in order to erect buildings before the coming of cold

[7] William J. Newsome, *Indian-Pioneer Papers*, LXVI, 460.

weather and to break the sod and prepare the ground for planting in the spring. Consequently fuel for heating was not required at first but by the time a home and outbuildings had been constructed the "eager and nipping air" warned the settler that winter was fast approaching and provision must be made to keep the family warm once its icy winds began to sweep the prairies.

Also, from the first, fuel was required for cooking and in most cases was not easy to obtain. In preparing the timbers for framing the new home some scraps of wood were inevitably left and these were carefully saved to be burned in the cook stove. These were too few to last long, however, and it became necessary to utilize the only fuel which the prairies afforded. This was "prairie coal" as buffalo chips or cow chips were commonly called. These had been largely used for campfires on the westward journey once the edge of the treeless plains had been reached and were equally dependable for burning in the cook stove or fire place of the sod house or dugout. They made a hot, though somewhat smoky fire that was reasonably adequate for cooking the meals and keeping a room fairly warm in mild winter weather. Cow chips formed the principal fuel of many settlers during the first two or three years of life on a prairie claim.[8] During the early years of the settlement of Nebraska, Kansas, and western Oklahoma a common sight was a homesteader slowly driving a team hitched to a farm wagon across the prairies while his wife and children walking beside it, picked up cow chips and tossed them into the wagon box until it was filled to overflowing despite the fact that it was equipped with "sideboards." Once back home the family unloaded the wagon, stacking the "prairie coal" in a neat rick beneath a

[8] Allie Wilson, *op. cit.*, and Vera Best, *Indian-Pioneer Papers*, VII, 467.

hay-covered shed where it would remain dry for wet cow chips persistently refused to burn. Moreover, even when perfectly dry it was almost imperative to have some wood to mix with them so additional trips to the school section, unoccupied lands of the public domain, or Indian reservations where some timber might be found were necessary.[9]

As more settlers came in the supply of "prairie coal" eventually became pretty well exhausted and if trees could be found only at a great distance the problem of fuel became increasingly acute. Corn cobs, corn stalks, and sunflower stalks were all utilized as fuel, for cooking the food, and in some cases wisps of twisted hay provided enough fire to boil coffee and fry bacon and hot cakes. One stanza of the old song, "The Little Old Sod Shanty on My Claim," refers to this as follows:

> And when I left my eastern home
> So happy and so gay
> To try to win my wealth and fame
> I little thought that I'd come down
> To burning twisted hay
> In the little old sod shanty on my claim.

In some parts of Nebraska, Kansas, western Oklahoma, and other prairie states a stove was sometimes fitted out as a "hayburner." The equipment consisted of several metal cylinders half the length of the fire box and open at one end. Inside each was a coiled wire spring attached to the closed end while the walls of the cylinder near the open end were pierced with a number of large holes. The spring was pushed down by packing the cylinders tightly with hay and two were placed in the fire box of the stove with the open ends

[9] Newsome, *op. cit.*, states that settlers in the Panhandle of Oklahoma hauled firewood thirty to forty miles.

together and the hay lighted at one of these holes. As it was consumed, the springs pressed a fresh supply into the fire and when it had all been burned, the cylinders were replaced with fresh ones. Another type of "hay-burner" had a large drum filled with hay above the fire box of the stove and this was fed into the fire by a coiled spring. In either type a hot fire could be produced but almost constant attention was required to keep it burning.[10]

When more bountiful crops were produced, some people in the remote prairie regions of the North burned corn at times when the cold was intense and corn prices low while those of the southern plains occasionally used cottonseed for fuel.[11] The feeling was common, however, that it was immoral to burn commodities so much needed for food by hungry persons and animals throughout the world. In consequence, it is doubtful if any considerable quantity of corn and cottonseed was used for fuel except in case of a grave emergency.[12]

Scarcity of wood for construction and fuel were only two aspects of the problem faced by the prairie settler because of lack of timber. A third and very serious question was the age-old one of enclosures. Once he had chosen and settled a tract of land, he was faced with the problem of restraining his own domestic animals and as soon as fields had been plowed and crops planted, some means must be devised of protecting them from his livestock and that of his neighbors

---

[10] *Ibid.*, pp. 461–462.

[11] George C. Neeley, *Indian-Pioneer Papers*, LXVI, 212–213; also G. R. Bellenger, *Ibid.*, VII, 76.

[12] The author's father has told of occasionally burning corn in northeastern Nebraska in severe weather and Dean E. D. Meacham of the University of Oklahoma states that corn was sometimes used for fuel in his father's home in Western Oklahoma.

as well as from cattle of the ranchmen who still lingered in the region even after the coming of many homesteaders.

In the wooded area the pioneer had no such problem. Once a field had been cleared the branches were trimmed from the tree trunks with an axe and used to construct a "brush fence" about the clearing which served reasonably well until such time as enough rails could be split to replace it with the more stable and permanent "worm fence" properly "staked and ridered." Lacking any suitable material for fencing, the prairie homesteader must adapt himself to his environment in this as in so many other things. If he had only a team of horses and a milk cow, the animals could be picketed out with long ropes and the stake pins moved every day to insure fresh pasturage. The rope soon became as much of a necessity to the prairie pioneer as the axe had been to his ancestors of the forest regions. In the summer a mother would sometimes tie one end of a rope about the waist of the two or three year old toddler and stake the youngster out on the prairie where he could play unharmed while she did her washing and other household tasks.

The prospect of herding the cows and staking out the work animals indefinitely was an appalling one, however, and many homesteaders planted hedges of bois d'arc commonly called "Osage orange" about their fields. Since it would be at least two or three years before these had grown sufficiently to protect crops, the settlers of most communities promptly voted a "herd law" requiring all persons owning livestock to restrain their animals and to pay for any damage resulting from their failure to do so. Ranchmen grazing their herds on the public domain complained bitterly but usually without effect.

In addition to planting hedges about their fields, most

settlers also set out young trees, or cottonwood slips, near their homes. Congress tardily recognizing the need of the prairie farmers for more trees enacted the timber culture act granting an additional hundred and sixty acres of land to any homesteader who would plant forty acres of trees and care for them ten years.[13] Nebraska, due to the efforts of J. Sterling Morton, made provisions for "Arbor Day" specifying a certain day each year on which its citizens were urged to plant trees.[14]

Moreover, "necessity is the mother of invention" and the great need of the prairie settlers for more adequate means of fencing their lands eventually brought about the invention and manufacture of barbed wire. J. F. Glidden of DeKalb, Illinois, before 1875 had perfected a barbed wire which became the pattern for most types and by 1885 the new type of fencing was widely used throughout the West.[15] For some years there was much prejudice against this type of fence, however, and even after it had become generally accepted, many poor homesteaders lacked the money to purchase wire. In addition, posts to which it must be nailed had to be secured and this added to the settlers' problem of finding more timber. Eventually, however, barbed wire fences replaced the hedges but often not until the trees of the latter had grown large enough to make posts. Even today one can see many hedge fences, or the remains of them, in Kansas, Nebraska, and some other western states.

Apart from the practical need of timber for improving the

[13] *U.S. Stats. at Large*, 17, pp. 605–606. The bill was introduced by Senator Phineas W. Hitchcock of Nebraska. (Fred A. Shannon, *The Farmer's Last Frontier*, pp. 58–59.) The act was amended and liberalized the following year. 18 *Stats.*, 21–22.

[14] James C. Olson, *J. Sterling Morton* (Lincoln, 1942), pp. 163–164.

[15] Earl W. Hayter, "Barbed Wire Fencing—A Prairie Invention," *Agricultural History*, XIII (October, 1939), 189–207.

homestead and for fuel, the complete absence of trees must have had a profound psychological, or spiritual, effect upon the prairie settler. He missed the fine old oaks and elms of his ancestral home quite as much as he missed his old friends, perhaps more than he missed his own and his wife's relatives! When the summer sun beat down relentlessly on the brown prairie, the pioneer women especially must have longed for the shade of the great trees that grew about the old homestead. The monotony of the landscape where one "could look farther and see less" than in any other region they had ever known must at times have proved most depressing. On no other basis can be explained the feverish energy with which so many of these people planted trees and the solicitous care with which they cared for them. On the first Arbor Day over a million trees were planted in Nebraska.[16] One who reads the impassioned plea for tree planting made by J. Sterling Morton in his article in the *Omaha Herald* for April 17, 1872, must feel that this subject was almost a religion to the great founder of Arbor Day.[17] This can be better understood by viewing a picture of his birthplace— an attractive little home surrounded by trees, or when one remembers that his youth was spent among the wooded hills of Michigan.[18] It was only the second generation of prairie pioneers, born and bred on the level plains who loved them intensely and felt themselves shut in and stifled when they visited the wooded areas from which their parents had migrated. Many of the first generation endured the prairies but zealously sought to break the monotony of the landscape by planting trees.

[16] Olson, *op. cit.*, p. 166.
[17] Quoted in Olson, *op. cit.*, p. 166.
[18] Olson, *op. cit.*, p. 10.

Grave as was the prairie settler's problem of securing fuel and timber for constructing buildings and enclosures, that of providing sufficient water for domestic use and livestock was equally acute. While not much fuel was required in the summer months, water must be available every day of the year. For the first few weeks of life on the homestead this almost certainly had to be hauled in barrels sometimes as much as eight to ten miles and this period of time might be extended to several months or even years.[19] In some favored localities an adequate supply of pure water might be had by sinking a well to the depth of from twenty to forty feet but on the high plains of western Texas and portions of western Oklahoma, Kansas, Nebraska, and some other states, it was necessary to drill a well to a depth of from three hundred to six hundred feet or even more to reach water. The cost of such a well was, of course, prohibitive for the average pioneer settler and he was forced to haul water from the nearest source of supply. The author as late as 1907 found an old gentleman in the Panhandle of Texas hauling water for household use and livestock nine miles. When asked why he did not drill a well, he replied that it was "just as near to water one way as the other" and he preferred to get his "along horizontal rather than perpendicular lines!"

Under such circumstances water was a precious commodity and must be used as sparingly as possible. Domestic animals could, of course, be made to travel to the source of supply under their own power and many a housewife found it far easier to load wash tubs, kettles, and soiled clothing into the wagon and take them to water and do her washing there rather than to bring water for that purpose to her home.[20]

---

[19] George C. Neeley, *op. cit.*
[20] Alice Neeley, *Indian-Pioneer Papers*, LXVI, 207–208.

If the latter were done, however, the soap suds might be used to scrub the floor if it were of wood, which was not often the case, and children were bathed in the tub of water in which the clothes had been rinsed.

Even if water were found by drilling or digging a well, it was in some areas likely to be impregnated with mineral, usually gypsum, and so unfit for human consumption. "Gyp water" was a sore trial to many a family, while livestock often died from the effects of drinking "alkali water."[21]

Obviously, the first settlers of a region had no idea at what depth water might be found and were puzzled as to the exact spot where the well should be dug. Sometimes a neighbor supposed to be peculiarly gifted at "finding water" would be summoned to give advice. Such an individual would walk about grasping in his hands the two ends of a forked switch until it curved down and pointed at a spot where water presumably could be found. In some areas of western Oklahoma where it was necessary to sink a well to a depth of a hundred to two hundred feet settlers, since they had no money to employ a driller, dug wells with a pick and shovel which must have been a laborious and even dangerous task.[22] In many small towns the problem of securing an adequate supply of water was an acute one. Water sold at twenty-five cents a tub in Woodward, Oklahoma, for a time and at an equally high price in Lawton during the first three or four months of the town's existence.[23] Towns that derived their

---

[21] Cornelia Newman, *Indian-Pioneer Papers*, LXVI, 398, who removed from Nebraska to Oklahoma soon after the first settlement of the latter area, speaks of bad water and the lonely life of the women of this region.

[22] William J. Newsome, *op. cit.*

[23] T. G. Netherton, *Indian-Pioneer Papers*, LXVI, 349. The author was at Lawton in August, 1901, and lived for a time with some "commercial water haulers."

water supply from shallow wells were frequently swept by typhoid fever which in some cases assumed epidemic proportions. In the early 1900's the author assisted in analyzing samples of water from nearly a hundred wells of a small town in western Oklahoma and found eighty per cent of them contaminated by typhoid. Even in the rural districts of the "shallow water" areas typhoid was often very common in earlier days.

Difficult as were the twin problems of securing an adequate supply of wood and water on the prairie plains, the passing years eventually saw their solution. Railroads were rapidly penetrating the entire prairie plains area. These brought in coal, lumber, and farm machinery. With a market for grain established at the little towns along these railway lines, the settlers increased their wheat production and with the money obtained from its sale purchased coal. They also were able to buy lumber and the sod house or dugout was replaced by a modest frame or box structure of two to four rooms. With a shingle roof over his head the prairie farmer in the "bad water" areas often placed gutters under his eaves, acquired cement and constructed a cistern thus insuring an ample supply of pure water for household use. Also if a suitable spot could be found on the farm, an earthen dam was thrown up to impound the rain water and so form a pond. Improved well drilling equipment soon began to be brought to the plains and many of the more prosperous settlers had wells drilled and erected windmills. These pumped water for domestic use and into a steel or wooden stock tank in the pasture or corral. The trees of the groves and hedge fences within a few years had grown large enough for fence posts, thus not only giving the homesteader a supply of "home grown fuel" but making it possible for him to cut down the hedges and replace them with wire fences as barbed wire came into general use.

Eventually came the opening up of oil pools in the Mid-Continent Area and the eager search for oil further promoted improvements in well drilling machinery. Also many gas wells were opened and for many people oil and gas became available for fuel as numerous pipe lines were constructed. Oil stoves were installed in many homes to be used in cooking, especially in summer.

As the settlers grew more prosperous through the greater production of grain and livestock, many of them constructed a new home sometimes securing additional funds for that purpose by mortgaging their land to which they had by this time received a patent in fee thus making it possible to use it as collateral for a loan. A large two-story farmhouse was accordingly built and water piped to it from an elevated steel tank set up near the windmill. An oil burning furnace was sometimes installed in the basement since oil was a cleaner and more satisfactory fuel than coal. In regions where natural gas was available, it was used both for heating and cooking. Rural electrification became common in some areas and electric lights and equipment were installed in those homes near a "high line." An electric motor or gasoline engine in some cases was acquired to pump water to the house for domestic use and the windmill used only to provide a supply of "stock water." The era of sod houses and dugouts, of "prairie coal," and wood hauled for twenty to thirty miles, or of hay burner stoves, and water brought in barrels from some distant spring had largely passed away.

The visitor to the Prairie West today who drives his car along one of the many broad highways that traverse that region will often slow down to admire a big two-story white farmhouse standing beside the road in the midst of a grove of noble trees. If he looks closely enough, however, he may sometimes note, a short distance back of it, an ancient, un-painted structure of rough lumber consisting of two or three rooms probably used for storage and a short distance beyond that the ruins of an old sodhouse or dugout. These three represent the stages of the farm owner's economic progress, and the observer of a philosophical turn of mind may wonder in which one of these homes this family found the most happiness.

There is little shortage of fuel and water in the prairie states today. At least a few trees have been planted on virtu-ally every farm and even the "shelterbelt" activities of the United States Government some years ago which brought considerable criticism from many people have in some areas been remarkably successful.[24] In those communities where the people depend for a water supply upon shallow wells and ponds long periods of drought may bring inconveniences but not nearly to the extent of earlier years. An occasional farmer, on marginal or submarginal lands, may still load his water barrels into a wagon and fill them at the well of one of his more fortunate neighbors or in years of crop failure be hard put to find enough money to buy his winter's supply of coal, for "the poor we have with us always" even in the Prairie West. Largely speaking, however, the twin problems of wood and water which proved so difficult for the settlers of the prairie plains half a century or more ago are now only a memory.

[24] The "shelterbelt trees" in parts of western Oklahoma where the soil is sandy have made a vigorous growth.

The Romance of the Range*

The business of herding or live stock raising is one of the most ancient and honorable of all industries. The Bible is filled with allusions to pastoral life, and the strife of Cain and Abel has been characterized as the first example of warfare between range and grange.

Not only is herding one of the earliest pursuits of mankind, but there has ever clustered about the business and those engaged in it something of the glamour of romance, of daring deeds and high adventure. Badger Clark in his poem "From Town" has expressed this in picturesque fashion when he says:

"Since the days when Lot and Abram
Split the Jordan range in halves
Just to fix it so their punchers wouldn't fight.
Since old Jacob skinned his dad-in-law of six years crop of calves
Then hit the trail for Canaan in the night,
There has been a taste for battle
Mongst the men who follow cattle,
And a love of doing things that's wild and strange,
And the warmth of Laban's words
When he missed his speckled herds
Still is useful in the language of the range."[1]

Since that time many rival ranchmen have "split a range in halves" to keep down strife among their punchers; more

* Published in *The Cattleman* (November, 1929), 33–40.
[1] Badger Clark, *Sun and Saddle Leather.*

than one enterprising young man has "skinned his dad-in-law" of a liberal share of various crops of calves, the taste for battle has manifested itself in many places resulting in "wild and strange doings," while not a few men who have missed a portion of their "speckled herds" have resorted to language even more forceful and picturesque than was included in the vocabulary of the ancient Laban.

Men engaged in pastoral pursuits seem, moreover, to be peculiarly favored by Divine Providence. Mohamet was a herder and a camel driver before he became the founder of the religion of Islam. To a band of herdsmen of Northern Spain appeared the mighty light which led them to the body of St. James the Elder, and caused the founding of the shrine of Santiago, de campostella, while to shepherds watching their flocks by night came the Angel of the Lord bringing "good tidings of great joy."

It is not in the old world alone, however, that the herding industry has been crowned by a halo of romance. The business in America has not been lacking in that respect and the rise and fall of the range cattle industry on the western plains constitutes one of the most remarkable epochs in all American history.

Ranching has existed in the United States as a frontier pursuit since very early times. Almost the first English settlers along the Atlantic seaboard brought cattle with them, and as the better lands along the coast were taken up and planted to crops, men owning a considerable number of animals removed farther west in order to find pasture for their herds on the unoccupied lands of the wilderness. Thus once agricultural settlement was well started in its westward march across the continent, there was to be found along its outer edge a comparatively narrow rim or border of pastoral life.

For a century and more it was there, slowly advancing as the area of cultivated lands advanced, a kind of twilight zone with the light of civilization behind it and the darkness of savagery before. The ranchmen could not push too far out into the wilderness because of the fierce tribes of Indians that inhabited it. On the other hand they could not linger too long on their original ranges or they would find themselves crowded and hemmed in by the men who depended upon cultivated crops for a livelihood. The American people had become "that great land animal." They pushed eagerly westward, occupied lands formerly devoted to grazing, cleared fields and planted crops, thus forcing the live stock growers again and again to move on to "new pastures."

Strange as this century long westward march of an industry may appear, the final phase is even more startling and has no parallel in the economic history of any other nation in the world. Soon after the Civil War this comparatively narrow belt of grazing hitherto fairly constant as to width and area, suddenly shot out into the wilderness and spread with amazing rapidity until it covered a region larger than all that part of the United States devoted to crop raising.[2] This region became the so-called "cow country" where ranching was carried on for several years upon a scale vastly greater than ever before until the homesteaders advancing slowly, but steadily westward, had at last invaded nearly every portion of it and taken over all of the lands suitable for cultivation.

A number of factors influenced this sudden rise of the "cow country." The close of the Civil War released from

[2] Nimmo gives the area devoted to cattle raising in the U.S. in 1885 as 1,355,000 square miles. See Joseph Nimmo, *The Range and Ranch Cattle Business of the United States* (Washington, 1885), p. 1.

the armies many young men who came west in search of adventure and fortune. Over the western plains roamed countless herds of buffalo, a potential source of food, clothing and shelter for the fierce Indian tribes that occupied that region. Buffalo hunting became at once a popular and profitable pursuit. Within two decades the great herds had been exterminated, and the Indians finding their food supply cut off removed more or less willingly to reservations set aside for them where they lived to a great extent dependent upon the bounty of the federal government. The plains were thus left open to occupation by herds of the cattlemen and the latter were not slow to take advantage of the opportunity presented to them.

Even so, ranching could not have spread so rapidly had there not existed a great reservoir from which animals might be drawn to stock these western plains. That reservoir was the great State of Texas. Even from the earliest times everything in Texas seemed to promote live stock raising. Range, climate, and the land system were all distinctly favorable to grazing. The early Spanish settlers brought with them cattle of the lean, long horned type that the Moors had raised on the plains of Andalusia for a thousand years. These increased rapidly and American settlers coming into Texas brought with them cattle of the North European breeds. These crossed with the original Spanish type produced animals that were larger and heavier than the Spanish cattle, and yet with the endurance and ability to take care of themselves so necessary on the open range.

Spain, and later the Republic of Mexico, gave out large grants of land to individuals and later the Republic of Texas continued this liberal land policy. Also when Texas was admitted as a state it retained possession of its own unoccupied lands, and these the state sold in large tracts and with liberal terms of payment. Thus at the outbreak of the Civil War Texas was, largely speaking, a region of great landed proprietors, nearly all of whom owned herds of cattle.[3]

The war came and the Texans, "ever eager for a fight or a frolic," and sometimes willing to regard the fight as a frolic, hurried away to join the armies of the Confederacy. For four years they fought bravely for the Lost Cause, proving their mettle upon many a bloody field. During all this time Texas was less touched than any other state of the Confederacy by the ravages of war. While Virginia was devastated by the armies of both sides, while Sherman's army ate a hole fifty miles wide across Georgia; and while the fields of Mississippi and Alabama lay fallow or grew up in bushes and briers for want of laborers to till them, the cattle on the broad plains of Texas grew fat and sleek and increased rapidly under the favorable conditions of range and climate. The result was that when the war closed and the Texans returned to their homes they found their ranges fairly overflowing with fine, fat cattle for which there was no market, though cattle and beef were selling at high prices in the north.[4] Stock cattle could be bought on the Texas prairies in 1866 at from one to three dollars a head while fat beeves sold at from five to six or seven dollars. Even in 1867 three-year-old steers were quoted as having an average value of $86.00 in Massachusetts,

[3] *The Census of 1860* gives the total number of cattle in Texas at that time as 3,534,678. *Eighth Census of the United States, 1860, Agriculture*, p. 148. Census figures are very unreliable, however, when applied to an industry of this nature.

[4] In 1866 round steak retailed in New York at 20 to 25 cents a pound, sirloin at 25 to 35 cents, and rib roast at 28 to 30 cents. On the live stock market of eastern cities, cattle brought as high as $10.00 per hundred weight, this price being refused on the Albany market December 21, 1866, for a choice lot of Illinois steers. (*New York Times*, December 22, 1866.) Also *New York Tribune*, June 23, 1866.

$68.57 in New York, $70.58 in New Jersey, $40.19 in Illinois, $38.40 in Kansas, $46.32 in Nebraska, and $9.46 in Texas.[5]

Out of this condition grew the so-called "northern drive." The Texas soldiers from the Confederate armies mostly reached home in the summer of 1865, too late to attempt to drive their cattle to market that year. In the spring of 1866, however, large herds were collected preparatory to starting north as soon as spring was sufficiently advanced to make the venture practicable. Most of these herds belonged to Texas ranchmen who were themselves driving them to market, though in some cases northern men came to Texas and purchased herds to drive up the trail.[6]

The start was usually made late in March or early in April. The usual route followed by these earliest drovers was north from Central Texas passing just west of Fort Worth, and on past Denton and Sherman to Red River. Beyond that stream the line of travel was north across the Indian Territory past Boggy Depot, thence northeast past Fort Gibson to the Kansas line near Baxter Springs.

Just how many cattle were started north from Texas in the spring and summer of 1866 is uncertain, but estimates made a few years later place the number at 260,000 head.[7] The drive proved on the whole disastrous in the extreme. Immuned as the Texans were to privation and hardship and accustomed as they were to handling cattle, few had at this time much experience in driving herds for long distances on the trail. Accounts left by some of these early drovers are little better than one long wail of trouble and misery. Rain,

[5] Monthly reports of U.S. Department of Agriculture, 1867, pp. 108, 109.
[6] See George C. Duffield's Diary in *Annals of Iowa*, Vol. XIV, No. 4, pp. 243–262, for an account of one of these drives.
[7] McCoy, *Historic Sketches of the Cattle Trade*, p. 23, or Nimmo, *Range and Ranch Cattle Traffic of the United States*, p. 28.

mud, swollen rivers, stampedes, and hunger, and dissatisfied men are but a few of the difficulties of which they complained before Red River was reached. Beyond that stream there was added to all these miseries endless annoyance from Indians who demanded payment for grass consumed by the cattle, stampeded herds at night in order to collect money for helping gather them again, and in other ways proved themselves a constant source of worry and vexation.[8] The war had but recently closed and conditions along the border and in the Indian Territory were lawless and unsettled. White thieves and outlaws, together with pilfering Indians, stole horses, mules, and cattle and made it necessary to be watchful at all times. When the drovers reached the Kansas or Missouri line they found themselves confronted by fresh difficulties. The settlers along the border of these states had suffered losses from Texas fever when some small herds had been driven up from the South just before the war, and were determined not to risk a repetition of such loss. Armed bands of farmers met the drovers at the border and warned them that they would not be permitted to proceed at least until cold weather had come to lessen the danger.

The question was complicated by the mysterious and subtle nature of the disease, Texas fever, which the northerners professed to fear. We know now that it is a malady to which southern cattle are immune, but which they carry to northern cattle by means of the fever ticks which drop from their bodies and attach themselves to other animals. The Texans asserted that their cattle were perfectly healthy and that it was absurd that they could bring disease to others. The Kansans declared that absurd or not when Texas cattle came near their own animals the latter sickened and died

[8] See Duffield's Diary, *Annals of Iowa*, Vol. XVI, No. 4.

though they were forced to admit they did not understand why.

Yet numerous theories were evolved. It was declared that a shrub of Texas wounded the feet of the animals and made sores from which pus exuded to poison the grass. Others asserted that the breath of Texas cattle upon the grass brought disease to other animals, a kind of bovine halitosis which no scruples of delicacy prevented the Kansans mentioning in no uncertain terms. Some felt that cattle ticks might be responsible, but most people ridiculed such a theory.[9]

The northerners did not, however, concern themselves much with theories. It was enough that their cattle had died in the past and might die in the future. They were fixed in their determination to take no chances.

There were conflicts in some cases. Sharp conflicts in which the Texans far from home and the support of their friends and kindred were foredoomed to failure. Drovers were assaulted and beaten, some were killed and in a few cases small herds of animals were shot down and killed to the last animal.[10] Some turned back into the Indian Territory and moved westward until far beyond all agricultural settlements, then turned north and continued until opposite their destination in Iowa or St. Joseph. Some of these succeeded in some measure, but the long drive and heavy losses seldom left them with enough animals to make the venture profitable. Of the 260,000 head of cattle driven north in the summer of 1866 very few reached a profitable market.[11]

[9] See *Second Annual Report of Missouri State Board of Agriculture*, pp. 16–18, or *Prairie Farmer*, August 15, 1868, for statements as to these theories of the cause of Texas fever.

[10] J. T. Botkin in *Topeka Daily Capitol*, February 6, 1915. See also McCoy, *Historic Sketches of the Cattle Trade*.

[11] Nimmo, *Range and Ranch Cattle Business of the U.S.*, p. 28.

The Texas ranchmen were almost in despair, but the following year was to see a solution of their problem. At this time the Kansas Pacific Railway was building west up the valley of the Kaw and had reached the town of Salina. In the spring of 1867 Joseph G. McCoy, a prominent and wealthy cattle feeder of Illinois, came to Kansas City and journeying westward in this railway to Abilene in Dickenson County, decided to establish there a great cattle depot and shipping point.[12]

Abilene was far west of all agricultural settlements. Here McCoy built a hotel and large shipping pens. He made with the railway a contract by which he was to have a share of the freight receipts from Texas cattle shipped to Kansas City and then sent a rider south to seek out herds on the trail and tell the owners to bring them to Abilene. From Abilene they might be shipped to Kansas City, and thence to Chicago or any other market that seemed desirable.

The advantages of this plan of reaching market were soon apparent. The route followed was far to the west of the old trail to Baxter Springs, and so avoided the wooded and mountainous areas of Eastern Oklahoma as well as most of the Indians, and above all the hostile agricultural population of Eastern Kansas. Late in the season as the project was started, 35,000 head of cattle were shipped from Abilene in 1867, while the following year, or 1868, 75,000 head were brought up the trail. By 1869 the number had risen to 350,000 and in 1871 the best estimates indicate that no less than 600,000 head were driven from Texas to the cow towns of Kansas.[13]

Abilene was only temporarily the great Texas shipping

---

[12] McCoy, *Historic Sketches of the Cattle Trade*, p. 44.

[13] The figures are from Nimmo, *Range and Ranch Cattle Business of the U.S.*, p. 28.

point. As the settlers began to come in to take homesteads near it, the cattle trade shifted farther west. New railroads were building and new cow towns sprang up. Among these were Newton, Ellsworth, Wichita, Caldwell, and especially Dodge City. Ogalalla, Nebraska, on the Union Pacific, also became an important shipping point.

Most important of all the "cow towns" was Dodge City which for ten years was the greatest cattle market in the world.[14] To it flocked the gamblers, saloon keepers and lawless riff-raff of the underworld to meet and prey upon the Texas cowboys who arrived with their summer's wages in their pockets and a thirst accumulated during the months of toil on the hot and dusty trail.

Dodge City's first jail was a well fifteen feet deep, into which drunks were lowered and left until sober, and ready to leave town. Two grave yards were early established, "Boot Hill" on one side of town where were buried those men who died with their boots on, and another cemetery on the opposite side for those who died peacefully, in bed. The latter cemetery remained small, but "Boot Hill" soon came to have a large and constantly growing population.[15]

The first trail drivers who took herds from Texas to the cow towns of Kansas, or the northern Indian agencies to fill beef contracts frequently knew little of the region to be traversed and had little to guide them. Yet no trail boss ever turned back. He merely set his wagon each night with the tongue pointing to the north star and the next morning pushed on with a grim determination to make his ten or fifteen miles that day. In a real sense he "hitched his wagon to a star," and did not shrink from difficulties and dangers.

[14] See Wright, *Dodge City, the Cowboy Capital*, for an account of this town and its importance as a cattle market.
[15] *Ibid.*

In time, however, certain well defined trails were established. Prominent among these was the Western Trail, crossing Red River at Doan's store and extending north past Fort Supply to Dodge City. East of this was the famous Chisholm Trail, following roughly the line of the present Rock Island Railway across Oklahoma. Still farther east was the West Shawnee Trail, and beyond that the East Shawnee Trail, that crossed into Kansas near Baxter Springs.[16]

During the two decades following the Civil War a vast stream of Texas cattle poured northward over these trails. The drive to the Kansas cow towns, moreover, frequently became but the first half of a drive from Texas to ranges on the northern plains. The possibilities of that region for ranching became apparent to many men very soon after the close of the war. Some men with small herds established themselves along the line of the newly constructed Union Pacific Railway. Others living near the overland trail established small herds through the purchase of lame and foot sore cattle from emigrants.[17] The development of mining camps in the Rocky Mountains brought in men with cattle to furnish beef to the miners while the government made contracts with cattlemen to supply beef to the Indians on northern reservations and large herds were driven up the trail for that purpose.

As the buffalo disappeared from the plains, however, leaving large areas of attractive pasture lands without animals to consume the grass, many men began to establish ranches in various parts of Wyoming, Colorado, Dakota and Montana, and these frequently purchased herds in the Kansas cow towns to stock their new ranges. The cattle industry was

[16] Charles M. Harger, "Cattle Trails of the Prairies," *Scribners Magazine*, June, 1892, p. 732.
[17] Baillie-Grohman, *Camp Fires of the Rockies*, pp. 351–353.

spreading with marvelous rapidity. It was found that the animals grew fatter and heavier on the Northern Plains than they did in Texas. As a result the mature animals from that state were shipped to market for slaughter, but tens of thousands of younger cattle were sold to northern buyers to stock ranges on the north plains. Eventually the drives came to consist largely of young steers for this purpose.[18] A division of labor was growing up. Texas, because of its low altitude and warm climate came to be regarded as a great breeding ground, while the high plains of the north became a great feeding and maturing ground. Cattle feeders from the Corn Belt began to purchase western steers for their feed pens. Profits grew and the ranch cattle business grew proportionately.

By the late 70's an interest in the range cattle of the United States had extended itself to Europe. In 1875 Timothy C. Eastman of New York began the shipment of dressed beef to England. Eastman had purchased outright the patent for the new "Bate Process" of refrigeration, by which beef was hung in refrigerator rooms and kept at a temperature of about 33 degrees Fahrenheit by means of cold air circulated by fans.[19]

The first shipment by Eastman was in October, 1875. In that month he sent 36,000 pounds of beef to England to be followed by the same quantity in November, and by 134,000 pounds in December. By April, 1876, his shipments had risen to over a million pounds a month; by September to over two million, and in December to more than three million.[20] Other

---

[18] A record made of 164 trail herds aggregating 384,147 head showed them to consist of yearlings, 124,967; twos, 116,824; threes, 66,078; fours, 43,257; dry cows, 30,060; cows with calves, 2,972. *Tenth Census*, Vol. III, p. 21.

[19] *Report of the Commission of Agriculture, 1876*, p. 314.

[20] *Ibid.*, p. 320.

men in New York as well as some in Philadelphia, took up the business. In 1877 the shipments of dressed beef to Europe, mostly to England, was nearly fifty million pounds. In 1880 this had risen to eighty-four million and in 1881 to a hundred and six million pounds.[21] This trade was accompanied by the annual shipment of many thousand head of live cattle.

As the trade grew, markets for American beef were established in many British cities and as the supply grew in volume the English and Scotch cattle raisers became alarmed as they saw their business threatened by this competition of American meat.

In 1877 the *Scotsman*, a Scotch newspaper devoted largely to the agricultural interests of North Britain, sent to America James McDonald, a prominent writer on its staff, with instructions to investigate the live stock business of the United States, and make reports in the form of a series of articles for publication. These articles described the great ranches of the West, and told in glowing terms of the great profits of the industry which it was stated averaged in most cases as much as 25 per cent annually.[22]

The interest of the British government was aroused and in 1880 it dispatched two commissioners to the United States to study and report upon the range cattle industry. The men chosen for this mission were Clare Read and Albert Pell, both members of parliament. They spent several months in the West and reported that the profits of the range cattle industry ordinarily averaged about 33⅓ per cent a year.[23]

Canny Scotch and British business men had already seen the possibilities of ranching in America as a field for invest-

[21] *Report of the Commissioner of Agriculture*, 1876, p. 320.
[22] McDonald, *Food from the Far West.*
[23] Read and Pell, *Reports from Commissioners and Inspectors, 1880*, Vol. XVIII, Serial 856.

ment. In 1870 the Scottish-American Investment Company had been founded by W. J. Menzies. It financed a number of cattle companies in the Great Plains area including the Wyoming Cattle Ranch Company and Western Ranches, Limited. Another great Scottish syndicate formed quite early was the Scottish-American Mortgage Company which established the Prairie Cattle Company, one of the largest enterprises in the West.[24]

The articles of McDonald and the report of Read and Pell served to increase greatly the interest of Scotch and English investors in cattle raising in America, and during the next three or four years many companies were formed and a vast stream of Scotch and British capital was poured into the West to promote the range cattle industry. Besides the cattle companies previously mentioned Scottish capital founded numerous other ranch enterprises. Prominent among these were the Matador, the Hansford Land and Cattle Company, the Texas Land and Cattle Company, the Swan Land and Cattle Company, and numerous others.[25]

By 1882 it was asserted that not less than thirty million dollars of English and Scotch capital had been invested in ranching on the western plains.[26] Not a few of the investors came over to give their personal attention to the business, and with them came others from the continent of Europe. Prominent among the latter were the Marquis de Mores, a French nobleman, and Baron von Richthofen, ancestor of the famous German ace. De Mores had married a New York girl and established with his father-in-law's money a ranch near the border of Montana and Dakota where he built and named

[24] See John Clay, *My Life on the Range*, or Richthofen, *Cattle Ranching on the Plains of North America*, for an account of these enterprises.
[25] Richthofen, *Cattle Ranching on the Plains of North America*, p. 55.
[26] *Report of Wyoming Stock Growers Association*, 1882, p. 19.

for his wife the town of Medora. Among the English and the Scotch were the Adairs, Murdo McKenzie, John Clay and a host of others.

Along with the foreigners there came to the western plains an ever-increasing swarm of enterprising young men from the eastern part of the United States. Young college men, among whom Theodore Roosevelt may be mentioned as a conspicuous example, hastened west to engage in the cattle business.[27]

An enthusiasm for ranching amounting almost to a craze swept over the country. United States senators, representatives, and judges were financially interested in range cattle, as were bankers, lawyers and manufacturers. A machinery was built up for financing the business. Great cattle exchange banks and loan companies were established. The great stream of Texas cattle flowed steadily northward in spite of quarantine regulations and fluctuations in prices and spread itself over the northern plains until the most remote ranges had been occupied. By the middle 80's the cattle business had reached its zenith and the vast cow country reached from the western edge of agricultural settlements to the Rocky Mountains and far beyond.

So came into existence the "cow country." A pastoral empire greater than any of its kind the world had ever seen, on whose broad plains grazed millions of cattle, cared for by men whose lives and deeds will be heralded in song and story as long as the American nation shall endure.

Throughout the whole vast region conditions of life and work were somewhat similar, yet the industry rose so rapidly

[27] See Herman Hagerdorn, *Roosevelt in the Bad Lands*, for an account of Roosevelt's ranching operations.

and suffered such a speedy decline that it never became entirely standardized. As a result generalizations are always difficult and are never more than approximately correct. An extremely technical business that was little understood except by those actually engaged in it, myths and misunderstandings with respect to ranching have been all too common.

Democratic as were the men of the cow country, that region nevertheless presented the picture of a curious kind of "American feudalism," in many ways not unlike that of medieval Europe. The great ranchman built his ranch house or headquarters which might be compared to the baronial castle; his cattle roamed over an area larger than that of many a principality of Europe; his bold riders were as numerous as were the men at arms of many a petty German princeling. The brand of X I T, the spur, frying pan or J. A. were more widely known perhaps than were the bleeding heart of the Douglas, the clenched hand and dagger of the Kilpatricks, or the white lion of the Howards. The raids of Indians, or white cattle thieves, strife with fence cutters or episodes like the "Lincoln County War," furnished quite as much excitement as did the forays of the moss troopers along the Scottish border; the live stock associations bore some resemblance to the federations entered into by groups of old world nobles, and while the tilt or tournament did not exist, the rodeo or roping contest furnished a very fair substitute.

Yet with all of these similarities to feudal Europe, there were striking differences. There was little of show, formality or ceremony and complete democracy was the universal rule. Cattle baron, cow puncher, cook and horse wrangler rode, ate, worked and played together upon terms of absolute equality. Circumstances had made one the boss and the other the "hand" today, but tomorrow or next month or next year the situation might be reversed.

Little has been written about the great leaders of the cow country and yet their influence upon American history has been enormous. They were men of vision and they had the energy and strength of purpose to be willing to endure all manner of privations and dangers in order to make their dreams come true.

As for the cowboy, that most picturesque figure among all the children of the Great West, he has received better, or at least more voluminous treatment at the hands of writers. Yet it must be admitted that much which has been written about the cowboy is untrue. He is sometimes pictured as a sort of modern Sir Galahad, a knight without stain and a champion without reproach, who rode about slaying villains and rescuing damsels in distress. By others he is described as a rough, wild, and lawless creature, crude and uncouth in speech and manner. Both views are equally distorted and incorrect. The cowboy was much like Kipling's "Tommy," who said:

> "We ain't no them red 'eroes
> And we ain't no black guards, too,
> But single men in barracks
> Most uncommonly like you."

"Just folks," remarked an old cowboy. "Just common ever day bow-legged humans! That's cow punchers."

The description fits. The cowboy was after all not unlike any other young man who lived in the open, an active and at times a somewhat hard and adventurous life. For while his work sometimes brought long periods of comparative ease and leisure, it also brought periods of terrific exertion, of hardship and privation, of exposure to cold and rain and the "bright face of danger." Such being the case he learned to take life as it came. Complaints could not change conditions, so why complain? Unconsciously he became a philosopher. He ate thankfully the flaky sour dough biscuit, and juicy beef steak in time of plenty, and tightened his belt with a grin in time of famine.

Happy-go-lucky and full of the joy of living, he sang and whistled at his work and play whether it was a bright morning in spring when he cantered over the green flower spangled prairies to make a friendly visit, or a cold, rainy November night when he must crawl from between his wet blankets at the glad hour of 2 a.m. and circle slowly around a restless herd until daylight.

Much has been written about cowboy songs, and they were indeed of infinite variety. There was the plaintive, mournful song so commonly regarded as typical like "Bury Me Not On the Lone Prairie," and there was the light lilting one as:

> " 'Twas in the fall of '71—
> I thought I'd see how cowpunchin' was done.
> The boss said cowpunchin' was only fun;
> There wasn't a bit of work to be done
> All you had to do was just to ride
> And go a-drifting with the tide.
> The son-of-a-gun, Oh, how he lied
> In seventy-one!"

Then there were the songs in which love formed the theme as: "Remember the Red River Valley and the Cowboy That Loved You So True," and frequently a deeply religious note crept in as in this:

> "Last night as I lay on the prairie
> Looking up at the stars in the sky

I wondered if ever a cowboy
Could go to that sweet bye and bye.
I wondered if ever a cowboy
Could go to that sweet bye and bye.
"Some day there will be a grand roundup
Where cowboys like cattle will stand
To be cut out by the riders of Judgment
Who are posted and know every brand.
To be cut out by the riders of Judgment
Who are posted and know every brand.
"The road that leads down to perdition
Is posted and blazed all the way
But the pathway that leads up to Heaven
Is narrow and dim, so they say.
"Whose fault is it then that so many
Go out on that wide range and fail
Who might have honor and plenty
Had they known of that dim, narrow trail."[28]

Such songs are folk lore, and are typically American. They reveal the very heart and soul of the cowboy. He was light hearted and frivolous at times, and he was often lonely. His reverence for pure womanhood is too well known to require comment. He was religious, too, after a fashion and according to his own way. He lived in the open air in God's big out of doors. He had seen men die with their boots on in most unpleasant fashion, and the thought of death and the world beyond grows strongly familiar when one lives close to it for so many years. This deeply religious nature is expressed in a little poem written by a Texas cow puncher, which has in it the majesty and beauty of real poetry:

"Oh Lord, I never lived where churches grow

[28] John A. Lomax of Texas, has done a great work for the preservation of cowboy folk lore. His two volumes, *Cowboy Songs*, and *Songs of the Ranch and Cattle Trail*, are well known.

I like Creation better as it stood
That day you finished it so long ago
Then looked upon your work and called it good.
I know that others find You in the light
That's sifted down through tinted window panes,
And yet I seem to feel You near tonight
In the dim, quiet starlight of the Plains."

The words of but few cowboy rhymes rise to such heights of poetic grandeur as this. Many of them deal with the life and work of the rough riders. Some men formulated tunes as well as words; they improvised, they sang parodies on the then popular songs of the day. Carrying still further the comparison to feudal Europe it may be noted that some men with good voices and a great repertoire of songs became almost famous throughout large sections of the cow country. They were welcomed gladly at every camp and round up wagon because of their ability as entertainers. They were minnesingers of the range, troubadours, wandering minstrels, and their songs were of wide variety. Many were of the type just described; some were ballads dealing with certain individuals that had lived beyond the law, but who had possessed personal qualities much admired by some of these wild riders of the prairies:

"Jesse left a wife
To mourn all her life
Three children they were brave
But a dirty little coward
Shot Mr. Howard
And laid Jesse James in his grave."

Another almost as well known dealt with the exploits of Sam Bass:

"Sam Bass was born in Indiana

263

It was his native home
And at the age of seventeen
Young Sam began to roam
He first came out to Texas
A ranger for to be.
A kinder-hearted fellow
You seldom ever see."

Outlaws, as they were the heroes of these songs, had many admirers. Legends not unlike those that cluster about the names of Robin Hood, Rob Roy, and Captain Kidd were associated with them.

Picturesque as was the life of the cow country of the middle eighties, it was doomed to a speedy passing. Its rise had been spectacular but its decline was hardly less spectacular, and certainly was much more tragic. The year of 1885 is the high water mark of the business. During the summer of that year President Cleveland issued a proclamation ordering all cattle to be removed within forty days from the lands of the Cheyenne-Arapaho Indians, in what is now Oklahoma.[29] These 210,000 head from this great reservation were thrown upon already overstocked ranges nearby and the following winter saw heavy losses.[30]

Prices were still high in the spring, however, and the drive north out of Texas was heavy. Tens of thousands of head were moved up the trail and spread out in the most reckless fashion imaginable over the already heavily stocked ranges of Wyoming, Montana and Dakota.

Winter came early and laid his icy hand upon the northern prairies. A terrific blizzard bringing sleet and snow came roaring out of the north and the thermometer went down as though it would never stop. The cattle drifted before the

[29] Proclamation of July 23, 1885. *Twenty-four States*, p. 1023.
[30] See Wright, *Dodge City, the Cowboy Capital*, p. 313.

bitter winds into ravines and coulees where they died by thousands. Heavy snows fell and intense cold continued throughout the winter. Hunger maddened cattle gathered along the little streams, and gnawed the bark from the willows as high as they could reach before they at last gave up the struggle, and lay down to die.[31]

Spring came to find every cattleman on the northern plains flat broke. Swan, Sturgis, Kohrs, Granville Stuart, Dickey Brothers, Worshams, the Continental Cattle Company, and a host of others failed or were in the shakiest possible condition. Theodore Roosevelt quit the cattle business, leaving his range thickly strewn with bones.[32]

No such winter had ever before been known in the history of the cow country. Charlie Russell, the cowboy artist, was in charge of a herd of five thousand head belonging to a group of eastern capitalists. Toward spring his employers wrote him a letter asking how the cattle were doing. Russell's painting which he sent as a reply has become famous. It is a picture of a gaunt and lonely old cow in the midst of great snowdrifts, standing with drooping head like a bovine peri at the gate of Paradise, and in the corner Russell had written the legend, "The Last of Five Thousand."

Most of the northern ranchmen never recovered from the effects of that frightful winter. Losses of 50 and 60 per cent were common. Eighty and ninety per cent were hardly exceptional. Many lenders who had been financing the industry were panic stricken. In a desperate attempt to pay interest and to liquidate a part of their loans ranchmen poured a stream of lean and unmerchantable cattle into the markets.

[31] See John Clay, *My Life on the Range*, pp. 177, 178, for an account of the losses of the tragic winter.
[32] *Ibid.*

Prices went down until cattle would hardly be accepted as a gift, especially since the summer of 1887 was very dry and crops throughout the Corn Belt almost a failure.[33] There was no demand for feeders and the range cattle were too thin for slaughter. A great industry was prostrate and recovery was slow and uncertain.

As a matter of fact the range cattle business never again rose to the heights it had attained in the middle eighties. Its glory had departed forever. The cow country was changing. Trunk lines of railroads heading out from the great markets had penetrated Texas making it possible to ship cattle to market by rail. The great drives began to lessen in volume. A realization that the northern ranges had been overstocked, the competition of the railroads, the stringent quarantine laws of Kansas, and the general depression of the industry all served to check the northern drive.

Pioneer settlers in prairie schooners were moreover drifting westward in large numbers and taking up homesteads in the range cattle area. Their little dugouts and sod houses appeared much like almost over night on the more fertile lands in various parts of the cow country. Thus Indian lands of Western Oklahoma were opened to settlement and a great area changed from grazing to crop growing.

Brief periods of prosperity came to the ranching industry at times, but the magnitude of the earlier operations steadily declined. Some of the big ranches began to subdivide their holdings and sell out lands in tracts to suit the purchaser. Fenced pastures, winter feeding and small scale production became the rule.

[33] *Breeder's Gazette*, September 15, 1887, p. 434. In 1882 good Texas steers brought $5.50 a hundred and above. In 1887 they sold at $1.90 to $2.50 and could scarcely be marketed at any price. *Ibid.*, September 29, 1877, p. 514.

The range was shrinking, cattle disappeared from many regions, and farmers armed with hoe and spade sprang up on all sides as though an unseen hand had planted dragon's teeth on every hill and in every valley. Steadily the ranchmen were forced out of the agricultural lands and pushed back into the barren deserts, the hills and mountains, or onto forest reserves and Indian reservations. Here the business still exists though large scale operations are about gone, and the life at its best or worst, depending upon the viewpoint, is only a faded and washed out copy of the life of the earlier days.

The men who once rode the boundless ranges of the Great Plains, or who followed the long herds up the dusty trail are with few exceptions no more. Gone with the things of long ago they have, to quote their own language, "passed up the dim, narrow trail to that new range which never fails, and where quarantine regulations do not exist.[34] Gone it is true, but I trust never to be forgotten. For if it is true that,

> "You may break, you may shatter
> The vase if you will
> But the scent of the rose
> Will cling to it still."

So it is also true that you may enclose the green prairies and plow up the sweet wild flowers, you may build towns and cities on sites once occupied by the cowboy's dugout and branding pen, but always something of the fragrance of the romance of those early days will cling to the region which the bold range riders once called their own, to remind us of those picturesque days now gone forever.

The period of the range cattle industry constitutes in a sense the heroic age of the great West. Those of us who

[34] Minutes of the Texas and Southwestern Cattle Raisers Association.

know something of it at first hand look back upon its passing with a tinge of regret. Yet we realize that society is never static, never still. The cowboy has given place to the settler, the city builder, the manufacturer, the merchant, the scholar. The tale of their rise in the West is another story, but there, too, lies romance.

Cowboy Cookery*

A cow outfit no less than an army moves like a snake—on its stomach. As a matter of fact, any man responsible for the accomplishment of a task requiring the services of many people for a long period of time quickly learns how important is good food for the preservation of morale and the smooth functioning of the human machine whose parts are the men who must get the job done.

This is as true of cowhands as it has always been of the army and navy, a crew of lumber jacks, a railway construction gang or any other body of men engaged in hard manual labor. Those who must work long hours at tasks involving much physical effort have little interest in knick knacks, nor is it necessary to tempt their appetites by dishes served in attractive forms. What they want is an ample supply of good, nourishing food that is clean, well cooked, and of a type calculated to "stick to the ribs" through long periods of arduous labor.

This every ranch foreman, trail boss or round-up captain, as well as every cook, who was worth his salt, sought to provide. True, some outfits were notorious for the poor fare they served their men just as others were famous for excellent food but when the fare was hopelessly bad, responsibility for it usually lay with some owner or general manager who operated from a distant office in a town or city rather than

* Published in *The Hereford Journal* (January, 1946), 1–7.

with an experienced range man who rode and ate with the men themselves.

The cowboy's work a generation ago consisted largely of driving cattle on the trail, sharing in the round-up, or riding the range. In the case of the first two, he ate at the wagon such food as was prepared by the cook, and in the last named, he lived in camp and ate his own. Every cowboy was a cook of sorts and the great majority developed considerable skill, though obviously some were far better than others.

A good cook in the cow country, as everywhere else, was regarded as a real treasure. Usually he commanded wages of at least $5 to $10 a month higher than the riders even when the latter were top hands. On the trail or with the round-up he drove the four horses or mules that pulled the chuck wagon, prepared the meals, washed the dishes, loaded up the wagon each morning and was something of an autocrat second only to the boss in importance.

Every chuck wagon was equipped with bows and a canvas cover to protect the supplies and bed rolls of the men from rain. Fitted into the wagon bed at the rear and held firmly in place by wagon rods extending through it was the chuck box. This was usually some four feet high with its front wall perpendicular while the rear one sloping outward from top to bottom, was hinged at the base so it could be let down to form a cook table supported by a sturdy leg. This leg was attached to the outer edge by a small hinge so it folded flat against the outside when the box was closed.

Shelves and perpendicular partitions divided the interior of the chuck box into compartments. The lower ones were large and held the sour dough jar or keg as well as the larger pans and tin plates, cups, knives, forks and spoons. The middle ones of smaller size were for sugar, syrup, lard, rice, beans or dried fruit, while the smaller ones at the top held salt, pepper, baking powder or other less bulky commodities. Most things were usually put in tin cans with close fitting lids and these were placed in compartments of a suitable size so they could not overturn as the wagon jolted over the rough and bumpy prairie.

It is doubtful if any better camp kitchen has ever been devised than the well-built chuck box attached to the rear of every trail or round-up wagon. By unscrewing the wagon rods, it could be lifted out and nailed to the wall in one corner of the range rider's dugout camp and so become the usual kitchen cabinet of the cow country. Naturally, on the trail or during the round-up only lighter articles and a supply of the more bulky groceries sufficient for a day or two were carried in the chuck box. The major part of the flour, beans, bacon, beef, dried fruit, sugar and coffee was in the wagon bed while a rack was built beneath it to carry the big Dutch ovens, pots, spade, axe, camp hooks, and other large and heavy utensils.

On the trail the cook ordinarily had the job of providing three square meals a day for about a dozen men, most of them with surprisingly healthy appetites. Reaching the spot designated by the boss, usually by the bank of a stream, he unharnessed and hobbled the team, brought up wood and a pail of water and after excavating a short, shallow trench, built a fire in it. On this he put the lids of the big Dutch ovens and then let down the back of the chuck box to form his cook table and set to work at the task of preparing dinner, or supper as the case might be, for the dozen hungry men some miles to the rear slowly moving the herd along the trail.

Ordinarily the first job was making bread. There is a tradition that the owners of the first herds driven north out of Texas frequently started with little in the way of food except corn meal and salt and so ate corn bread for most of the journey. If this is true, it must have been only during the first year or two after the close of the Civil War for the staff of life throughout the cow country during most of its existence was sour dough biscuits. At their best sour dough biscuits are about the final word in food made from flour but it must be admitted that at their worst the less said about them the better. In any case, however, they were the staple article of diet throughout the entire length and breadth of the American frontier for a generation or more.

Their basis is the sour dough which is made by filling a stone jar or small keg nearly half full of lukewarm water, adding a handful of sugar and then stirring in flour with a flat wooden paddle to make a batter as thick as it can be stirred. The jar is then set in a warm place and within 48 hours, or less, it has become sour and has increased to twice its original bulk. The cook merely filled a large tin pan two-thirds full of flour, and pushed it back from the center to leave a depression in the middle into which was poured half the contents of the sour dough jar. A teaspoonful of soda was then dissolved in a little lukewarm water, put into the sour dough, and a little salt and lard or bacon grease added.

The flour was then worked in from the sides, care being taken that the dissolved soda was well distributed throughout the mass. The table was thickly dredged with flour and the dough lifted on to it and kneaded thoroughly for several minutes. A large spoonful of lard or some bacon fat had been placed in the Dutch oven and melted and pieces of the dough about the size of an egg or slightly smaller were pinched off, rolled into balls, and placed in the Dutch oven and turned over in order to give to the entire surface of each a coating of grease so that they would not stick together. When the oven was full it was placed near the fire or in the summer time, set out in the sun for half an hour or more so that the biscuits might rise while the rest of the meal was being prepared.

The huge coffee pot with a wide base and usually well blackened was brought out and nearly filled with water. A generous supply of coffee was ground on the mill attached to the side of the chuck box and dumped into the pot which was then placed on coals shoveled from the fire. The coffee used was often one of the standard brands put up in one pound packages and an enormous quantity was required, for the cook firmly believed that there is no such thing as strong coffee but only "weak people" and the men for whom he must provide were surely not of that type!

The next step was the preparation of the meat. Usually a fat heifer was slaughtered every few days and the quarters of beef after being hung up overnight to cool were packed in the wagon. Half a quarter was brought out and the meat cut in fairly thick slices with a sharp butcher knife. A couple of big skillets were placed on a bed of coals and in each was put a generous handful of suet cut into small pieces.

While this was frying out, the steaks were cut into liberal-sized pieces and pounded with a hammer if there was any suspicion that the meat might be tough. Each piece was then sprinkled with salt, dredged with flour, and the suet "cracklings" were lifted out or pushed aside and the steaks dropped into the sizzling hot fat which should ordinarily be half an inch or more deep. A tin lid was often put on each skillet which kept out the dust and kept in the steam and flavor.

The oven of biscuits was then put on a few coals and covered with the hot lid lifted from the fire with a camp hook. Coals were placed on top and the cook could then devote himself to turning the steak and at the same time keep an eye on the coffee, and lift the lid from the oven once or twice with the camp hook to be sure that the biscuits were browning properly. The secret of baking bread in a Dutch oven is to see that there are not too many coals below and plenty above so that biscuits may be produced with each one having a deep brown upper and lower crust enclosing its delicious, soft, spongy interior.

Correct timing was necessary in order to have everything ready when the herd appeared and was spread out along the stream to water and graze while all the men except a couple left to "day herd" came in to eat. If they were a little slow, the cook took the bread and meat off the coals but placed them near the fire to keep warm.

At the last minute all of the steaks were put into one skillet and into the fat of the other was stirred a couple of tablespoonsful of flour. Salt and water were then added and the mixture briskly stirred until it had boiled sufficiently to produce a thick gravy commonly known as "sop."

A jug or can of syrup was then set out together with a stone jar or tin pail full of dried apples, peaches or apricots, which had usually been stewed the night before. When the men appeared, the more persnickety ones washed in a tin basin and each loaded up his plate and sat down cross legged on the grass to enjoy a meal which food experts might not regard as properly balanced but that was nevertheless very satisfying.

None of the three meals of the day—breakfast, dinner, and supper—departed very much from this standard pattern. Bacon cut in thick slices and fried to a golden brown might replace the beef, and beans boiled with bacon or salt pork were often served—and rice at times—but the name "moon-shine" by which the latter was commonly called is evidence that it was not regarded very highly as food for a real he-man.

As has been indicated the cook was an important man who was always treated with a considerable degree of respect, and the old cowboy saying: "Only a fool argues with a woman, a mule or the cook," is significant. Often the boss felt it necessary to stop the herd for a few days to allow the cattle to rest and graze. Upon such occasions the cook had ample time and opportunity to exercise his talents. Moreover, the riders had a good deal of leisure since only a couple of men were usually required for day herding.

This leisure they sometimes employed in fishing, often bringing in a string of perch or catfish and dressing them to be fried and so breaking the monotony of the daily fare. Also they would help the cook by dragging up dry wood with a rope or do other minor chores about camp, while in some instances they spent hours in gathering pecans, walnuts, or, in the summer, wild plums and grapes. Also it was upon such occasions that a beef was slaughtered, sometimes a fat stray for there is some element of truth in the saying that: "No cowman ever liked the taste of his own beef."

Relieved for a few days of the task of harnessing and unharnessing the team, loading the men's bed rolls and of driving for several miles each day, the cook often took advantage of the opportunity to prepare some especially delectable type of dish which he thought the men would like. One of these was beef and dumplings. Pieces of fat beef were placed in a pot and simmered slowly over the fire until perfectly tender. When the biscuits were put in the oven a good-sized lump of dough was put aside to rise for some three-quarters of an hour. Bits of this the size of the end of the finger were snipped off and dropped into the pot with the beef and cooked for a few minutes. A little flour was then dissolved in half a cup of water and added to the contents of the pot in order to thicken the gravy. The small lumps of dough puffed up to three or four times their original size and a plate filled with this tender beef and light dumplings swimming in rich gravy was about all that was required for a meal which was truly "soothing, sustaining and satisfying."

When a calf or other young animal was killed the cook sometimes made the favorite dish of the cowboy which in his more polite moments he called "son-of-a-gun-stew" or merely "son-of-a-gun." No recipe for it can be given for the reason that every cook had his own and in consequence there were as many ways of making it as there were cooks. Ordinarily the tongue, sweetbreads, heart, brains and perhaps the liver of the freshly killed animal were chopped into small pieces and put into a big kettle. If more meat was needed, a choice cut also chopped fine was added. In cowboy parlance, you "put in everything except the hide, horns and holler."

The meat was covered with water and any vegetables available were added. Some cooks put in chopped potatoes and onions, a can or two of tomatoes, a couple of cans of corn, or whatever could be had. In fact, it might be said of "son-of-a-gun," as the colored man replied to the query of how the soup was made, "We don't usually make it at all; it just sort of accumulates."

The "accumulation" in the kettle of "son-of-a-gun" was covered with water and boiled slowly for a long time. In fact it was commonly said that "the longer you cook it the better it is" and also "if you can tell what's in it you know it ain't made right."

On the whole the man who supplied the gastronomic needs of a bunch of cowhands had no easy task and few doubted that he earned every dollar of his wages. In pleasant weather his job was not too difficult but when it rained and the soaking wet wood refused to burn in anything like adequate fashion, his patience and temper were both sorely tried. Even in clear warm weather he must rise long before day to prepare breakfast and rouse the sleepy men with loud yells of: "Roll out, you waddies! It's getting daylight. Come git it 'fore I throw it in the creek."

Fortunately, he was not expected to provide pies, cookies and doughnuts as do many of the cooks in the camps of the lumberjacks of the northern woods. Plain food and plenty of it was demanded by the cowboys but, as has been said, they did not expect any frills or fancy fixin's and in most cases, would have been astounded if anything of the sort had been set before them.

The diet of the cow country on the whole rested upon seven pillars—flour, beef, bacon, beans, coffee, syrup and dried fruit. With these essentials—plus salt, sugar and soda—any man whether a regular cook or a cowhand in some remote line camp, which he occupied all alone or with a single companion, could prepare tasty and nourishing meals with a surprisingly wide range of variations. True, a few cases of canned tomatoes or corn helped a good deal as did a keg of pickles, or a few onions and potatoes from time to time, but not many men expected these as a regular part of their fare.

With the basic materials so few in number it was highly important that every dish be prepared with care and made as nearly perfect as possible. The biscuits must be brown and light, the beef well cooked and tender, the beans properly seasoned and thoroughly done. Unlike the person seated at a well loaded dinner table where if one article of food is not pleasing something else can be selected, the cowhand had no choice and expected these as a regular fare. If any article of food were badly cooked, the entire meal was ruined.

As a rule the cook for a dozen or more men seldom had either the time or inclination to experiment, but the lone cowboy in his line camp often tried out new things, sometimes with surprising and even disastrous results! Yet, there was always an ideal to be sought for in the preparation of these basic foods, and the making of good biscuits was one art that was to be cultivated at all times.

Every cowhand literally loved sour dough bread. Baking powder biscuits he would eat upon occasion without too much complaint but they were commonly considered as not healthful as a steady diet. The buttermilk biscuits affected by the nesters, and that he occasionally got at headquarters if the foreman had a wife who demanded a supply of milk and butter, he admitted were good though still somewhat below the sour dough variety. Corn bread he disliked as a rule and baker's bread, often called "wasp nest bread," he abhorred. Moreover, the finest of homemade "light bread" did not appeal to him.

Buck Rainey who had been visiting for a day or two with a friend whose wife was well known locally for the quality of her homemade bread could see nothing about it to admire. When other visitors expressed enthusiasm for the big snowy loaves that came from the oven, Buck only remarked plaintively: "Yes, I guess it must be fine but somehow it don't seem to do me the least bit of good."

In fact the making of such bread was a mystery to most cowhands. A ranchman's wife has related that when Johnnie Thompson dropped in Saturday afternoon to spend the weekend with the family she served him homemade bread for supper. The next morning he was up early and came out to the kitchen just as she was starting breakfast. "Miz Brown," he said hopefully, "I'll help you get breakfast and let's not cook no light bread for breakfast this mornin'—what do you say?"

The essential thing to remember in making sour dough biscuits is to use only half of the contents of the sour dough jar and to add to what is left lukewarm water and flour to make a very stiff batter. As a result the degree of acidity will be about the same when the time comes for the next meal and one can know just about how much soda to use. Moreover, the technique of making baking powder biscuits is exactly the reverse of that employed in preparing those made with sour dough. In the latter case, little shortening is required, the dough is kneaded thoroughly, and the biscuits allowed to rise for some time. They are then baked in a moderately slow oven. On the other hand the dough for baking powder biscuits should be made with very cold water and plenty of shortening, handled as little as possible, and baked in a very hot oven.

In addition to the methods of cooking beef already mentioned there were many others. Sometimes a sort of pot roast was prepared by salting a large piece of beef, dredging it lightly with flour and putting it in a Dutch oven with a cup or so of water to bake slowly for half a day. When it was nearly done some peeled potatoes and onions were added, upon those rare occasions when they were available, and more coals put on top of the lid to bake them to a golden brown. Such a dish, with biscuits, syrup or dried fruit, made a full meal.

There were several schools of thought with respect to

cooking steak, but on two points there was universal agreement. It must be well done and must be fried—broiled steak being virtually unknown in the cow country. Also it should never be fried in lard except as a last resort but in beef fat secured from a little chopped suet. From this point on, differences of opinion crept in. Some asserted that it should first be dredged with flour. Others declared that this was not only unnecessary but undesirable. Still others went even farther and insisted that each piece of meat should be dipped in butter before frying. Some wanted it cut thin and others thick, some wanted it served with pan gravy made from the hot fat and a dash of water, while others insisted on "sop." All agreed, however, that it should be fried in suet and must be well done.

Steak and sour dough biscuits were the twin essentials of cowboy diet. Even a man who accompanied a trainload of cattle to Kansas City or Chicago would walk into a restaurant, look the bill of fare over from top to bottom and passing up the fish, oysters, lobster and other strange delicacies at last say: "Guess I'll have a nice steak." Once in a great while one might be found with sufficient imagination to order ham and eggs but this was most unusual!

It is true that most men who rode the range agreed that bacon had its points and a skillet full of thick slices fried brown was not to be despised. Plenty of bacon was essential in the cow country for it was not only fried but also boiled with beans, and boiled beans and bacon would stay with a man throughout a hard day of work. In fact, Badger Clark voiced a fundamental truth when he wrote:

> "You always came in when the fresh meat had ceased
> And the road of the pathway of empire was greased
> By the bacon we fried on the way."

After a few days of bacon as the only meat, however, the cowhand began to pine for beef and cast about for a suitable animal to slaughter. In case he must eat bacon a considerable length of time he began to devise ways and means to change the flavor and so make it more palatable. Thick slices of bacon or salt pork were often parboiled for a few minutes and then rolled in flour and fried. It was still bacon or pork but at least the taste was different!

Deeply respected as was the cook, the boys would occasionally indulge in a bit of good natured joking at his expense, but this always stopped short if he showed the least indication not to take it in good part. "Don't you go to squattin' and snortin' at Sim's biscuits," remarked a cowhand when one of his companions had declared that these were "mighty firm biscuits." "Every one of them biscuits is about two pounds lighter'n it looks."

Milk and butter were of course virtually unknown in the range area except once in a while at headquarters and were, as a matter of fact, articles of food from which the average old-time cowhand shied as does a range horse from corn. Upon rare occasions a few cans of condensed milk might be seen but this was seldom. Sometimes a newcomer would complain bitterly, and one tenderfoot from the hills of Arkansas after a month on the range insisted that he was going back home where he could get some milk and butter instead of staying any longer "in a country that had nothing in it but cows!"

Since he was needed to do certain chores about camp, the boys at last rounded up an elderly brindle longhorn with a young calf and put her in the corral as a milk cow. After the first milking she was promptly dubbed "Old Sahara." For a week the men risked life and limb each night and morning in the perilous task of attempting to secure a little milk. Then they decided that two or three cupsful a day were not worth the effort, to say nothing of the danger, and in disgust turned Old Sahara out on the range again.

In planning and preparing a meal few cooks felt that it was necessary to provide any dessert except the inevitable dried fruit stewed with plenty of sugar. Even this was sometimes lacking and the dinner or supper was merely "topped off" with syrup. This might be sorghum, ribbon cane, sugar drip, corn syrup or any one of half a dozen other varieties. The fruit was usually dried peaches, apples, apricots or occasionally prunes or raisins.

Sometimes a bread pudding was made by soaking cold biscuits in warm water and adding sugar and raisins. After the mass had been beaten to a pulp, it was poured into a well greased Dutch oven and baked to a golden brown. With some sugar syrup poured over each serving it was not bad, though of course not so light as is the bread pudding made with eggs. It was often called "slumgullion" though this is a somewhat elusive term applied to beef stew in some parts of the cow country.

As has been indicated, a lone cowboy in some remote line camp had more time and opportunity for experimentation in the culinary art than did the professional cook who must prepare three meals a day for a crew of hungry men. Sometimes such a cowhand had a companion, the two men riding out from camp in opposite directions each morning, but in many cases he was all alone. Every cowboy was judged in a great measure by the way in which he kept his camp. Contrary to common opinion, he was in most cases an excellent housekeeper. The dirt floor was sprinkled and carefully swept every day with a broom made by tying a large bunch of long grass to the end of a stick. The pans and tin plates were scoured and polished until they shone, and the bed was carefully made up each morning. Only a bum, it was asserted, was willing to live in the midst of dirt and disorder. Moreover, he was usually clean and orderly in his cooking as he was in everything else.

About once a month a wagon came out from headquarters bringing him the staple articles of food previously referred to, except beef which he ordinarily supplied himself by slaughtering a young animal in time of need and hanging up the quarters in a tree if one were near camp. While beef and bacon were the standard meats, he often had a shotgun at camp and would at times kill a few quail, prairie chickens, wild turkeys, plovers or ducks to vary his fare. Quail were skinned, drawn and split into halves. They were then salted, rolled in flour and fried in fairly deep fat with a lid turned over the skillet. For a change they might be stewed and dumplings made from small pieces of biscuit dough dropped in when the birds were tender. Prairie chickens were unjointed, rolled in flour and fried, or boiled with dumplings, or in some cases baked in a Dutch oven with a stuffing made of bread crumbs. Drop dumplings were made with baking powder and flour stirred into water to make a stiff batter which was dropped into the pot a teaspoonful at a time.

Sometimes wild blackberries or dewberries were found along the streams and an enterprising cowhand might decide to try his hand at making a pie. Lard, flour and water were mixed to make a "pie dough" and a deep tin plate was floured and lined with this. The berries that had been stewed and sweetened were then poured in, a top crust added, and the pie baked in a Dutch oven. If it proved successful, others might be attempted with a filling of dried apples, peaches or apricots.

Some men even declared that a cake made by kneading sugar and raisins into a lump of dough, made up as for sour dough biscuits, was quite good. Others asserted that sugar could be added to the biscuit dough and after this had risen a little, strips could be cut off, made into twists, and fried in deep, hot fat to make quite tolerable doughnuts.

Once started on such experiments the ambitious cow-puncher found few limits to his ingenuity in devising tooth-some delicacies. Fried pies, or turnovers, were easily made and were especially delicious. Dried apples, peaches or apricots were stewed until quite tender and then crushed to a pulp and sweetened to taste. Pie dough was made by taking a lump of lard twice the size of an egg, putting it in a hole in the middle of a pan of flour, and adding half a cup of water. The flour was worked in from the sides to form a lump of dough which was lifted onto a well floured board and rolled out thin with a bottle in lieu of a rolling pin. This was cut into disks about the size of a saucer with a large tin can and the top of the disk thickly sprinkled with flour. The sweetened fruit pulp was then spooned out onto one side of the disk, the edges wet with a finger dipped into water, and the dough folded over the fruit to form a half-moon shaped turnover.

The edges were firmly pressed together with a fork and it was then carefully lifted off the board and dropped into a kettle or deep skillet of hot fat. Three or four could be fried at a time and when deep brown, were lifted out and placed on a newspaper which absorbed some of the grease. By frying up a couple of dozen at a time, some containing one kind of dried fruit and some another, an excellent dessert for several meals was insured.

Potatoes were seldom a regular item in the cowboy's bill of fare because they were bulky and would freeze in winter or rot in summer. When they were available a favorite way of cooking them was by frying. They were peeled, cut in thin slices, and dumped into a skillet containing half an inch of hot bacon fat. Salt was added and a lid placed on the skillet to retain the steam. From time to time the slices were turned over with a broad bladed knife. When they were tender and part of them browned, they were scooped out on tin plates, and a generous serving of fried potatoes plus three or four slices of bacon, some biscuits, and coffee made an excellent meal.

Apples were sliced with the peelings left on and fried in exactly the same way except that they were sprinkled with sugar instead of salt. Canned corn was also fried in bacon fat, sometimes with a little water added, while canned tomatoes were stewed and some crackers or crusts of bread broken up and cooked with them.

Hot cakes or "flapjacks" were a standard article of food in every cow camp. They could be made with sour dough by adding soda, a little salt, and enough water to make a batter of the proper consistency. It was better to let the batter stand for half an hour in a warm place so that bubbles would form, making the cakes lighter. Flapjacks were also made by mixing a liberal supply of baking powder with flour and stirring this gently into a pan of cold water to make a batter. Care was taken not to beat the batter since this made the cakes tougher. If the cook had some condensed milk and could use one part of this to three parts of water, so much the better.

Hot cakes should be baked on a griddle or in a skillet very

lightly greased with a bacon rind rather than fried in a considerable quantity of grease. They were served with a spoonful of bacon fryings on each one in lieu of butter and a generous supply of syrup. If the flavor of the latter had begun to pall, sugar syrup was often made merely by boiling two or three cups of sugar with a cupful of water.

Maple syrup was of course virtually unknown but an ingenious cowhand would sometimes stew dried fruit with a considerable quantity of water and then pour off the surplus juice, add to it two or three cups of sugar, and boil for several minutes. In this way syrup could be made with apricot, peach or apple flavor which was an agreeable change from that made merely with sugar and water. Also preserves were made by soaking dried peaches or apricots overnight, adding an equal bulk of sugar and a cupful of water, and boiling until the fruit was tender and a thick syrup had been formed. The result appealed greatly to the taste of many.

If the supply of sugar was low, a man would sometimes prepare what was called "fried molasses." Three or four slices of bacon were fried in a skillet and after they had been lifted out, a pint of sorghum was poured into the hot bacon fat and boiled briskly for five or six minutes. The change in taste is surprising and no matter how tired a man had grown of the same old sorghum three times a day he usually found the "fried molasses" extremely good with hot biscuits or flapjacks.

Returning to the subject of coffee which was regarded as an essential accompaniment of every meal, it is only necessary to say that the pot two-thirds full of cold water was placed on the coals and the coffee ground and dumped in. When it had boiled for three or four minutes, a dash of cold water was added to settle the grounds. So made it was clear and of excellent flavor if the quality of coffee used were good. The only requirement was that it be strong, for as Bill Jones once remarked: "It seems that a lot of people never realize how little water it takes to make good coffee!"

Lacking dried fruit, the enterprising range rider might decide to try his hand at a vinegar pie. This was made by adding half a cup of vinegar to a pint of water and dissolving in it sugar to taste. A lump of fat two-thirds the size of an egg was melted in the skillet and a heaping tablespoonful of flour stirred into it as though to make gravy. The tangy vinegar mixture was then poured in, slowly stirring the contents of the skillet all the time. When it had boiled a few minutes and was beginning to thicken the liquid was poured into a tin plate lined with pie dough and more strips of the dough criss-crossed over the top. It was then set into a hot Dutch oven and baked until the crust was a rich brown and the filling had congealed into a soft jelly. Vinegar pie may not sound attractive but when properly made it is delicious and most people will want to go back for a second helping.

It is impossible to give any complete list of cowboy dishes since the food varied with the season, the region and the source of supply. Many ingenious cowhands devised new ones. Beef ribs were barbecued over a bed of coals by placing them on an improvised grill made of peeled green poles. Canned corn and tomatoes were stewed together. Potatoes were sliced and fried with onions. Sometimes in the spring a rider in a remote camp would feel a hunger for fresh vegetable food and gather some form of wild greens, as poke salad or lambs quarter, to be boiled with a slab of bacon or salt pork.

Wild onions, a favorite food of some Indian tribes, might be pulled and fried in bacon grease. Biscuit dough was rolled thin, cut into strips, and dropped into smoking hot fat to make fried bread. In rare cases a wild turkey's nest might be found and the extraordinary treat of eggs enjoyed. There are even instances of a cowpuncher's finding, along some timber-bordered stream, a bee tree which was cut and a supply of honey added to the resources of the camp. Such cases are, of course, exceptional. Ordinarily the seven standard food staples named were the chief dependence of the cow country and with these available few men complained of any lack in either the quality or variety of their daily fare.

Most dietitians would probably hold up their hands in holy horror over both cowboy food and cookery. They would doubtless assert that so much starch and protein and the constant consumption of fried foods must inevitably cause grave digestive disturbances and result in bad health and a weakened physical condition. But there is nothing so tragic as a beautiful theory assassinated by a fact!

No hardier, healthier or more robust men ever lived than were the riders of the cow country. Digestive troubles were virtually unknown among them. On the fare described they rode from dawn until dark and often far into the night, day after day, in heat and cold, rain or snow, or worked at the hard labor of branding calves all day and never seemed to tire. Upon occasions they would ride all day and dance most of the night and then get back to camp a little sleepy perhaps but ready and willing to tackle the day's work.

The chief value of a knowledge of the past is its application to the present. The man planning a hunting or fishing trip which will take him into the woods or mountains for several days will find some study of cowboy foods and cookery of great value. It is even possible that some housewives who have been faced with problems of points and shortages may find such study useful in helping them to devise wholesome and satisfying meals for their families.

Unfortunately the average housewife has, in recent years, found some difficulty in securing an ample supply of some things which the cowhand had in abundance—especially meat, fats and sugar. Even so, the ingenuity shown by these range riders in making the most of their scanty resources can hardly fail to prove an inspiration to the busy wife and mother who so often complains of not being able "to think of anything to cook." No doubt her husband and children would be delighted with some of the dishes that a generation ago were commonplace to the riders of the cow country.

Moreover, the male guest who drops in to dinner and lavishly praises her caviar, canapes and "tossed up salad" would, in all probability, infinitely prefer sitting down to a platter of thick steaks fried in suet, flanked by a generous bowl of "sop" made with milk, plenty of sour dough biscuits, and a dessert of hot fried pies instead of raspberry sherbet or anemic looking blanc mange.

Food habits, like everything else in the world, are subject to change, but the nature of man remains essentially the same.

The Passing of the
Range Cattle Industry in Oklahoma[*]

An old Texas buffalo hunter once said that the American bison on the southern range disappeared with a suddenness that was almost startling. Each spring the hunters would go westward to the plains and there slaughter the animals by thousands, sending back the hides stacked high on the large freight wagons. When winter came on they abandoned their work and returned to the little frontier towns, there to pass the cold days in comfort and to "waste their substance in riotious living."

One spring they went to the hunting grounds as usual and met with the usual success. Apparently the great herds were just as large as ever, apparently the thousands which they killed could not be missed from the seemingly limitless number of these animals that roamed the prairies. Winter came and the hunters returned to the settlements. Their money, so easily acquired, was lavishly spent, and when the warm days of spring had come they started west again to replenish their empty purses.

They reached the plains and found that the buffalo had disappeared. One or two small bands were found and quickly slaughtered; but that was all. The great herds had vanished into thin air and the men who for years had depended upon this work for a livelihood must now turn their hands to other employment.

[*] Published in *The Cattleman*, XI (November, 1924), 9–17.

This incident has been related because what was true in the case of the buffalo hunters is also largely true of the cowmen of Oklahoma. The cattle industry had flourished there for many years. Ever since the coming of the first white men, the region had been a cattle country, and few of these early settlers realized that it might by any possibility ever be anything else. They bought and sold large herds, improved their ranches, made plans for the future, and waited for the settlers who were gathering about them to "starve out" and leave the country. But at last one fine morning they awoke and discovered that they were no longer in a cow country but a farming community, that the mule and the plow had displaced the bronco and the saddle, and that if any emigrating was to be done, they themselves were to be the travelers and not the hardy and patient homesteaders.

The awakening had come late but it was none the less thorough. Those who were wise saved themselves as best they could, accepted the changed conditions, disposed of their cattle as quickly as possible and "grabbed land" wherever they could find it. Those who were foolish hung on as long as possible, tried to make a gradual change, or went further west seeking for something almost as visionary as the "Fountain of Youth," a region where they could hope to spend their lives in the range cattle industry. Unlike the ten virgins, however, the wise and foolish were by no means equal in number. The foolish had an overwhelming majority.

To tell something of the cattle business as it was carried on during its last stages in this region, and especially to explain the conditions that wrought such a sudden transition, is the purpose of this sketch.

During the late nineties western Oklahoma was rapidly changing from ranching to agriculture and by the first years of the twentieth century the transformation was about complete.

Western Oklahoma was at this time a very peculiar country. The general impression, even in the West, seems to be that Oklahoma was settled almost in a day. Strictly speaking, this is not true, and the stories of the great "rushes" are in some cases misleading. The newspapers of the time told of the great crowds gathered along the border, of how when the gun was fired at high noon on the day appointed for the opening, these people dashed across the line and staked their claims, two or three men sometimes locating upon the same tract of land, so the casual reader is likely to get the impression that the entire country was taken up in this way.

This is quite erroneous. While it is true that the lands near the towns and the more fertile plains and valleys, especially in the eastern part of the Territory, were settled in this manner, it is also true that there were hundreds of acres of fertile agricultural land not settled until years after these "openings." This is particularly true of the western part of the Cheyenne and Arapaho reservation and of the Cherokee Outlet, opened to settlement in 1892 and 1893, respectively. In 1898 the author rode across this part of the country on horseback, and while there were settlements along the streams and in some cases on the level upland plains, yet it was possible to travel ten miles or more without seeing a house, though all of this land, except a little in each township, reserved for school purposes, was subject to homestead entry.

The greater part of this region was grazed over by the herds of the cattlemen. The manner of handling these cattle varied somewhat in different localities, but these differences were not important. In the southwestern portion of Oklahoma lay the large Kiowa-Comanche Indian reservation of about three million acres. Nearly all of this was leased to cowmen and fenced in large pastures. Many of these men were Texans who also owned ranches elsewhere and handled cattle on a very large scale. They were the real "cattle kings." Among them was W. T. Waggoner, who had one pasture of six hundred and fifty thousand acres on this reservation besides several smaller ones, and probably kept, at times, more than a hundred thousand head of cattle. Others were Burnett, Herring, Silverstine, Ikard and Kell, besides many cattle companies, such as the "Lone Star Cattle Company," "The Mule Shoe Company," and half a dozen others.

It is not my intention to describe the operations of these men, although their business was interesting enough. Their ranges were well fenced so they simply turned their cattle into these pastures and allowed them to grow and fatten in peace. "Line camps" were built at convenient places and in each of these little cabins or "dugouts" lived one or two men who rode the fences in order to keep them in good repair. These men also rode about over the range as much as possible, visiting the water holes and dragged out any cow or steer that happened to be mired down in the mud. They killed a wolf whenever opportunity offered, watched carefully for prairie fires at certain seasons of the year, kept a sharp lookout for cattle thieves, watching the Indians especially closely, since they were very fond of beef, and not at all scrupulous as to how it was obtained, and sought in every way to guard the interests of their employers.

Three or four times a year these camps were visited by a wagon from headquarters, bringing a load of flour, bacon, coffee, sugar, beans and dried fruit. The life of these men was lonely but not especially hard.

In many ways more strenuous and in every way more

vexatious was the life of the smaller cowman whose herds ranged the vacant lands in the regions already opened to settlement. It was to this class that nearly all of the cattle owners in Oklahoma belonged.

Each of these men would locate his headquarters on, or near, some stream, for in this business water was just as essential as grass and in Oklahoma decidedly scarcer. He would usually take a homestead and perhaps lease a school section if one was near. There were from two to four sections of school land in each township of this Territory and the lease at this time was only about forty dollars a year for each section, so it was not very expensive grass. Then if one or two of his cowpunchers were "old hands" who had worked for him some years they would often take a homestead near-by. They had, of course, to swear that they were taking it for a home and expected to live on it and improve it, but that did not matter. Cowpunchers' consciences were sufficiently elastic to admit of that. If the ranchman had a relative or two, uncle, aunt or cousin, who could be induced to take up a claim in the immediate vicinity, so much the better.

With a school section or two and three or four homesteads under his control, the rancher had an excellent location, provided, of course, that he had plenty of water. All about him lay the vacant government lands which the law prohibited him from fencing, but he would fence these homesteads and school land, build there his house and corrals, fence a horse pasture and perhaps a meadow, and let his cattle graze upon the open range. In some cases a location was selected near Indian allotments. These locations were good ones because the Indians always chose lands along the streams, and the water, timber, and rich meadow lands were very valuable to the cowmen. These Indian allotments were never farmed and could always be leased at low figures, thus giving complete control of a larger area.

In every case the boundaries of each man's range were pretty definitely agreed upon. If the ranchman owned but a few hundred head of cattle or even a thousand or two, and kept but two or three cowboys in his employ, the men might all stay at the ranch house and ride out each morning to look after the cattle. If his herds were larger than this, he would probably erect a camp or two near the border of his range and let a man or two stay out there, especially during the summer. In the winter the cattle were not permitted to scatter quite so much but were drawn in nearer to headquarters, and the poorest ones were sometimes fed a little hay or other rough feed.

As has been indicated, the life was not easy. Easterners have often expressed surprise that a man could turn a couple of thousand head of cattle out on the range to graze over an area of two or three hundred square miles and not lose a large part of them. As a matter of fact, they lost very few. In the first place, these men rode hard. With only one or two thousand head of cattle, three or four men, riding out each morning and keeping the saddle until dark, would see the greater part of them every day. Then, too, all of these cattle were branded in large, plain letters and every man helped every other. If your neighbor saw some of your cattle on his range he "turned them back" or "sent you word," for he knew that you would do as much for him should opportunity offer. The ethics of the range were very clear. It was considered in the highest degree dishonorable not to look after a neighboring ranchman's cattle just as carefully and conscientiously as after your own. Above all, these men had most remarkable memories, cultivated to a wonderful exactness by years of work on the range. I have seen men buy three hundred head of perfectly "strange cattle," drive them one day, and if one escaped during the night, they would, on the following morning, look over the herd, discover that one was gone, and describe the missing animal exactly. A "tenderfoot" can hardly count even three hundred head of cattle in open herd on the prairie and get the same result twice in succession.

These same men could tell of every strange animal they had seen on the range for weeks, describe it in detail, giving all brands and just when and where they had seen it. Of course this was the result of practice, but such a memory was invaluable to the cowboy or ranchman. Each fall and spring were held the "roundups," when all the cattle in a large region were driven together into one herd and all the cowmen for many miles in every direction came and "cut out" their own.

In pleasant weather this work was all agreeable enough but in cold or rainy weather it was very trying. The cowboys were a happy-go-lucky set of fellows, generous, big-hearted, reckless and improvident. They were usually paid from twenty-five to thirty-five dollars a month, and were given, in addition, their board and horses to ride. A full "mount" of horses was ten, but in the later years of the business few men had a full mount. Perhaps the more ordinary number was six or seven, and with that many good horses a man could do very fair work. The work of driving cattle on the trail was often paid for by the day at prices ranging from a dollar and a half to three dollars and a half per day. The food was coarse, but plentiful and well cooked. Every outfit on the trail had a cook who also drove the "chuck wagon" in which was hauled the food and each man's roll of bedding. Cooks were paid about the same wages as "punchers" and in some cases a little more. Many of the men were more or less dandies in matters of dress and all rode fine saddles. The joke of a "fifty-dollar saddle on a twenty-five dollar horse" was frequently not a joke at all but a reality. Very good cow horses were often sold for no more than twenty-five dollars, while a good saddle cost from thirty-five to sixty-five. The days of leather chaps and belled spurs were about gone by the late nineties, but most of these men, whether wealthy cattle owners or common hands at twenty-five dollars a month, wore shirts of soft, fine wool, white Stetson hats, gloves of white buckskin, and the finest of shop-made boots with dainty high heels.

Under favorable circumstances the profits of the cattle industry were enormous. But circumstances were often not favorable, and this was especially true about 1898 when settlers began to flock into this region in large numbers. They came from every direction, though by far the greater number came from the states of the Middle West, such as Iowa, Illinois, Nebraska, Kansas and Indiana, or from the Southern States of Texas and Arkansas. Nearly all of the settlers from the latter states came singly, while many of those from the former came in colonies and established little settlements or communities. The bond of union for these groups or colonies was sometimes a common religious belief, sometimes a common nationality, and in still other cases apparently only the tie of former acquaintanceship. Thus there were Mennonite settlements, Lutheran settlements, German, or Bohemian, settlements, and others known as the "Missouri settlement" or "the Indiana colony."

Of course, by no means all these settlers from the north came in colonies, many of them came singly, while practically all of those from the south came singly. Almost without exception these settlers, regardless of where their former homes had been, were very poor. Nearly all of them had been renters or common farm hands. Their worldly goods usually consisted of a poor team of horses, an old wagon, and a few household goods and farming implements. Each settled the best quarter-section of land he could find, built a rude sod-house or "dugout" in which to live, broke out a tract of land and planted a crop.

Naturally, there was but little sympathy between these people and the ranchmen, though the bitterness of feeling that is often said to have existed between them has been greatly exaggerated. The tendency at the present time, even in Oklahoma, is to criticise the cowman of the earlier days most harshly. He is usually held up to scorn as the man who tried in every possible way to hinder the development of that region, who sought to discourage settlement and even resorted to lawless methods to drive out the honest pioneer settlers. This is most unjust. Naturally the settler and the rancher did not understand each other in the least. Their ideas were totally different, their viewpoints were as unlike as they could well be. But there are two sides to the story and doubtless each class had some just cause to complain of the other.

It had been frequently urged that the ranchmen knew perfectly well the splendid agricultural possibilities of this region and that they sought to discourage settlement for purely selfish reasons. This is little short of absurd. The ranchman was not a fortune teller. He could not foresee any more than others the wonderful development of this region, that was to come within the next few years. Farming had never been thoroughly tested in this part of the country. The cowman had never attempted to raise more than a garden or a little feed, and his experiences had not been encouraging. When he said that the region was not, and never would be, an agricultural region, he was only voicing the belief of nearly every man in the east or north who was fortunate enough to own a tract of land. It was only those who were too poor to own land in an established agricultural region who would come to this western country and take up government land in the hope that it might some day have a real value. The rancher said that when a man plowed up the grass of these prairies he plowed up the best crop the land would ever produce. Time has shown his mistake, but twenty-five years ago he believed this, honestly and sincerely. Of course, such statements as this did not please the settler who was staking his all upon a homestead.

Moreover, the settlers disliked and in some cases feared the ranchmen. To them these cowpunchers were a rough, reckless set who rode hard, swore hard and feared neither God nor man. They did not realize that the business was one that required hard riding and at times almost seemed to require hard swearing. Also the settlers insisted that the cowmen often made no attempt to restrain their cattle, but allowed them to break into the farmers' fields and destroy his crops; that they tried in many ways to discourage settlement and would doubtless be glad to see every homesteader "starve out" and leave the country.

The ranchman retorted in kind and "a good deal more." He said that he rode after his cattle and tried to take care of them, but that the farmer depended upon a fence consisting of "one wire and a dog" to protect his crops and that naturally cattle would break through sometimes. He said further that the settler often did not give him square treatment, that his cattle "were shot if they even looked through the fence at the farmer's crop" and chased with dogs if they came near his house. He said that the settlers could not stay in the country at all were it not for the cowmen who bought their surplus feed and furnished them cows to milk, and yet these farmers showed no appreciation whatever, but charged them three prices for any little crops which the cattle might destroy, "churn-dashered"[1] their calves and seemed to think it perfectly legitimate to wring every possible dollar from a ranchman, by fair means or foul.

Doubtless both were partly right and partly wrong. There were some ranchmen who made no attempt to watch over their herds and to prevent them from destroying the crops, but the majority of them were honestly doing the best they could. Nearly all of them, however, had a most lordly and profound contempt for the "kafir-corner" as they called the settler. He was regarded as inevitably a man of "small ideas" because he was bound to a petty hundred and sixty acres of land, walked and plowed, demanded payment of travelers who spent the night with him, and he knew nothing of what was going on in the world as he did not get a dozen miles away from home more than two or three times a year. Of course his ignorance of live stock was almost alarming. He climbed upon a horse like a man going up the side of a battleship, had not the least idea of how to use a rope and if he owned a saddle at all it was an antiquated structure, the very sight of which moved the "punchers" to spasms of laugh-

[1] Many of the pioneer settlers obtained cows to milk from the ranchmen. In the west calves are never weaned while little. They are kept in a lot or corral during the day and in the evening when the cows are milked, these cows are left in the corral overnight while the calves are turned out to graze. If the calves are not allowed to have much milk they are said to be "knocked in the head with the churn-dasher or briefly, "churn-dashered." Men coming for cows to milk have often asserted that they would not churn-dasher the calves but would give them half the milk.

ter. The ranchmen themselves almost lived on horseback. They were here today and fifty or sixty miles away tomorrow and even the common hands often went to Chicago or Kansas City during the shipping season.

But worst of all, the homesteader, if from the north, was nearly always a believer in the "herd law," and this to the cowman was the unpardonable sin. This question of herd law or free grass was a burning issue at various times in certain sections of Oklahoma. Reduced to its lowest terms, the question is: Shall each man fence his field or his pasture land? That is, must he keep his crop or his live stock under fence? The rancher with hundreds of cattle and only a garden in cultivation said, quite naturally, that not one acre in a hundred in the entire region was in cultivation, so as a matter of course the crops should be fenced. The homesteader, owning a pair of ponies and cultivating forty acres of land was just as positive that each man should restrain his animals and allow the fields to be left unfenced.

Herd law was usually voted on separately in each municipal township and thus there soon came to be certain "herd law settlements" in various parts of the Territory. Herd law was the "Kansas system" while free grass was the "Texas system." Therefore, the settlers from Texas and Arkansas were on better terms with the cowmen than were the settlers from the north.

These herd law settlements increased the difficulties of the cattle business. When a man driving even a small herd of cattle across the country came to one of them he was almost obliged to go around it if possible. Should he attempt to drive across it at any time during the crop season he was sure to repent his temerity in sackcloth and ashes. There were no fences and the corn, kafir corn and vegetables were planted up to the very edge of the road. Before he had gone a mile, a half dozen "Dutch farmers" were out, mounted on plow-horses, and armed with pitchforks, helping him to hurry the cattle along, demanding damages and no doubt thirsting for his life.[2] One such experience was always sufficient.

As more and more settlers came into the cattle country these herd law communities increased in number and became larger, while individual settlers came in and took up claims on various parts of the range. Naturally they selected the best lands, the valleys and the level prairies with fertile soil, and each man broke out a field and fenced as much of his land as he was able. But good soil produces good grass and vice versa, consequently the damage done to the range was out of all proportion to the acreage enclosed. At first the cattle-men did not realize this fact. There was apparently still an abundance of open range, though it consisted largely of the rougher and less fertile uplands, covered in many cases with coarse bunch grass. It was hard to comprehend at first just how much the cattle interests had suffered by the fencing and breaking of these comparatively small areas of rich valley land.

It became more apparent, however, after one or two severe winters. The winter of 1898–99 was one of the worst ever known in the southwest, and cattle died by thousands. The winter following, 1899–1900, while not so cold, was very wet. Heavy rains fell early in the autumn, thus, in the language of the range, "washing all the strength out of the grass" and the loss was almost as great, in some localities, as it had been the preceding winter. These losses were largely due to the fact that the cattle must depend upon the coarser

[2] There were many German settlers in this region. They often came in colonies and all favored the herd law.

upland grass for food; previous winters had been almost as severe without one-fourth the loss. Ranchmen began to realize the importance of these bottom lands and fertile valleys, that had been fenced by the settlers, and discovered that cattle must now be fed a little each winter or many of them would die.

During 1899 and 1900 settlers came into this region in ever increasing numbers. A new line of railroad had been built into the Territory about this time. It was a great convenience to many ranch-men because it afforded better shipping facilities. But, it also furnished an easy ingress for homesteaders. Heretofore, many of the pioneer farmers had traveled long distances in wagons in order to reach good lands in Western Oklahoma. Now men in Illinois or Iowa would charter a car, load into it wagon and team, household goods and farming implements, and come to Oklahoma. Upon reaching one of the little towns in the western part of the Territory the car would be unloaded, the furniture and tools packed in the wagon, the team hitched to it and the new settler would drive out into the country and locate upon the first good tract of vacant land to be found.

Some of these men had a little money, at least enough to fence the hundred and sixty-acre homestead, and those who did not, fenced as much as they could. Nearly all of them had "Eastern ideas." They had never before owned a single acre of land and they were bitterly intolerant of the cowmen. This hundred and sixty acres of land was theirs, soil, grass and water—if there happened to be any. They wanted the entire benefit of it and, of course, they were entitled to it; but the ranchman thought they often went to extremes. The Texas settler was usually perfectly content to fence his field and allow the rancher's cattle to graze over the rest of his land. He himself had no live stock, why should he object to the cattle eating the grass which he could not use? The northern settler had no such ideas. He was accustomed to "No Trespassing, Police Take Notice" signs. This free and easy method of doing business did not appeal to him in the least. He might not be able to use the grass himself but if it was worth real money to the stockman, the latter ought to be willing to pay for it.

The cow-man was to him the embodiment of wealth and aristocracy. The settler felt toward him very much as the average citizen feels toward a great corporation such as a railway company. Railroad men in Texas in the early days before the roads were fenced, often remarked that though Texas long-horned cattle ranged the prairies by thousands none were ever killed by their locomotives. Those killed were always the finest of Jerseys and Holsteins.

The ranchman felt that the average Yankee settler dealt with him in the same manner. If a few cattle broke into the fields and destroyed a little kafir corn or some pumpkins, the heaviest of damages were at once demanded. Moreover, as these poorly fenced fields multiplied, the difficulties of keeping the cattle out increased. The coarse bunch-grass did not satisfy the animals when tempting fields of corn or kafir corn were scattered all about. No matter how hard a man might ride or how conscientiously he might watch his herds, crops would be damaged and heavy bills have to be paid. The life of the cow puncher became a "dog's life." His troubles and vexations, great enough at best, became almost unbearable.

Worst of all his cattle did not fatten. The coarse "stemmy" grass was poor food and frequent chasing about by the settlers helped to keep the animals poor and thin. Cattle that in

August and September should have been fat were in only moderately fair flesh. When shipped to market the returns were most disappointing. Those that were to be kept over the winter were thin and in bad condition to endure severe weather, before winter had really begun.

Of course, these cattle sometimes looked to be in very good shape but every cow-man knows that cattle frequently look fat when they are not. Range cattle will sometimes appear almost as fat the first of July as they do the first of September but the scales will usually tell a very different story. Cattle the first of July are only "full of grass." Two months later, if the range is good, this apparent fat is real and the cattle weigh heavily. In these later days of the business cattle seldom got beyond that stage of "merely looking fat."

So far I have discussed only those troubles of the ranchman on the range. He had other troubles off the range; however, that were perhaps even worse. The financial side of the cattle industry is a subject upon which comparatively little has been written and yet it was most important. Nearly all of the cattle men in Oklahoma at this later period carried on the business largely on borrowed capital.

Chicago, Kansas City, St. Louis and every other important cattle market had scores of firms of live stock commission merchants to which the shipments of cattle were consigned. These firms also loaned money. They began perhaps by making loans to feeders; then the business was later extended to include men engaged in the range cattle industry, and soon practically every cow-man was handling more or less of this "commission money."

It was easy to obtain. The commission men tempted by large profits were eager to make loans to any man who had a fair location, reasonable ability as a cow-man and a very little collateral, provided his reputation for honesty was fairly well established. They were all the more eager since they were, in nearly all cases, lending other peoples' money. Had the conservative Eastern and Northern bankers realized the risks that were being taken with their precious dollars, they would have doubtless passed some sleepless nights; but this was a case where ignorance was bliss. The commission men were sometimes retired cow-men or western bankers. They sent out agents or "loan inspectors" to the cattle country who took up their quarters in the little frontier towns and from there looked after their employers' interests. In some cases detectives were sent out also.

The ease with which money could be obtained tempted many a cow-man to enlarge his business at the very time when the conditions of the cattle country demanded retrenchment. Often a man with a good range and ten or fifteen thousand dollars worth of cattle would decide that it was a great pity not to have sufficient cattle to stock that range and would hasten to Kansas City or Chicago and borrow money. If his reputation were good and he had fifteen thousand dollars worth of cattle, he could probably borrow twelve thousand dollars on them. With this twelve thousand he would buy more cattle and immediately proceed to put them up as a collateral for a loan of ten thousand; the cattle bought with this furnished collateral for a loan of eight thousand and these for six thousand, etc.

If his reputation were exceptionally good, he could sometimes borrow money to buy cattle without furnishing any collateral at all except the cattle to be bought. The author knows one man who borrowed seventy thousand dollars for which he gave no security whatever except the two thousand head of steers which he proposed to buy with the money, and this too was at a period of considerable financial stringency.

Thus the man with ten or fifteen thousand dollars capital would soon find himself in possession of a hundred thousand dollars worth of cattle or even more. If everything went well, his profits were great; but things were not going well about this time and if they went badly, if prices dropped or a cold winter brought heavy losses, nothing could save him from ruin.

As an illustration of the immense profits to be made under favorable circumstances, a friend of the author bought in the autumn of 1897 two thousand head of two-year-old steers at twenty-one dollars a head. They were delivered to him at Bowie, Texas, the 15th of October. He immediately drove them to his range in Oklahoma, not more than a hundred and fifty miles away. Here he held them on the open range, with the aid of two or three men at twenty-five dollars a month, until the following August, when they were shipped to Kansas City. They weighed one thousand pounds each and sold for $3.75 per hundred or $37.50 per steer, a gross profit of $16.50 per head. The loss had been nothing, the expense for help but a few hundred dollars. After the freight to Kansas City and the interest on $42,000 commission money had been paid, he had still made a good deal more than twenty thousand dollars in ten months, or fifty per cent on his investment. He was lucky. Two or three years later he lost it all and twenty thousand dollars more in even less time on a single unfortunate deal.

By 1898 nearly every ranchman in this region was running his business on just this kind of system which has been described. The men with three or four thousand dollars original capital had fifteen or twenty thousand dollars worth of cattle; those with ten to twenty thousand dollars had in many cases from a hundred thousand to two hundred thousand dollars worth. The money was usually loaned from six to twelve months time, eight months being the ordinary period. The interest was from eight to ten per cent, with some times an additional three or four per cent, paid separately and called a "commission."

The commission firm's method of doing business was very similar to that of the ranchman. It would lend him money, taking his note and mortgage on his cattle. This note and mortgage, after being indorsed by the commission firm, would be sold to an Eastern banker at about its face value, or it would be given as collateral for a loan of almost its face value. The money obtained by this sale or loan would be lent to another cow-man and the process repeated as an endless chain. Thus there grew up in the West that large class of securities known as "cattle paper."

The business of the commission firm, like that of the rancher, of course, soon became terribly inflated. A smash at the bottom meant a smash all along the line and this is just what happened. Forerunners came in the form of isolated failures of single individuals who had gone "too deep." One of the most noted of these was that of Grant G. Gilette, the Kansas "cattle plunger," whose failure nearly ruined half a dozen commission firms and banks. This was but a solitary case however which came early in the game. As a matter of fact the whole structure that had been built up was becoming shaky, it was a bubble which would break at a touch. A house of cards had been erected and the least breath would send the whole structure tumbling down about the ears of its builders.

The severe winters before mentioned removed the last prop and rendered the situation truly desperate. The losses of the ranchmen in Western Oklahoma during the winter of 1898–99 were terrible. Twenty-five to thirty per cent was common, forty, fifty, even sixty per cent and more was hardly exceptional. Men saw all of their little original capital and much of their borrowed capital lying scattered about on the frozen prairie, food for the wolves. Spring came, and the time to renew their eight-month notes that were falling due. What was to be done? The gaunt and famished spectres that were left to them would in many cases not have sold for half the amount of money due. In hardly any case were they anything like sufficient collateral for a renewal of the loans if sound business principles had been adhered to.

But sound business principles had never been adhered to in this industry. The commission men realized that the loss had been heavy, but in most cases they had not the remotest idea how heavy. Loan inspectors do not ride the range much when there is a foot of snow on the ground and the thermometer is hovering around zero. They leave that to men whose interests are more vitally concerned, and these men, for obvious reasons, did not publish their losses from the house tops. The commission firms, moreover, had no desire to close the ranchman out and take the cattle, if it could be avoided. They themselves were not in the cattle business, and their own position was entirely too precarious to make them anxious to "start anything." They would take the cattle, of course, as a last resort, but only as a last resort.

A few of the ranchmen had enough cattle left to make a very shaky and uncertain collateral for a renewal of their paper. A few others "lay down" in their own language and told the money lenders to take what was left. Others "managed" for a renewal of their loans as best they could. It was not difficult. The hair on the cattle was long and shaggy in the spring and concealed the brands, while many of the commission men's agents were cattlemen only "in theory." It was easy to take the average loan inspector out, show him their own cattle and those of two or three of their neighbors', and then go back to town and swear that they had a certain number "to the best of their knowledge and belief."

They should not be judged too harshly. They hoped for the best. Profits had often been great in the past, why not in the future? To quit now meant ruin and bitter poverty. It meant sometimes that a son must come home from college, or that the plans for educating a daughter must be given up. They knew no other business. They would have to go to work for wages as common hands or fall into the ranks of the despised "kafir corner." Moreover, they doubtless tried to soothe their conscience by trying to think that it was best for their creditors also. They could not nearly pay out now; their failure might ruin some of the commission men, too. A little later, with some good fortune, they might be able to pay the last dollar. And so they would hold on as long as possible.

It must not be supposed that all of these men adopted such a policy. Many of them honestly confessed their failure and turned in their cattle, and yet some of them did not, and we must admit that their temptation was great.

Such methods only further undermined the already tottering structure. The lax business methods, the scarcity of grass, the hemming in of the settlers, and the severe winter all had been enough; but when to these was added an attempt to bolster up the business by dishonesty and perjury, when men gave their cattle as security for the renewal of loans of two or three times their value, the outcome was rapidly becoming obvious to the dullest mind.

Settlers continued to pour into the country, and the next

winter was the rainy one already mentioned. Cattle died in almost as great numbers as the preceding one, and when spring came many men, weary of the struggle against such overwhelming odds, decided to give it up and ask their creditors to take charge of their cattle. The money lenders took the cattle, but knew not what to do with them. They were not cattlemen; and even if they had been, they could hardly hope to succeed where the ranchman had failed. Nor was there any better range to be found elsewhere. All they could do was to throw the cattle upon the Chicago or Kansas City markets. Poor and thin as they were, they seldom brought anything like enough to pay the notes for which they were collateral. The bankers turned to the commission merchants from whom the paper had been purchased for the remainder.

It was the beginning of the end. The commission firms turned to the other ranchmen to whom they had made loans and demanded their money as fast as the notes fell due. But where should they be sold? The neighboring cowmen, even those in the best of circumstances, no longer had sufficient range. They were so hemmed in by settlers that they were already shipping half fat cattle upon the market in order to reduce their herds, thus pushing the market prices steadily downward. Everyone wanted to sell, no one was in a position to buy. There was nothing for the man who must raise money to do but rush his cattle upon the market also, and that, too, as quickly as possible before prices went even lower.

A hurried scuffle ensued to get to market. Trainload after trainload of cattle, most of them entirely unfit to ship, came pouring into Chicago, Kansas City and St. Louis. The market sagged, broke, and at last went to smash altogether.

The tremendous slump in prices still further frightened the holders of cattle paper. They became clamorous in their demands for their money, and to supply it, men who had owned thousands of head gave up even the last milk cow. The saddle horses, mules and "chuck wagon," and often the headquarters and the house in town, all went, and in many cases all proved insufficient. If the ranchmen had sinned in trying, even by dishonest means, to hold out as long as possible, many of them amply atoned by the completeness of their surrender when it did come. Pet ponies belonging to the children, household goods, everything went, and strangely enough, the ranchman who had been for years a wealthy and influential citizen, now faced the world with only his two hands with which to earn a living for himself and family.

And, strangest of all, it was a new world which he faced. Like Rip Van Winkle, he awoke to find all changed. The cattle had disappeared as if by magic, and farmers armed with hoe and spade had sprung up on all sides as though an unseen hand had planted dragons' teeth on every hill and in every valley. The days of the cowman were over. This strange community in which he found himself was a farming country.

The Cow Country in Transition*

Rivalries serve to explain many things in history. The rivalry between Athens and Sparta, Rome and Carthage, and England and Spain are all familiar Old World examples, while that between North and South, the industrial East and the agricultural West, and New York and Boston are equally familiar for the New. Similarly, rivalries have often existed not between cities, nations, or geographic regions, but between groups or certain social, economic, or racial orders within the same region. When the Anglo-American civilization struck the Spanish culture of the Southwest, when the English colonists came in contact with those of the French in Canada, or when the New England Puritans met and mingled with the German settlers of the Old Northwest, a struggle ensued as to which racial element and which type of social order should prevail.

Out of this mingling of two societies came first conflict and eventually a fusion producing a new order unlike either of the first two, but with some of the attributes of both. So developed a regional society, growing from two stems, which continued for generations and which still bears fruit of a hybrid variety showing certain characteristics of both parent stocks.

* Read by the author as the presidential address before the Mississippi Valley Historical Association in St. Louis, Missouri, April 29, 1937. Reprinted from Edward Everett Dale, *Cow Country* (New ed., Norman: University of Oklahoma Press, 1965), pp. 215–236.

If "it is a wise child that knows his own father," so is it a wise society which knows both its own father and its own mother, or the two dominant roots from which it sprang. Obviously, these are often more than two in number, but perhaps in most cases two are so much more important than the others that they may logically be called the parents of the existing society. The father of the present social order in most of that part of the western prairie states settled within the last two generations was the wild, roaring "cow country" of earlier days, while the mother might be said to be the agricultural society of the homesteaders coming from the wooded, or partially wooded, crop-growing region of small farmers farther east. The story of their introduction to one another and the ripening of their acquaintance until "these twain became one flesh" is a story which, so far as the writer knows, has never been told with any detail. Yet it is a most significant story which, if the figure of speech may be continued, proves conclusively the truth of Kipling's famous statement that "the female of the species is more deadly than the male." It indicates, too, that the bride did all the pursuing and having won her mate by strong arm methods, she eventually imposed upon him and upon the family most of her own ideas and ideals. The wild, roistering days of his youth were left behind. He and his children in time joined the wife's church, adopted her way of life and settled down as sober, respectable citizens. Only occasionally does the offspring show an outcropping of that paternal wildness which had made its father a bit notorious in earlier years.

It is true that during the period of the honeymoon the groom made a more or less determined effort to induce his spouse to accept his guidance as to the conduct of their daily affairs of life, but in this he met with scant success. She was an obstinate and head-strong wench and he soon became impressed with the truth of the old rhyme:

> A wedding is the greatest place
> For folks to go and learn
> He thought that she was his'n
> But he found that he was her'n.

This union was to bear fruit in the years following the Civil War when a vast stream of cattle flowed north out of Texas and spread over the central and northern plains, while agricultural settlement hesitated for a time at the eastern edge of the great prairies. Even a half decade after Appomatox the states and territories forming the second tier west of the Mississippi were comparatively thinly peopled. At that time their unsettled area included nearly all of the Dakotas, the western three-fourths of Nebraska, two-thirds of Kansas, virtually all of Indian Territory except for the Five Civilized Tribes of Indians in its eastern one-third, and the western two-thirds of Texas. Much of this region was potentially valuable for the growing of crops and all of it, together with the broad expanse of more arid lands farther west, was wide open to occupation by cattle. Within two decades after the close of the war the range cattle industry had spread over virtually all of this vast territory and had reached the point of its greatest extent and the height of its importance.

So came into existence that vast pastoral empire commonly known as the "cow country" in which society had for its economic basis, cattle and the native pasturage upon which they fed. Like every pastoral society, it was mobile, with the people who composed it far less fixed as to abode than were the crop-growing farmers farther east. True, some ranchmen owned in fee at least a part of the lands occupied by their herds and had built permanent homes where they lived with their families. Most of them, however, occupied temporary ranges upon the public domain or on Indian reservations where their tenure was most precarious and uncertain. In such cases improvements were of flimsy and temporary construction, and the headquarters was merely the administrative center of their business. As conditions changed, these men would, in a few years, shift their operations and establish new headquarters, or in some cases remove all or a portion of their cattle to new ranges quite remote from the original ranch. As for the cowboys who carried on the business, they seldom had any fixed abode which could properly be called a home. They occupied temporary line camps along the borders of a range. Here they might remain for only a few months after which they would be transferred to some other camp. They followed the round-up wagon in the spring or autumn, accompanied herds of cattle on the long drive up the trail, left one outfit after a few months or a few years to seek employment with another, and were in general a wandering and restless group seldom occupying, for any considerable length of time, a fixed habitation.

Since the cattle business requires comparatively few persons for its successful operation, the cow country was very thinly peopled and the society primitive and rough. The cowboy who is, however, often pictured either as a Sir Galahad or a wild semi-outlaw was as a matter of fact, neither the one nor the other. He was in most cases a young man who worked hard, lived according to his code, and who maintained toward his employer or the brand an intense and whole-hearted loyalty. That some were wild and rough cannot be denied, but they were by no means as black as they have been painted, or as they at times saw fit to paint themselves. The average cow-puncher was a sane and reasonably sober individual who lived a lonely, but not unhappy life. In bad weather he might endure considerable hardship, but this was forgotten when the sun shone bright and warm and colorful wild flowers sprinkled the green prairie. He liked his work, was proud of his job, and like every man on horseback whether he be called knight, *chevalier*, *Ritter*, *caballero*, or cow hand felt himself distinctly superior to the man who walked.

By the early eighties an enthusiasm for ranching on the great western plains, amounting almost to a craze, had swept over the United States and had extended even to Great Britain and the European continent. By this time, also, a curious kind of "American feudalism" had grown up in the Far West bearing certain similarities to the society of medieval Europe. The great ranchman often occupied a range larger than was the territory claimed by many a petty German princeling. His riders were quite as numerous as were the knights and men-at-arms of some of the Old World barons. His brand, the X.I.T., the Pitchfork, Frying Pan, or Long X, was as widely known as had been the bleeding heart of the Douglas, the white lion of the Howards, or the clenched hand and dagger of the Kilpatricks. The ranch house, where he dispensed a generous hospitality to all comers, except that it often shifted as to place, was somewhat of an equivalent to the medieval castle, and if the cow country had no tilts or tournaments, the rodeo or roping contest furnished a fairly satisfactory substitute.

The range area was peculiarly a man's country. One range rider has recorded that during a year's work he did not see a woman for nine months and the writer as late as 1904 visited a ranch in western Texas where the ranchman's wife asserted that she had not seen another woman for over six weeks. Since women were so few in number, they were held in high esteem and treated with an almost exaggerated respect. Many a quick-witted cowboy known for his gay conversation and clever repartee with his own kind became a tongue-tied, stuttering moron when in the presence of a woman with whom he was but slightly acquainted. Yet some few of the ranchmen had wives and daughters who gave a feminine touch to their homes and who would occasionally arrange social affairs which people traveled long distances to attend. These were, in most cases, dances with few girls and many "stags" where the "square dance" or quadrille was the rule. Music was furnished by one or two fiddlers, assisted at times by some one to "beat the strings" with two heavy knitting needles or pieces of wire. If the home boasted a cottage organ and some one could be found to "second on the organ," so much the better. The dance often lasted all night with supper served at midnight. "We danced the last set after sunrise" was a proud boast meant to indicate a remarkably good time. Since girls were so few in number, some danced virtually every set, and after breakfast mounted their horses to ride fifteen to thirty miles to their homes.

Such dances furnished the average cow hand with almost his only opportunity for the society of women. His pleasures were few and simple. He sometimes had at his camp a few books or magazines and of course played cards if he had a partner, or if some stray rider dropped in to spend the night. If on his rare visits to town he sought solace in a game of poker or a few drinks, he should be pitied for the loneliness of his life rather than blamed for his weakness or folly.

Into this rough, masculine society of the cow country eventually began to be projected a far different social order.

Men from the settled regions to the east, eagerly seeking for "level land" upon which to establish homes, came in with their families in covered wagons, bringing not only strange tools and household goods, but even stranger ideas and ideals. Choosing one hundred sixty acre homesteads on the fertile plains, these men set to work to build homes, plow up the prairie sod, fence fields, and plant crops. Into a region of long-horned steers, hard riding men, boots, spurs, branding irons, saddles, ropes, and six shooters, they brought plows and hoes, pitchforks, churns, cook stoves, rocking chairs, feather beds, pillows, dogs, cats, pigs, and chickens, but most important of all, wives and children.

To a region of sour dough bread, beef steak, bacon, dried apples, beans, flapjacks, and coffee were brought salt rising bread, buttermilk biscuits, pies, cakes, doughnuts, preserves, jellies, custards, and fresh vegetables. To a vast area covered with cattle, these newcomers, curiously enough, brought milk and butter, articles of food from which the average cow-puncher shied as does a range horse from corn.

Most significant of all, these people brought the home, the school, the church, and the Sunday school to compete with the camp, saloon, dance hall, and gaming table. With all of these things they brought what was to the cow country a new conception of life and of society—a new set of objectives to be attained.

The effects of the impact of this sober, settled, industrious farming population upon the more primitive pastoral society of the cow country were at once apparent. The range riders regarded these intruders with some contempt and suspicion, not unmixed with active hostility. They must inevitably be men of small ideas, since each was bound to a petty one hundred sixty acres of land, walked rather than rode, and worked at such menial tasks as plowing, milking cows, and feeding chickens. The ignorance and general wrong-headedness of many a newcomer were, moreover, alarming. He climbed on a horse like a man going up a ladder, could not read a brand, and if he owned a saddle at all, it was an antiquated structure the very sight of which moved the punchers to spasms of laughter. His methods of doing business were mysterious and past finding out. The fence, designed to protect his field, consisted of one wire and a dog, and he possessed a "one way pocket book" wherein he hoarded diligently his few hard earned dimes.

"I guess old man Johnson's maybe a nice old feller enough," said cow hand, Bill Jones, "but he don't know nothin' at all about business. Why, he's savin' as hell."

"That's right," answered his companion. "You know th' other day he gave me a letter to mail and two copper cents to buy the stamp. I told him that nothin' less'n a nickel goes in this country."

"Just like him," replied Bill. "He may be all right in his way, but damn his way."

So spoke Bill Jones, and so spoke the cow country as a whole. The homesteader, commonly called the "nester" might be all right in his way, but it was a far different way from that of the range region, and the latter disapproved of it whole-heartedly. His penny pinching tendency was but one of many unpleasant characteristics, but that alone was bad enough. Any man who had been known to refuse a respectable traveler a couple of meals and a night's lodging, or even worse, to demand payment for such a trifling courtesy, was beneath contempt.

The range riders regarded themselves as far above any such petty meanness. In fact, until the coming of these homesteaders, such behavior was an unheard of thing. A rider might stop at any cow camp certain of food and shelter and a cordial welcome. If the cowboy stationed at the camp happened to be absent, it did not matter. No lock was on the door and any hungry traveler passing by was expected to go in and prepare himself a meal or spend the night if he wished, courtesy only requiring that he wash the dishes before leaving. The cow hands drew fair wages, had no families to support, and took very little thought of the morrow. Money, if they had it, was to spend. They bought drinks for the crowd, candy by the pound, wore expensive hats and gloves, and paid enough for one pair of boots to shoe the numerous issue of the homesteader for a whole year with something left over. If they wanted to shoot craps or play poker for high stakes when they were in town, who was to say them nay? It was their own money. If they lost it, they were sure of food and a place to sleep at any ranch or line camp in the whole great pastoral empire that was the cow country. Such minor courtesies as riding thirty miles to restore a strayed horse to the owner, lending a friend half a month's wages, or taking him a quarter of beef were a part of life. Would not anyone do the same? Of course he would, unless he happened to be one of those blue-nosed nesters!

The cow hands observed that their boss, who owned the ranch, carried on his business on the same basis, and they felt it must be the correct basis since he was a wealthy and successful man. His hospitality was boundless. Any stranger was welcome at the ranch and might stay as long as he liked. They had seen the ranch owner feed and care for from fifty to a hundred head of some neighboring ranchman's cattle all winter until the latter could come and get them. With many thousands of dollars in the bank he would give a common puncher a book full of checks signed in blank and start him out to buying steers, certain that every check would be filled out for exactly the correct amount required in each purchase. They had, in some cases, seen him play at dice for fifty dollars a throw and there were rumors of valuable ranches or an entire brand of cattle won or lost in a single poker game. They knew that he had borrowed or loaned thousands of dollars with no collateral involved except the name and reputation of the borrower.

"I've been doing business with you for some time now," an old ranchman once wrote to a friend who had met with misfortune. "We've bought and sold back and forth, and I think we're about even. You figure it up and if I owe you anything, let me know what it is and I'll send you a check. If you owe me anything, just forget it." With such examples before him, it is not surprising that the cowboy was lavish with his money, nor is it strange that both he and his employer had nothing but contempt for the economic ideas of the settler. As a matter of fact, the business methods of the range area might be satisfactory enough so long as every one practiced them, but once brought into competition with the methods of the new society that was fast coming, they were nearly certain to bring ruin to those who could not or would not change.

If the range rider disliked the way of the pioneer settlers, however, the latter returned that dislike with full measure "pressed down and running over." The cowboy had, of course, no fear of the homesteaders except the fear that their presence might threaten the security of the only business the ranchman knew. The nesters, on the other hand, both feared and disliked the cow-puncher. To them the cowboy was a wild, reckless type who rode hard, swore hard, and feared neither God nor man. The nesters regarded the cowboy as a swaggering swashbuckler, who carried a gun, had little regard for horse flesh, and who seemed at all times to be "jealous of honor, sudden and quick in quarrel." He probably never attended church or Sunday school and would not, even if he had the chance. He spent his wages foolishly and was strongly suspected of playing cards and other sinful games. He wanted the region to remain a cow country, favored "free grass" and would doubtless be glad to see all the settlers "starve out" and depart for the region from whence they came. His ways were not their ways, nor his thoughts their thoughts, and his interests were certainly not their interests. The nesters wanted more settlers so that they might have a school and preaching at least once or twice a month as well as more and nearer neighbors. The cowboy asserted the grass was the best crop this land would ever produce and that the region would never be a thickly populated farming area; whereas on the hope that it would be just that, the first settlers had well nigh staked "their lives, their fortunes, and their sacred honor." Eager for more neighbors, they wrote letters to friends and relatives in their old home urging them to come west. Some yielded to their entreaties and came, occupying homesteads near those of the first comers. Sod houses or dugouts sprang up—or down—as the case might be, and little communities of settlers began to be formed that were like small islands of crop growing in the midst of the vast area of grazing lands that formed the pastoral empire of the cow country.

These small groups of settlers were but the advance agents of a great population that was soon to follow. In the two decades from 1870 to 1890, the population of the Dakotas increased in round numbers from 14,000 to 719,000, that of

Nebraska from 122,000 to 1,058,000, Kansas from 364,000 to 1,427,000 and Texas from 818,000 to 2,235,000. Making due allowance for inaccuracies in the census returns, these figures are still truly startling, but the full significance of this westward advance can be understood only after an examination of the census returns from some of the central and western counties of such states as Kansas and Nebraska, many of which show a population increase of a hundred fold in a single decade. During the next ten year period, from 1890 to 1900, the increase in population in the western counties of the states mentioned and in the next tier of states to the west was also very great; while Oklahoma Territory with only 61,000 people in 1890 had increased to 400,000 by 1900. Even in the first decade of the twentieth century Oklahoma, western Texas, and portions of other states in the range area show enormous increases in population.

Distrustful and contemptuous as the cowboy was of these earliest settlers upon the range, the time came when he could not entirely ignore them. Eventually the loneliness of life in his line camp or innate curiosity prompted him to stop at some homesteader's dugout or sod house to ask for a drink of water or to inquire about a stray horse. Here he in all probability made a discovery. The nester had a daughter—a comely young woman of eighteen or twenty years who even though she belonged to a despised order was nevertheless amazingly attractive! In a region where there were so few women, the coming of a new girl was regarded as an event of major importance. Too shy to talk much or remain long upon the occasion of his first visit, it was not many days until the cow hand returned bringing his offering in the form of half a quarter of fat beef, of uncertain origin, slung across his saddle.

The settler was suspicious of the Greeks when they came bearing gifts, but the family which had subsisted for weeks on a diet consisting largely of corn bread and buttermilk, warmed a bit to the giver. The wife urged that they could surely do no less than invite him to stay for supper. A kind of *entente cordiale* was established which, if tinged with distrust on both sides, did not perhaps differ so materially from similar arrangements made by nations of modern times. Away from the homesteader's family the cow-puncher sometimes felt a bit conscience stricken over his fall from grace and paid a visit to the daughter of some ranchman thirty miles away. Here he must meet the intense competition of a dozen other buckaroos and this, plus the memory of a pair of bright eyes, eventually brought him back to fraternize once more with this family outside his own caste.

The young woman's father spoke wisely and warningly of these wild cowboys and extolled in glowing terms the virtues of the hard working farm boy on the adjoining claim, but it was plain that the daughter did not altogether agree with him. This is not surprising. After all, the callow granger lad in his overalls, ninety-eight cent wool hat, and heavy plow shoes did not compare favorably with a dashing figure on a spirited horse who rode a fifty dollar saddle, and wore ornate shop made boots, "California trousers," a white Stetson hat, and soft gloves of the finest buckskin. As for the younger children of the household, they made no attempt to conceal their enthusiastic admiration. A man who could ride a bucking horse, rope a steer, and who carried a gun, wore jingling spurs, and gave you half a dollar merely for opening a gate for him was someone to admire! They compared the two pound box of candy which he handed out so carelessly with the skimpy dime's worth brought from town by their father or the neighboring farm youth to be divided among four or five children, and it began to be plain where their affections lay.

It was not long until they began to imitate their hero. The father found his two younger sons trying to rope the dog with an improvised *riata* made from their mother's clothes line, or staging a rodeo back of the barn with the milk pen calves playing the rôle of bucking broncos. They played cowboy and whittled pistols from wood long before a certain public enemy, who found such a contrivance useful, was born. Sent on an errand to the little store and post office that had been established in the new community, they lingered to listen to the conversation of the cow hands who had dropped in to inquire for the mail or to lay in a supply of tobacco. After remaining as long as they dared, the lads at last returned to their home with the best alibi they could muster and a vocabulary vastly enlarged even if not exactly enriched. The old songs brought from the East as the "Gypsy's Warning" and "Silver Threads Among the Gold" were apparently forgotten and the Sabbath stillness of the settler's home was shattered by such mournful productions as the "Dying Cowboy" or "Bury Me Not on the Lone Prairie." The mother, torn between a natural feminine love for a romantic figure and fears for her daughter's happiness, began in time to yield a somewhat reluctant admiration to a generous and attractive young man.

After several calls upon the young woman, the cowboy summoned up courage to ask her to accompany him to a dance, but unless in the northern zone of settlement where the German or Scandinavian element was large, he in all probability met with a courteous but uncompromising refusal. Dancing in many regions seems to be at the two

extremes of civilized society. The primitive and the sophisticated both dance, but the in-betweens will have none of it.
The girl made it plain that she was a member of the church
and dancing was taboo. They were building a little school
house in the neighborhood and expected to have preaching
at least once a month. If he cared to go with her to church or
literary society or even to a social or play party at some
settler's home, perhaps it could be arranged, but a dance was
not to be considered. Even if she were willing to go, her
parents would object and she was a dutiful and obedient
daughter. So a play party or social it must be, attended
largely by sons and daughters of the nesters. Here such
games as "Miller Boy," "Down to Rowsers'," and "Shoot
the Buffalo" were played by the young people, while their
fathers and mothers, who thought dancing the invention of
the devil, looked on with smiling approbation. Later when
the school house was finished, he accompanied her some
Sunday to church and sat throughout the sermon in a state
of painful self-consciousness which was considerably accen-
tuated when she whispered to him her wish that he, too,
might make "Heaven his destination."

As more settlers came in, the school house became something of a social center. Here were held singings, literary
society meetings, and box suppers. At the last named, the boxes
were sold at auction and young men would bid vociferously
against one another for the box of some particularly attractive
girl. After the boxes had all been sold, a cake was often
given to the most popular young lady. Votes were usually
one cent each, and in most cases there were but two leading
candidates. One of these represented the range riders' interests—usually some ranchman's daughter who was clever and
witty, an excellent dancer, and commonly known as "good

company"—whatever that might mean. In opposition to her the homesteaders would nominate a young woman who taught a Sunday school class, led the singing at church, and was known to be "good to wait on the sick." The two girls were conducted to the end of the room and seated near the teacher's desk where everyone could see the candidate for whom he was voting, and the contest began. As votes were called out and the money passed to the cashier, tellers checked on the blackboard the number of votes. In such cases the cowboys—even those who had shown some attention to a nester girl—usually rallied to the colors, while the granger lads and their fathers were equally determined to elect their nominee and vote *that girl* down! Eventually it became more than a contest between two personable young women. It was a conflict between two social and economic orders. To many of the settlers it was a struggle of the forces of evil against good, of darkness against light, of the past against the future. "Let us elect our candidate and prove to all that this is a progressive, God-fearing community, that the reign of the wild cow-puncher is over, that civilization is mighty and will prevail." Quite often the cow hands, who drew some thirty dollars a month in real money, were able to pay for more votes than could the poverty stricken settlers. Reckless with their money as in all else, the range riders did not hesitate to pay out their last dollar for votes, but the homesteaders did their best and if they went down in defeat, they felt that this was merely another example of the triumph of might over right and of money over principles. They were certain that their day was coming and that it would not be long delayed.

In this they were not mistaken. Settlers continued to pour

into the cow country in ever increasing numbers and take up homesteads along the streams and in the more fertile areas of the wide prairies. The ranchmen were forced back into the rougher uplands sometimes remote from an adequate supply of water. Good land, however, produces good grass, while barren hills and thin soils afforded poor grazing. For a time there still seemed to be an abundance of pasturage. The cow men did not at first understand how much their range had suffered by the homesteading and fencing of the more fertile lowlands. Then they began to realize that their cattle did not fatten. They looked about for additional pasture lands, but they were not to be found. The range was steadily shrinking. Indian reservations were opened to settlement and a flood of homesteaders poured in, still further reducing the area that could be utilized for grazing. A village began to grow up about the first general store established in each community. Soon there came a second store, then a third, followed by a blacksmith shop, a hotel, and a church. Railroads began to penetrate the cow country and the village grew into a real town. Good land began to grow scarce. The homesteaders were soon very much in the majority in most parts of the cow country where there was sufficient rainfall for the growing of crops. Under such circumstances the fusion of the two social and economic orders went on rapidly. More and more cow-punchers began to call upon young women of the settler class. Dimly they began to comprehend how difficult it was for a man on a raw one hundred sixty acre claim to provide his family with the bare necessities of life. They saw the pitiful extremities to which the daughter of the household was driven to secure suitable clothing in order to keep herself attractive and to join in the social life of the community. Toleration took the place of the former antagonism and they began "first to endure, then pity, then embrace."

The homesteader, under the influence of closer association, found his prejudices beginning to melt. After all, these cowboys were not as bad as he had thought. Perhaps daughter might do worse. Unconsciously, his own conduct and psychology began to be at least slightly influenced by the customs of the range area. His horizon became wider. Finding he must travel greater distances than in the old home, he acquired another horse or two, secured a better saddle, and sometimes surprised his wife by the purchase of things formerly regarded as luxuries.

As the influx of settlers continued, church and school assumed a larger importance. An arbor was constructed and a revival meeting was held where cow hands who came to scoff sometimes remained to pray. Under the thundering sound of the minister's voice their thoughts turned to the sins of earlier days. They were strangely moved when the congregation sang "Almost Persuaded" or "Turn Sinners Turn," and they gazed with open mouthed awe while the three hundred pound wife of a settler gave a solo rendition of "Love Lifted Me," thereby furnishing uncontrovertible proof of the power of redeeming love! Seeing how much a deep religious faith meant to people who must endure the hardships and vicissitudes of pioneer life, they sometimes sought in religion consolation for their own fast multiplying troubles.

The ranchman, finding his range reduced, must purchase feed from the settlers or lease from them their surplus grazing land. Business relations once established paved the way for closer social relations. The old time hostilities and prejudices were passing. There were bitter-enders, of course, in both groups who found their dislike of the other class only intensified by association, but these were in the minority. Generally speaking, the reverse was true. If the examples, given largely in terms of individuals or single communities, should be multiplied by several thousand, a fairly correct picture would be presented of the cow country in transition.

As more of the range was settled and plowed, the ranchman found he must reduce his herds and began to ship all merchantable cattle to market. The settlers, once they had secured a majority in a community, usually proceeded to vote a herd law which forced the ranchmen to acquire land in fee and enclose it with wire fences. With reduced herds and fenced pastures, the rancher needed fewer men; cowboys of long experience found themselves out of a job and realized that it was impossible to secure one. Those retained, who had formerly scorned to do anything but ride, were forced to engage in such lowly work as building fences, plowing fire guards, and planting or harvesting forage crops —since with grazing lands so greatly reduced it had become necessary to feed cattle in winter. Some men out of employment rode farther west, seeking a region where they might hope to spend their lives in the cattle business, but it soon became apparent that there were not jobs enough for all. Many, especially those who had acquired a measure of tolerance for the new order, frankly accepted the changed conditions, married a nester girl, and took up a homestead. Here they grazed a few cattle, but it was not long until they began to plow and plant in awkward fashion and in time some became fairly successful farmers.

No doubt, most of these marriages were happy ones, though it is possible that a larger proportion were not successful than in the case of marriages between persons of less widely divergent backgrounds. Such a statement is impossible to prove, though some evidence exists that it may be true. Texas, with a population of slightly over three million in 1900, granted in the twenty year period from 1887 to 1906 over sixty-two thousand divorces, while Massachusetts, with a population of slightly less than three million in 1900, granted in the same twenty year period less than twenty-three thousand, and Pennsylvania, with a population of over six million, only thirty-nine thousand. Kansas, with a population of less than one and a half million, had nearly twenty-nine thousand divorces in the period from 1887 to 1906, while New Jersey, with a considerably larger population, had less than eight thousand. Colorado had nearly sixteen thousand divorces in this twenty year period, though the total poulation in 1900 was only slightly over half a million, while Connecticut, with a population nearly twice as great, had in round numbers only nine thousand. No doubt the greater ease with which divorce could be secured in a western state had its effect, but the very fact that divorce laws were more liberal in such states is in itself significant.

Not all cowboys who found their vocation gone would become farmers. Many who still hated the new order drifted to town seeking employment that would not put them into the class of the despised nesters. Three lines of business appealed to them and all three were doomed to speedy extinction. They could open a butcher shop in some small town, buying and slaughtering their own cattle; they could establish a livery stable and continue to work with horses; or they could open a saloon. With the coming of railroads and refrigerator cars, the great packing houses forced the local butchers out of business; the automobile destroyed the livery stable; and local option and later prohibition closed the saloon.

The ranchman fared no better in the midst of changed conditions than did his cow punchers. Some few who were wise accepted the inevitable, sold their cattle for what they would bring, bought a little land, and established a live stock farm. Others who were foolish tried to hold out as long as possible, borrowed money at ruinous rates of interest in order to rent pasturage or purchase feed, and in most cases lost everything. Their lax business methods might be satisfactory enough in a region where everyone else practiced the same code, but in a society which pinched pennies and drove hard bargains such methods could end only in disaster and financial ruin. The wrecks of many ranching enterprises that strew the one time cow country give eloquent testimony as to how far this is true.

The desperation with which some ranchmen clung to the old order is little short of tragic. Like the Indians of the Ghost Dance who believed that the whites would vanish from the earth and the plains again be covered with buffalo, some of these men with an almost religious fervor held fast to the belief that the nesters would eventually return to the old homes from whence they had come and that the region would once more become a pastoral empire as in days gone by. Their awakening came late, but in most cases it was thorough. Pasturage grew more and more restricted. Every portion of the range area suitable for crop growing—and much which it now seems was not suitable—was occupied. The cattle disappeared from the plains as if by magic and farmers armed with the tools of their craft sprang up on all sides as though some unseen hand had planted dragons' teeth on every hill and in every valley.

333

At last the cow man realized that the old order was gone and broken in fortune, in many cases, he accepted the inevitable and set to work at strange tasks often with only his two hands with which to earn a living for himself and family. One who knows at first hand the story of these men is likely to forget their shortsightedness and poor judgment and to think only of their courage. Occasionally one of these men who has not yet accepted the new order may still be seen. Such an individual stands like a blackened tree trunk in the midst of plowed fields, a mute reminder of a bygone era. Janus like, he looks in two directions—toward an old world that has gone forever and toward a new one which he does not even remotely understand.

Though the cow country has passed away and the social order it produced is largely a memory, its influence throughout the region where that order once prevailed is still apparent. It is not mere accident that the University of Texas calls its magnificent dining hall the "Chuck Wagon" or that the walls of one of its finest buildings should display the old cattle brands of the Lone Star state, while a similar building at Harvard has carved beneath its eaves quotations from the Bible or from the classics. It is not by chance that traveling salesmen avidly read cowboy stories or that thousands of staid, sober citizens attend each year the rodeos held at many places in what was once the cow country. It is significant that Rotarians purchase from mail order houses cowboy suits for their offspring and that thousands of people tune in each evening to hear some crooner render, with a Manhattan accent, "A Home on the Range" or "The Last Round-up." One finds a distinguished college professor decorating his office with a magnificent pair of steer horns and framed pictures of trail herds, round-up wagons, and other cowboy scenes. Throughout the West dude ranches have sprung up where college boys and girls, tired business men, and society matrons may for a consideration dress in leather chaps and ten gallon hats and ride the range under suitable guidance, returning in the evening to eat from tin plates about a mess table and to sleep in a glorified bunk house.

Occasionally, in a more civilized society, a bit of the wild lawlessness of other days crops out as a reminder of the code of men long since dead. Old man cow country has gone, but his spirit still lives on in a generation that never knew him in the flesh. He was a good old man according to the standards by which he lived. May his memory long remain green in the hearts of his descendants.

Memories of Frederick Jackson Turner[*]

My first meeting with Turner was at Harvard in September, 1913. I had landed in Cambridge only a few days before, with an A.B. degree awarded two years before by my own little state university, one of Harvard's Austin teacher's scholarships, a few hundred dollars in money, and an overweening ambition to secure a master's degree from Harvard. Twenty-five of my thirty-four years had been spent on the plains of southwestern Oklahoma, where I had seen that region grow, as Turner later expressed it, "from the picturesque wildness of those early days to the equally picturesque wildness of the present day."

According to the registration procedure of the time, the professors had assembled in a large room of one of the buildings on the Yard, where they sat at small tables scattered about the room to receive and advise with students who wished to register for their courses. I was directed to Turner's table, and with all the assurance of a westerner introduced myself and extended my hand in greeting. My memory of him is of a man with a strong, well-knit figure, bronzed complexion, a close-cropped mustache, and blazing blue eyes. He appeared to be something of an outdoor man, for he was dressed in a suit of rough tweed with sturdy tan shoes. When he shook hands I noticed that his hand was hard

* Published in *Mississippi Valley Historical Review*, XXX (December, 1943), 339–58.

as though he had been engaged in manual labor, which he had—if paddling a canoe on the lakes of Maine may be so designated.

One of his colleagues came past while we were talking and stopped to ask how he had spent the vacation period. "Up in the Maine woods," replied Turner, adding, a trifle wistfully, "and I wish I were up in the Maine woods now."

He talked to me for a few minutes and registered me for two of his courses, History 17, "The West," and 20K, "Individual Research." Both were full courses, extending throughout the year, and so constituted one-half of my first year's work at Harvard. With deep shame it must be confessed that at this time my knowledge of Turner was close to absolute zero. In justice to myself, it may be stated that neither his volume of essays, *The Frontier in American History*, nor his *Sections* had as yet been published in book form. I had read his *Rise of the New West* but apparently it had made little impression, while of his so-called "thesis" I was in total ignorance.

Turner's first lectures in History 17 opened up to me a new heaven and a new earth in the field of American history. Perhaps my abysmal ignorance of his theories and previous work was not without its advantages. I had no preconceived notions, no thin veneer of knowledge, to confuse me or obscure the crystal clarity with which he expressed his views on the subject so dear to his heart—the significance of the American frontier.

When Turner referred to the frontier of the hunter, the cowboy, and of pioneer agriculture, he was on ground which was to me strangely familiar. Had I not hunted and trapped wolves for two years, worked as a cowhand and small ranchman, and lived in a sod-house home, wringing a living of

337

sorts from the scanty soil of newly plowed prairie sod? When he talked of the successive stages of development in the West, I recalled seeing Oklahoma change from an almost unpeopled wilderness to a thickly populated land of homes, churches, schools, towns, and cities. I had seen towns grow, within a dozen years, from a few tents and shacks to attractive cities with all modern conveniences, dugouts replaced by white farm houses, straw-covered sheds grow to big red barns, and the scrawny sprouts of fruit trees to thriving orchards. I had observed the coming of rural mail delivery, trails widened to broad highways, the formation of consolidated schools instead of one-room box shanties; and had seen regions as large as some eastern states transformed in a decade from virgin prairie to stable civilization.

When he spoke of the frontiersman's lack of respect for the letter of the law and of extra-legal institutions evolved, I recalled ministers of the gospel who hauled wood from the lands of an Indian reservation, keeping diligent watch for United States deputy marshals as they cut and loaded the scrubby mesquite trees, nominally the property of the Kiowa-Comanche Indians. Yet these men were often called upon to adjudicate disputes between two neighbors who, in a region remote from courts of law, preferred such extra-legal methods of settling their differences to a more orthodox or conventional one.

References to Liberty, Equality, Fraternity, as frontier watchwords brought to mind the freedom from restraint afforded by life on the southwestern Plains, where we had no game laws, nor too much law of any kind, where the slogan of all social events was "everybody invited, nobody slighted," and where kind friends would assemble to work an unfortunate neighbor's crop, to nurse the sick, or bury the dead.

I had lived so close to all these things that they were conditions to be accepted as a matter of course. It had been impossible for me to see the forest for the trees, or the city for the houses. But Turner's lectures changed all this. It was with a distinct shock that there came to me the realization that what I had seen take place within the short space of a couple of decades in Oklahoma was, in miniature, an evolution of society—a development of civilization which in most parts of our country had required two or three generations and in the world as a whole a thousand years. Proof of virtually every theory which Turner advanced I had witnessed in practice, though at the time it had been meaningless.

That was a great course and a great class. George W. Stephenson, now of the University of Minnesota, was the assistant and gave lectures on the public domain several times when Turner was ill. Avery Craven, now of the University of Chicago, was a member—together with a number of others who have since achieved more or less fame in fields of scholarship, politics, or business.

In the research course known as 20K I met Turner for an hour each week. Here my sketchy preparation, or lack of preparation, for graduate work in history was at once painfully apparent. My desire was to write a history of my own state, and with painstaking care and supreme confidence I had prepared some twelve or fifteen topics, with the idea of developing all of them in such fashion that the completed work would be a fairly comprehensive history of Oklahoma. Turner looked at my topics, and smiled in a quizzical fashion as he said, "I think any one of these might prove quite satisfactory as a subject for research, but to work on all of them would be, clearly, quite impossible." A little dashed by this I gave up the original idea and set to work, with his approval, on the subject, "Conditions in the Indian Territory in 1888." Turner helped from time to time with suggestions and counsel—but the finished manuscript must have been pretty terrible. Yet he was always patient and kind, though he did not hesitate to point out blunders and weaknesses. "This is a dead thing," he said to me at last. "Are there no contemporary accounts that could be found in letters, diaries, or other personal manuscripts, that might add human interest? You have given the facts, but what we want is to see the wheels go 'round."

During the second half-year my problem was the "White Settlement of Oklahoma." As in the period of preparing the former study, Turner met with me for an hour once a week, and I am sure that we both looked forward to these conferences with some pleasure. He seemed to feel that an ex-cowboy should be able to give him some first-hand information, and in consequence asked me many questions and evinced a lively interest in the answers. At the same time he was frank as to my shortcomings. "You are an astonishing fellow," he once said to me. "At times I am amazed by your knowledge of things which I have no right to expect a college graduate to know, and at others I am equally amazed by your ignorance of things that I would have every right to expect a college-trained man should know."

Near the close of the year I was elected to an instructorship in history at my Alma Mater, the University of Oklahoma. This meant definitely giving up public school work and raised the question of my eventually taking a doctor's degree. Turner encouraged me, though he did not appear to think too much of the Ph.D. degree. "There is only one question," said he, "and that is your age. But you are far younger than your years would imply, and it seems to me that you should do it. My own doctor's degree was delayed for a good many years, but friends wanted me to take it, and I am glad that I did, but have never believed that my work or career would have been greatly different if I had not."

In consequence, it was with the definite intention of returning eventually for further graduate study that I started for home in June, 1914. The next two years were spent largely in teaching history and government to undergraduates. I was eager to do a dissertation on some phase of the history of my own state, preferably the ranch cattle industry. In the spring of 1916 I was awarded another Austin teacher's scholarship and made my plans to return to Harvard the following autumn.

Turner wrote, however, that he was taking sabbatical leave during 1916–1917 and so would not be in Cambridge during that year, but would be glad to learn from time to time how my work was progressing, though, of course, he could not undertake the direction of a dissertation while on leave. In consequence I spent this year at Harvard largely in course work with various professors and in preparing for the general examinations which were taken shortly before my return to Oklahoma in June, 1917.

The following year was spent in teaching—broken by various unsuccessful attempts to get into the Army—and in preliminary work on my dissertation which, it had been decided, should be "A History of the Range Cattle Industry in Oklahoma." Turner had approved the subject and during this year I had spent much time in planning and outlining the proposed study, aided by a great collection of the private papers of some important early-day ranchmen.

In the summer of 1918 I returned to Harvard to spend a couple of months in the library, and there completed a very detailed outline. Turner was spending his vacation at Hancock Point, Maine, where he had a summer cottage. As the time approached for my return to Oklahoma, I decided to go to Hancock Point for a few days' vacation to see Turner and talk with him about my dissertation. This decision was another example of my complete ignorance. Turner was on vacation and, of course, should not have been disturbed by the presence of an inquiring student.

But "fools rush in . . ."; so I traveled by train to Mt. Desert ferry and walked the two or three miles along the beach to the tiny village of Hancock Point. This consisted of only a summer hotel, one or two stores and shops, and two or three residences. Turner's cottage, together with half a dozen others scattered along the beach, was less than half a mile from the hotel. I was dressed in rough-weather costume— flannel shirt, tweed jacket, riding breeches, and puttees—and carried the barest necessities in a tiny bag. Since it was near the end of the season, the hotel was not crowded and it was not difficult to secure a room. This attended to, I walked to the cottage to call on the Turners.

They both seemed delighted to see me. Dorothy was married and living in Madison, Wisconsin. Turner and his wife had been alone, except for the maid, during the summer. Perhaps they were a little lonely and the quiet life of fishing and walking about the beach or over the hills had begun to pall a trifle on them, so that the presence of even an unbidden guest was welcome. At any rate, they received me very cordially, and Turner and I sat on the porch and talked about the dissertation as we went over the outline step by step.

"I like it," he said at last. "I believe you are going to have a good piece of work." He invited me to come back for dinner the next evening, and I left the cottage in high spirits.

When I returned the following evening, Turner was again very cordial, but slightly apologetic. He had been fishing and had some flounders in the icebox which he had planned to have for supper, but he had forgotten that it was the maid's afternoon out. Such being the case, they would have to take me to the hotel for dinner. This prompted me to offer a suggestion. I said, "Professor Turner, the first lesson which a cowboy learns is that he has two choices: he can either cook or starve. I have always preferred to cook, so if you would like to have flounders for supper it will be a pleasure to go into the kitchen and fry them and prepare supper."

Turner's face brightened. "Let's do it!" he said. "I think it would be fun." I repaired to the kitchen, donned an apron which Mrs. Turner provided, and proceeded to make a pan of biscuits—praying all the time that my hand had not lost its cunning—and to fry the flounders. They were all dressed and ready for cooking, and required only to be salted a little and rolled in flour and dropped in the skillet of sizzling hot fat. It was war time, and the Turner cupboard was a bit scanty on lard, but there was enough to do. Good fortune was with me. The biscuits came out of the oven light and flaky, and their rich brown color matched that of the fried flounders. I also made a pot of coffee and, with the addition of jelly and pickles, we sat down to a real feast. Turner was apparently in high spirits. When Mrs. Turner expressed regret that it was Mary Ann's afternoon out and, in consequence, the guest had to cook his own supper, Turner exclaimed, "I am glad she's gone. Mary Ann in her palmiest days never fried flounders or made biscuits like these!"

I stayed at Hancock Point for more than a week and saw

Turner every day with the exception of one when I crossed over to the island to visit Bar Harbor and climb the mountains back of it. He had a canoe with swelling sides which he called "The Mumps," and in this we paddled about the edge of Frenchman's Bay and fished for flounders. It was not very thrilling sport merely to bait a hook with a clam, lower it deep into the water, and pull up a fish when a slight tug was felt at the line. He taught me the elementary principles of paddling a canoe, which he explained were not too different from the strokes used in wielding a broom. Learning that I had never seen a sculpin he was not content until he had caught one of these evil-looking creatures for my inspection. Flounders were delicious eating, and when we had caught a number, for they were not large, we would pull back to the beach and build a fire of driftwood. Mrs. Turner would bring down from the cabin the necessary picnic equipment, together with bread and coffee, and we would have a wonderful "shore dinner." After the dishes had been washed and put away Turner and I would lie on the sand on the sunny side of a rock and talk, sometimes for hours.

He seemed interested in my frontier experiences as hunter, cowboy, clerk in a trading post, claim holder, deputy sheriff, and rural school teacher. This prompted me to relate numerous yarns of incidents, humorous or tragic, which I had witnessed in earlier years in a remote region from forty to eighty miles from the nearest railroad. He also related a number of his own. One of these was about going far up into the Maine woods on a fishing trip with a single companion. After going as far as they could by canoe, it was necessary to tramp ten or twelve miles to the cabin, carrying on their shoulders heavy packs of food and equipment. He said that both were fast approaching complete exhaustion long before they had reached the end of their journey, and made the last three or four miles only by constantly reminding one another of a bottle of a particularly delectable type of cocktail which they promised themselves to sit down and share the moment they reached their destination. When their lagging feet had at last brought them to the cabin, however, and they sank down on the ground and opened the pack, they discovered that as they clambered over some big rocks the bottle had been broken and the last drop of the precious liquid was gone. Turner said that this was one of the major disappointments of his life!

He inquired eagerly about the relations between the ranchmen and the settlers who came to displace them, which prompted more stories of my own experiences with this phase of frontier history. He also expressed considerable interest in the Indians of Oklahoma and was surprised to learn that the Kiowas and Comanches would never break their own horses to ride if a white man could be hired to do it for them. He observed, however, that he had always noticed that Indians were by no means daredevils, for he had, in some instances, seen white men in canoes running rapids which none of the natives would venture to tackle.

I expressed some surprise that Turner was not swimming every day, for the water looked very inviting. He remarked that it was a bit cold and that he did not often swim, but we would celebrate my visit with a plunge if I liked. I saw a twinkle in his eye and felt that he was challenging my hardihood, which made me determined to take a dip in the ocean even if it were necessary to break the ice in order to have that privilege. We accordingly donned bathing suits, walked down to the sea, and from the top of a half-submerged rock plunged into the icy water. The word "icy" is too mild. We

swam about for a few minutes; then Turner proposed that
we go out, and no second invitation was needed. I had fully
learned that the sea on the upper part of the Maine coast the
first of September is no place to enjoy a swim.

The following year was spent in teaching at Oklahoma
University, but in the summer of 1919 I was married and
returned with my wife to Cambridge, arriving just in time
to do a turn for law and order in the Boston police strike,
since before school opened I served as a volunteer policeman
in the South End. This brought me some notoriety through
newspaper publicity because I asked for and secured permission from the police captain to take my own 45 Colt's "six
gun," as well as the regular little police revolver when I
went out to walk my beat. During this year of 1919–1920
my entire time was given to the dissertation except for a half
course on manuscript materials in American history with
Worthington Ford. Memories of the florid fashion in which
my introductory chapter was originally begun still bring a
blush of embarrassment. The opening sentences were something like this:

The herding industry is as old as mankind. Abraham, Isaac, and
Jacob grazed herds of cattle, and the strife between Cain and
Abel has been referred to as the first conflict between range and
grange.

Turner's comment on this awful tripe was characteristic of
the tactful manner in which he dealt with all of my adoles-
cent vagaries in graduate work. He said: "You have fallen
into an error common to most amateurs. When I started my
dissertation on the early fur trade of Wisconsin I began with
some discussion of the fur trade among the ancient Carthaginians. It did not take my old professor long to tell me that
if he were writing on the early fur trade in Wisconsin he

would not concern himself too much about the fur trade of the ancient Carthaginians."

Turner always seemed to have time for his students. Perhaps it was because of this that Channing once remarked to me: "Turner is a dear fellow, but he has no idea of the value of time. He has never written any big books." I made no answer, but in my mind was the thought that this was not necessary. Turner could say more in one brief essay than most historians did in an entire volume.

Perhaps there is some truth, however, in the statement that Turner did not have sufficient appreciation of the value of time. At least he gave a great deal of it to my wife and me during that year. For example, we had Christmas dinner with the Turners and later they took us to dinner at a Chinese restaurant which they had discovered in Boston's Chinatown. Mrs. Turner spent much of the latter part of the winter in Wisconsin and during her absence Turner came to our apartment more than once to informal little suppers of "flap jacks" and sausage. He insisted on taking us to "Pop's Concert," on our spending an entire evening in his home after dinner at the Cockhorse Inn, and on one occasion dashed over through a heavy rain to spend an evening with me and an Indian visitor from Oklahoma who told lurid tales of his corrugated past.

My dissertation, like most, presented many difficult problems and eventually grew to a very considerable length. My wife did the typing, and Turner read every chapter with me and suggested corrections. It was not finished until the first of June—far too late for me to take my final examination. We said goodbye to the Turners and returned to Oklahoma, where I was to teach in the summer session.

My plan was to read American history and review all of

my previous work during the next year while teaching and to return for my final examination in approximately fifteen months, or early in the autumn of 1921. Our son was born late in August, 1920, however, and during the following year so much time was required for "day herding my students" and "night herding the offspring" that not too much time was left for study. Accordingly, I returned to Cambridge soon after the first of August, 1921, for a couple of months' intensive review before the final examination.

Professor and Mrs. Turner were away, presumably at Hancock Point, and I did not see them until school had opened, late in September. Since my wife and son had, of course, been left at home, I took a room and spent ten or twelve hours a day in hard study. On the morning of October fourth, which was the date set for the examination, a friend drove by and asked me to go with him to Quincy, where he had some errands to do, assuring me that he would get me back in plenty of time for the examination at four o'clock that afternoon. He was, of course, merely trying to curb my nervousness, for he did not return me to my room until two o'clock. I rested for a little while and then bathed and dressed in careful fashion—determined, like immortal Caesar, to "die with decency"—and set out for what seemed not unlike a rendezvous with death.

I took a seat in the entrance hall of the room in which the examination was to be held and my committee, consisting of Haskins, Turner, Hart, and McIlwain, eventually drifted in. Undoubtedly seeing my nervousness, Turner shook hands, giving me a grip which I recognized.

My showing on the examination was probably far from brilliant, but it was at least much better than had been the case in my generals some years before. At the end of two hours it was over, and I was sent into the hall while the committee conferred. Naturally I paced the floor, for what seemed to me a week, though the clock indicated it was only five or ten minutes before the members of the committee came out. Some days before, at Turner's request, I had given him four or five posed snapshots of myself in cowboy costume. When he came through the door he was putting these back into his wallet. Evidently he had been passing them around for inspection by other members of the committee during the time I was having chills and fever from thinking of the weighty deliberations that were going on as they pondered the question of my passing. Members of the committee all shook hands with me and offered their congratulations. Professor Hart asked me to go to dinner with him at the Harvard Club while Turner suggested that I go to his house and make some flapjacks while he stirred up a Welsh rabbit. Both of these invitations had to be refused, for I had promised a friend to have dinner with him at the Boston City Club—if I were still alive at six o'clock. So to the Boston City Club we went for a "Victory Dinner."

Before leaving for Oklahoma the following day, I called to bid Turner goodbye. There was no thought in my mind that we should not be meeting often in the future, but it was not to be, for I never saw him again. We corresponded, however, more or less regularly until a short time before his death. His letters, usually of an intimate, personal nature, seem to me quite revealing as to his qualities of heart and mind.

Early in 1923 Oklahoma's new governor became involved in a controversy with the state legislature as well as with certain individuals and organizations within the state. The governor attributed much of the criticism directed against him to the Ku Klux Klan, which was at that time quite powerful in Oklahoma. The general turmoil seemed to threaten adequate appropriations for our university and, while such threats fortunately never were translated into action, some members of our faculty including myself became a bit disturbed over the outlook. In consequence I wrote to Turner suggesting my willingness to take a position elsewhere, if a fairly good one were available. Turner wrote me as follows:

The Moorings
Hancock Point, Maine

May 27, 1923

DEAR PROFESSOR DALE:

I am sorry that you have been ill and that things go badly with the Oklahoma control and funds. I wonder just what is happening in the Southwest, for I hear the same reports from Texas. Perhaps Democracy is getting an *education*—expensively and with hardship to the faculties.

I shall let Dean Haskins know the situation, and shall keep you in mind myself. But I am retiring at the end of the coming academic year in order to write instead of teach—if I may; and I do not know of all the vacancies. I judge there may be one in. . . . It is rumored that . . . is leaving there; but don't quote me to that effect.

Your difficulty in any change is likely to be due to the fact that your salary is now higher than that in most of the openings —and the new crops of Ph.D.'s are accepting less. So if you can weather the storm and help to keep Oklahoma's course steady, it may be worth the unpleasantness. But you are the best judge.

We both send regards to your wife and yourself. I have been on sabbatical (working on a book) this half year; and came up here the middle of May, whereupon I was treated to a series of bilious attacks, from which I am just recovering, and [am] going back for a few days to Cambridge tonight. But this will be my summer address.

Yours sincerely,
FREDERICK J. TURNER

Fortunately, the political upheaval in Oklahoma was of short duration and early in the autumn I wrote Turner that everything was all right again and told him of my promotion and advance in salary, at the same time sending him a separate of one of my magazine articles on ranching. Turner replied almost immediately.

7 Phillips Place
Cambridge 38, Mass.

Oct. 31, 1923

DEAR DALE:

I am glad to learn that you have escaped the hands of the Klan and of the Governor both! Perhaps your experience on the Boston frontier, as a "two gun man" stood you in good stead. Coolidge ought to remember your services! Congratulations on your advance. I look to see your full paper published. The briefer article is well written and well organized, I think, and I am glad to have a separate. Perhaps you will donate one to the History 17 "Reservation" for the use of your successors. Good luck to you and Oklahoma!

We had a pleasant summer in our Maine home,—hated to leave and are already planning our return, for we hope to spend half of our time there. I think I may send the bulk of my library up there, and use the Wisconsin library in the winter,—Cambridge too expensive for my income!

Give our warm regards to the wife and boy. Don't fail to let us know when you come to New England. We like to see you.

Cordially yours,
FREDERICK J. TURNER

The Turners spent the winter of 1924–1925 in Madison, Wisconsin, and he wrote me once or twice, sending me a picture of his little home there together with brief greetings. About holiday season I wrote him and sent a few things including a song called "Pal O'Mine," for which I had written the lyric. There was also included a volume prepared by

351

one of our professors called an *Anthology of Oklahoma Verse*, which contained a number of my so-called poems; and finally, a copy of my *High School History of Oklahoma*. This last named had been offered to the State Text Book Commission for adoption, but had been rejected and I bewailed the fact in a somewhat doleful fashion. I also told Turner of my promotion to the headship of the Department of History and of being granted six months' leave of absence to do a study of the range cattle industry on the Plains for the Bureau of Agricultural Economics of the United States Department of Agriculture. Turner answered my letter as follows:

2214 Van Hise Avenue
Madison, Wisconsin

January 29, 1925

DEAR DALE:

It was a full meal and *intellectually* as pleasing as the homemade sausages in Cambridge, and the flounders at the Hancock Point beach were *stomachically*. Being a *retired* Professor of History, however, I can be quite frank at the expense of my professional properties, and admit that the poems went right to my heart and got first reading. They deserve a wide circle of readers. Every one of yours has a real quality and appeals to me. Mrs. Turner and I both are therefore happy to have on our piano your "Pal O'Mine" in its appealing musical dress. Tell the Pal it makes us want to show her the house and its contents.

"The Vagabond" is bully, but why not let your "Pal O'Mine" hike with you on the friendly road? "Butterside Down" is a joy forever—particularly the lines on the "shining crown."

You are in good company in the Anthology—though many of the best poems seem to spring from other than Oklahoma soil. I wonder if I don't know said soil; or if the poems are from eastern or Old World pens temporarily in the state; or if the state has so quickly passed through all the stages of growth— from green blade to over-ripe fruit; or if they are merely evidence of the capability of clever Oklahoma students to do the sort of thing that takes in New York.

Some other time I will write of History. Your book on Oklahoma looks as though it should have won out. I know how to sympathise with you, for once when I walked home from my seminar with one of my graduate students, he pulled out of his trousers pocket the check for his current quarterly royalty from his adopted state history. It was for more money than all my writings together ever brought me! But any one who can make and cook sausages and flapjacks is independent of fortune.

I am glad to hear of your promotion if it doesn't mean substitution of administrative duties for history writing. It is gratifying to learn that Oklahoma politics are quieter.

Our affectionate regards to you and Mrs. Dale and the Son. Please remember me to Wardell.

Cordially yours,
Frederick J. Turner

I see I haven't mentioned the fact that I think the Washington staff in Agriculture show their good sense in getting your aid. I know you will enjoy the work. Several of the group are former students of mine whom I like and admire. Remember me to them.

F. J. T.

On their way to the Henry Huntington Library in the winter of 1926–1927, the Turners stopped at Tucson to see my wife, who was visiting her sister at that place. My own work at that time had taken me to the wilds of Montana where I was trailing Indians, having been granted a year's leave of absence to serve on the Indian Survey staff of the Brookings Foundation, which was making a study of conditions among the Indians at the request of Secretary of the Interior Hubert Work.

After my return to the University of Oklahoma, other occasional letters from Turner reached me from time to time. These were usually brief, for his health was not good, and they were always written on a typewriter, in contrast to his former ones, which were invariably penned by his own hand. He always seemed interested in my work, particularly that with respect to Oklahoma. Early in the autumn of 1930 I wrote him of my success in securing a generous gift from Frank Phillips, a wealthy Oklahoma oil man, to enable me to assemble a collection of materials on western history, and at the same time sent him a copy of my recently published *Range Cattle Industry*. He replied as follows:

Henry Huntington Library and Art Gallery
San Marino, California

November 10, 1930

DEAR DALE:

I am very glad to hear from you and to know of your success. The study of Oklahoma and its region offers you a very splendid chance for collection and writing, and I am glad that you are finding the necessary funds. So much has been done in the way of the romance of the region that, I think, economic and social researches are now especially important. So far as I am aware, no adequate survey has ever been made of the rise of the oil industry there and its effects upon the settlement and industrial development of the region. It must have greatly changed the whole life.

Please give the regards of myself and wife to your wife. I should certainly like to see that ten-year-old boy. Your *Range Cattle Industry* I had the pleasure of taking a look at, by courtesy of the Huntington Library, and I shall be glad to make a thorough reading of it. I have no doubt that the content is fully up to the standard of mechanical workmanship, although that is impressive.

I suppose you know that I have been laid up for a couple of years, after an operation; and I am only doing part work, but am now going to the Library for an hour or two every day and am able to do some additional work.

Cordially yours,
FREDERICK J. TURNER

Later in the same year he sent me two or three lines in regard to the book, *Frontier Trails*, published a month or so before, which I had edited.

December 10, 1930

DEAR DALE:

My wife and I have been reading with excitement your Frank Canton, *Frontier Trails*. What a personality he was, and how fortunate you were in preserving his recollections!

Sincerely yours,

FREDERICK J. TURNER

The following year, in response to a letter mentioning my recent completion of a novel dealing with western life, Turner wrote me a note consisting of a single sentence: "Your work in history is fine, but I want to read your novel!"

These were the last words he ever wrote to me. In fact, not much more time was left to him. On March 14, 1932, very quietly we are told, came the end of his long and brilliant life. He had lived exactly four months beyond the three score and ten years traditionally allotted to man.

Much has been written about Turner, and when any two or three of his former students get together they are certain to speak of him—invariably with reverence and love. Not a few persons have asserted that Turner was never happy at Harvard, in spite of the fact that he was a member of the faculty for some fourteen years. Perhaps this is true, but during my long association with him, which included the major part of this period, no evidence of it ever came to my attention. To me he always seemed quite happy and satisfied, and he often spoke of the cosmopolitan nature of his classes and of the many interesting students he had in them. Certainly he loved New England, as is shown by his purchase of a summer home on the Maine coast and his plan to remove a part of his library to it and to live there half of each year after his retirement. Moreover, he never voiced to me the slightest dissatisfaction with his work at Harvard or life there, unless his statement that the cost of living in Cambridge was too high for a retired professor could be so construed.

Within recent years a number of historical scholars have sought to evaluate Turner's work and some of these have criticised his ideas in a fashion that, to my prejudiced mind, has seemed unjustifiable and unduly severe. It is significant that most of these have been younger men, generally from the East, who knew Turner very slightly if at all, and whose knowledge of the changing West is purely academic. Some of them have, in my opinion, put words into Turner's mouth which he never uttered, and credited him with ideas which he never had.

My notes on one of Turner's first lectures in History 17, "The West," show that he said:

This course is an interpretation of American History in terms of the westward movement. Many people have sought for a key to American History. Some have tried to find it in the two streams of migration which came to our shores—the Cavalier and the Puritan—but the key is not there. Others have sought it in the black man, but it is not there. It is found in neither of these because there is no key to American History. But the most important thing in our nation's history, and that which most nearly approaches the long sought key, is the westward movement. It lies in the fact that for centuries America was a land of beginning over again.

It seems clear, therefore, that Turner never claimed that the westward movement constituted a magic formula for an understanding of American history or that it was the only approach to the subject. He merely asserted that here was a phase of American history of enormous importance which

356

most scholars had hitherto largely overlooked, and with this assertion few will disagree. That there were other approaches he clearly recognized, but in this course as in nearly all of his work he chose the one in which he was most interested and to which he had given long and earnest study and profound thought.

A number of scholars who have been critical of Turner's ideas have given special attention to what they are pleased to call his "safety valve theory": that the free lands of the West provided a safety valve for eastern labor. They have pointed out at considerable length that few laboring men ever left the factories, shops, and mines of the older, settled regions to seek homes on undeveloped lands of the American frontier, and therefore insist that the labor problem of the East could not have been greatly affected by the peopling of the West.

I am quite certain that Turner never asserted, or believed, that any appreciable number of wage earners ever left their jobs in the industrial establishments of eastern cities to emigrate westward and carve farms from the American wilderness. That some agricultural laborers, or farm hands, did so migrate is unquestionably true, but if I have understood Turner correctly, he never claimed that western lands furnished an outlet for actual labor, but for *potential* labor. That this is true seems to me capable of abundant proof. As Turner often pointed out, the estates of the back country farmers, both in New England and the South, were comparatively small and their families large—a dozen children being hardly exceptional. As these children grew to maturity and overflowed the ancestral acres, the scarcity and high price of fertile farm lands in the East forced them to one or the other of two courses. They could go to one of the

357

fast growing industrial cities and secure a job, or could migrate to the West to acquire and develop a tract of virgin soil. Many of them, and perhaps most, preferred the latter alternative. In consequence, potential labor was drained out of the country, and to secure it for his fast expanding industrial enterprise, the manufacturer must import labor from Europe.

To see that this is actually what took place it is only necessary to survey the people of such western states as Texas, Oklahoma, Missouri, or Wyoming—mostly American born for generations—and to compare them with those of such industrial states as Pennsylvania, Massachusetts, or New York. Any such survey must convince the most skeptical of the truth of Turner's statement that "the West has always been the most American part of our country." If the "safety valve" of cheap western lands had not existed, it seems certain that the population elements of our industrial areas in the East would be considerably different from what they are today.

Not so long ago a brilliant young scholar gave before a group at an American Historical Association meeting a discussion of the so-called "Turner thesis." In preparation for this he utilized a typically American method of collecting misinformation by sending a questionnaire to a large number of Turner's former students and attempted to analyze and tabulate the results. Near the close of his discussion (I quote from memory) he said: "Several of Turner's former students have done him, in my opinion, the disservice of stating that he had no thesis." As one guilty, if that is the correct word, of such a statement, it may be observed that, in my judgment, not one of the former students of Turner so questioned ever even thought of seeking to do him either a service or the reverse. All that was sought was to give an honest expression of opinion. No scholar worthy of the name could do less.

As for his former students, I am sure they will all agree that Turner needs no service from us. His position in the very forefront of American historians is secure and his work will be remembered long after that of most of us, including his critics, has been forgotten. For so long as young hearts shall beat a little faster at the recital of the exploits and adventures of the trappers, argonauts, and cowboys, who were the advance agents of civilization on the American frontier; or so long as men and women thrill to the story of the pioneers driving their covered wagons out into the sunset to establish homes in a raw and untamed land; just so long will it be remembered that Turner first taught us the significance of these things and brought us to see that they were not merely isolated incidents or events, but an important, integral part of the great pattern of our country's history.

It is true that Turner never wrote any "big books," but he wrote great books nevertheless. For as a distinguished American scholar once said: "The volume of Turner's writing was comparatively small, but he had a greater influence upon the study and teaching of American History than did any other man of his generation."

The Prairie Schooner*

When I see a prairie schooner
  With the tongue a-pointing west
What a mighty nameless longing
  Always swells and fills my breast.
For it's headed toward a country
  I shall always love the best
Toward a land of stars and sunshine
  Toward the prairies of the West.

It's a wide and wondrous region
  Naught it's virgin beauty mars
Where the plains are strewn with blossoms
  As the sky is strewn with stars.
Where the air so keen and bracing
  Gives to life a joy and zest
Makes the pulses leap and tingle
  In the blood there runs the West.

And I know within the schooner
  'Neath it's cover worn and brown
There are hearts with hope a-tingle
  There is faith that will not down.
Though a man may meet misfortune
  Failure never is confessed
When he mounts a prairie schooner
  With the tongue a-pointing west.

So when from the ties that bind me

* From Edward Everett Dale. *The Prairie Schooner and Other Poems*
(Guthrie, 1929), 14.

I at last shall break away.
Leave each sordid task behind me,
  As I surely shall someday.
When I choose a craft for cruising
  Love or Fortune as my quest,
It will be a prairie schooner
  With the tongue a-pointing west.

The Piebald Steer*

Did you ever hear of the piebald steer
    That belonged to the "Lazy Z?"
He looked more queer, that piebald steer
    Than any I ever did see.

He was black and white, he was sure a sight,
    For he'd spots of red besides
And his temper grim was the worst of him
    When he comes the wise man rides.

He chased Bill Jones over sticks and stones
    To a friendly sod-house roof
From which safe perch, Bill left the church
    And cussed him from horn to hoof.

But our country's sons have weighty guns
    And Bill remembers well
So we all did fear that th' piebald steer
    To each must bid farewell.

How he came to go we do not know
    But his old haunts know him not,
And we all believe when he came to leave
    That Bill was on the spot.

So drop a tear for th' piebald steer
    Though Bill may guiltless be
But a spotted hide on his fence I spied
    With the brand of th' "Lazy Z."

* From Edward Everett Dale. *The Prairie Schooner and Other Poems*
(Guthrie, 1929), 49.

The Sooner*

Both Bill and me wuz campin'
  Along the Kansas line
Both seekin' Oklahomy land
  The spring of '89.
And on the 22nd
  When they told us all to go
I gave old Sorrel Top the rein
  And led the bloomin' show.
I knew the best location
  And I headed for it straight
I waved the crowd a fare ye well
  But kept the same old gait.
At last before my eager eyes,
  The chosen spot appears
And there wuz Bill a-plowin'
  With a yoke of spotted steers.
    Fer Bill he wuz a Sooner
    He had riz before the day
    And sneaked across and staked the Promised
      Land,
    And kept it too, By Ginger
    Spite of all that I could say
    So I took a farm of rocky hills and sand.
A little further down the creek
  Old Johnson had a claim
He had a mighty pretty gal
  Rebecca wuz her name.

* From Edward Everett Dale. *The Prairie Schooner and Other Poems* (Guthrie, 1929), 24.

And she an' me wuz sweethearts,
　But Johnson donned his gun
And said she couldn't marry me
　Till she wuz twenty-one.
And since it meant a year to wait
　I worked most awful hard
And fixed us up a dandy home
　With posies in the yard,
And then one mornin' early
　Her dad rode o'er the hill
To tell me that Becky had eloped
　With no one else but Bill
　　Fer Bill he wuz a Sooner
　　He had riz before the day
　　And promptly carried off and wed the gal,
　　And they lived together happy
　　Spite of all her dad could say
　　So I married Smith's red-headed daughter, Sal.
Now Bill an' me are older
　Than back in '89,
Perhaps another score of years
　Will see us o'er the line.
And now I tell my neighbors
　About that land o' light
Where is no pain or sorrow
　But all is fair and bright,
But when the Judgement mornin'
　At last comes rollin' round
And we our narrow prisons burst
　When Gabriel's trump shall sound,
I know that when we pass that gate
　To claim our rich reward
We'll find the central mansion staked
And Bill a-standin' guard.
　　Fer Bill, he is a Sooner
　　Just before the Judgement Day
　　He'll rise and stake the Tree of Life in haste

And keep it too, By Ginger
Spite of all the Lord can say
And make us pawn our wings
To buy a taste.

Butter-side Down*

When I was just a little kid and always in the way,
My Ma would spread a slice of bread and send me out
   to play,
I'd play about beneath the trees with marbles, bat
   and ball,
Or climb upon the orchard fence, or on the garden wall,
But if that bread should drop from out my little hand
   so brown,
It always struck the dusty earth,
                        Butter-side Down.

I grew a little older and to college went away,
I studied hard each lesson never taking time for play,
I burned the oil of midnight o'er my Latin and Greek,
I toiled both late and early through each long and weary
   week,
But when examination day at last came rolling round,
I always dropped, yes sadly dropped,
                        Butter-side Down.

I courted a fair maiden, her heart I hoped to win,
For candy, books, and flowers spent all my surplus tin,
She had another fellow, a tall and ugly guy,
With hair as red as blazes, and a wicked looking eye,
But just about the time I thought I had him done up
   brown,
She married him and let me drop,
                        Butter-side Down.

* From Edward Everett Dale. *The Prairie Schooner and Other Poems*
(Guthrie, 1929), 22.

And so it's been throughout my life, I've met Dame
    Fortune's frown,
For all of my investments went Butter-side Down,
I quite believe that when I leave this world of doubt
    and sin,
And reach that Golden City that the righteous enter in,
When that good old man, St. Peter, presents my shining
    crown,
I'll drop the everlasting thing,
                    Butter-side Down.